HOW TO TROUBLESHOOT, REPAIR, A

MOTORCYCLE
ELECTRICAL SYSTEMS

By Tracy Martin

motorbooks

First published in 2014 by Motorbooks, an imprint of Quarto Publishing Group USA Inc., 400 First Avenue North, Suite 400, Minneapolis, MN 55401 USA

Motorbooks titles are also available at discounts in bulk quantity for industrial or sales-promotional use. For details write to Special Sales Manager at Quarto Publishing Group USA Inc., 400 First Avenue North, Suite 400, Minneapolis, MN 55401 USA.

To find out more about our books, visit us online at www.motorbooks.com.

ISBN: 978-0-7603-4536-8

Editor: Darwin Holmstrom
Design Manager: Brad Springer
Layout Designer: Danielle Smith-Boldt
Cover Photography: Paul Markert

Printed in China

10 9 8 7 6 5 4 3 2 1

About the Author

Tracy Martin writes for *Motorcycle Consumer News*, *RoadBike*, *Friction Zone*, *PowerSports*, and *Dealer News* magazines. Author of three books, Tracy co-authored the *MSF's Guide to Motorcycling Excellence, Second Edition*. Published by Motorbooks, Tracy's latest book, *Motorcycle Electrical Systems: Troubleshooting and Repair*, is available at booksellers everywhere. His first book, *How to Diagnose and Repair Automotive Electrical Systems*, is also available at bookstores. In addition to writing, Tracy teaches the Total Control Advanced Riding Clinic with Lee Parks, author of *Total Control*. Tracy has presented riding skills and motorcycle suspension seminars across the United States and recently in England and the Russian Federation.

Contents

Introduction

If you are reading this you have bought my fifth book, or maybe you're online and thinking about it. This book on motorcycle electrical systems is different from my previous book on the same subject. It's more hands-on, with lots of photographs and graphics that I hope will explain what to do when something electrical goes awry with your motorcycle. Often when faced with an electrical problem, many owner's first step is to take their bike to a dealer and spend money. While this works most of the time, it's not without pitfalls. You have to get the motorcycle there, pick it up, and of course, spend money for someone else to figure out what's wrong. Just like performing your own oil and filter changes, or other maintenance, repairing your electrical system can provide owner satisfaction. Even if you ultimately have the dealer do the work, a little knowledge about what they are working on can go a long way toward getting the most for your money. In addition to how to fix electrical things that don't work, throughout the book there are many electrically related projects of all types and most are relatively easy to do. If you have ever wondered how to install a 12-volt relay (or even why one would want to), or how to read a factory wiring diagram, these subjects are covered as well.

I wanted to thank the people and companies that helped me with many aspects of creating this book. The motorcycle dealerships that kindly let me run amok in their service departments, asking questions and looking at factory manuals are all credited in the Sources section at the end of the book. Likewise, the companies that donated products that appear as electrical projects are also acknowledged in the Sources section. I had help with the photographs, and I thank Marc Connelly, Rick Haskings, Dennis Kreps, and Alan Lapp for taking a lot of the photos that ended up in the book. Thank you for all your hard work.

Dedication

I wrote this book for my son, who at the young age of 30 has had to make too many life-and-death decisions in his brave fight against cancer. His courage has been an inspiration to my wife and me as we watch him make it through each day of his treatment. Before his diagnosis, the term "cancer survivor" was only an ad slogan that I would occasionally read or see on TV, but after witnessing his struggle, it takes on a whole new meaning. I know that he will emerge from this nightmare intact and ready to move on with his life.

With all my love, Dad.

Chapter 1
Batteries

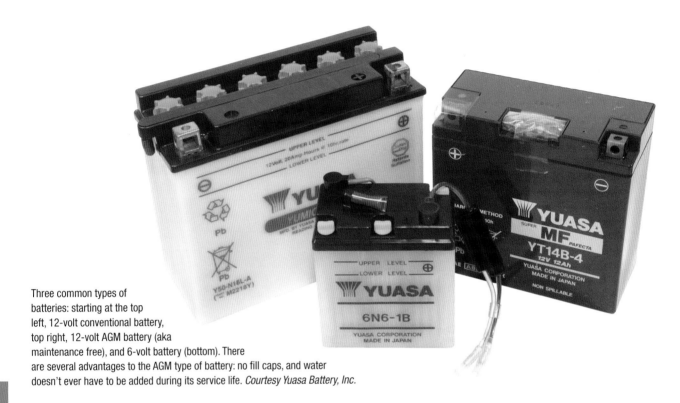

Three common types of batteries: starting at the top left, 12-volt conventional battery, top right, 12-volt AGM battery (aka maintenance free), and 6-volt battery (bottom). There are several advantages to the AGM type of battery: no fill caps, and water doesn't ever have to be added during its service life. *Courtesy Yuasa Battery, Inc.*

Here are the parts that make up a Yuasa absorbed glass matt or AGM battery. The polypropylene plastic case, cover, and filler caps form the "container" for the battery. The cell group (lower left) consists of positive and negatives plates with glass mat separators in between each plate. The three odd-shaped lead lugs are inter-cell connectors that attach the cell groups to the positive and negative battery terminals. *Courtesy Yuasa Battery, Inc.*

INTRODUCTION TO BATTERIES

Typically, most people don't spend a lot of time worrying about the battery in their motorcycle until the engine won't start; then it gets 100 percent attention. Fortunately, a jump start can get the engine going, but the bigger problem is whether it will start up again once the engine is shut off. In addition to not starting the engine, a weak or old battery can also lead to engine performance issues with electronically fuel-injected (EFI) bikes and cause problems with the charging system. Understanding how batteries operate and how to test and maintain them is simple. Basically batteries perform three jobs: (1) to provide electrical power to start the engine, (2) to supply additional current

The size, or displacement in cubic centimeters (cc), of a motorcycle engine determines the power required by the starter motor to spin it fast enough to start. This determines how much capacity the battery needs to have to provide the energy required to operate the starter motor.

Batteries are rated in amp hours (Ah) and cold cranking amps (CCA). The larger the CCA and Ah numbers the more energy it can produce. Larger motorcycle engines require batteries with higher CCA and Ah ratings. *Courtesy Yuasa Battery, Inc.*

when the charging system can't keep up with electrical demand, and (3) to act as a voltage stabilizer for the motorcycle's charging system.

A battery's primary job is starting the engine, and in this case, size does matter. Engine displacement is the determining factor for amperage requirements for engine starting and related battery capacity. The amperage required for starting an engine varies depending upon the type and size of motorcycle engine. For purposes of engine starting, batteries are rated in two ways, amp/hour (Ah) and cold cranking amps (CCA). Amp-hour rating is the battery's ability to deliver current for an extended period of time. Cold cranking amperage is the battery's ability to produce current in low temperatures. In general, larger batteries will have greater Ah and CCA ratings. There are some high-performance batteries where this is not true and physical size is not an indication of electrical cranking power.

A battery's second job is to supply current when the charging system is overworked. This usually occurs (though not always) when the engine is being operated at lower speeds. If the motorcycle's electrical system is creating a high demand—headlights on, heated vest and gloves, stereo in use, and so on—and the engine's speed is too low for the charging system to supply enough current for the power requirements of the motorcycle, the battery makes up the difference. This situation can only last for a short time, as the overworked charging system will not be able to keep the battery charged. Eventually there won't be enough electrical energy to run the engine's ignition and fuel system and the engine will stop running.

The last function of a battery is to act as a voltage stabilizer for the charging system. Charging systems need something to push against to keep from producing excessive voltage. A battery should never be disconnected when the motorcycle's engine is running because the charging output voltage could increase to more than 20 volts—enough electrical pressure to "take out" many (if not all) solid-state components such as ignition modules, computers, stereos, and so on.

Pictured is an AGM battery case with the top off. The plates and separators can from one of the six battery cells can be seen. Twelve-volt batteries have six cells that produce around 2 volts each; hence the six cells produce 12 volts. *Courtesy Yuasa Battery, Inc.*

Pictured are a group of battery plates and separators. One negative plate, a glass mat separator, and one positive plate make up the cells inside an AGM, or maintenance-free battery. The white glass mats between the plates absorb the electrolytic solution of sulfuric acid and distilled water. *Courtesy Yuasa Battery, Inc.*

These components make up a typical motorcycle-charging system. The stator (bottom) uses the rotating engine to produce alternating current, or AC. The rectifier (top) converts the AC current to DC (direct current), where it can be used to power everything electrical on the bike.

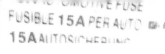

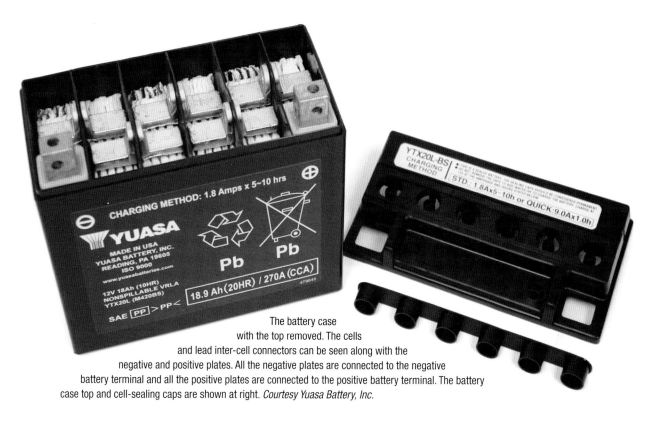

The battery case with the top removed. The cells and lead inter-cell connectors can be seen along with the negative and positive plates. All the negative plates are connected to the negative battery terminal and all the positive plates are connected to the positive battery terminal. The battery case top and cell-sealing caps are shown at right. *Courtesy Yuasa Battery, Inc.*

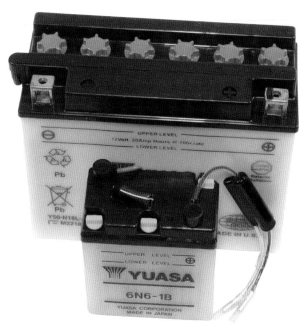

The 12-volt battery (top) has six fill caps, one for each cell. The 6-volt version only has three fill caps (yellow caps). Both of these batteries are of the "conventional" design and require periodic topping-off with distilled water. Both must be externally vented so harmful out-gassing does not corrode any metal parts near the battery. *Courtesy Yuasa Battery, Inc.*

This AGM battery never has to be filled with water. In fact, it doesn't ever have to be checked for water level as all the liquid inside the battery is absorbed in fiberglass mats. Some AGM batteries can be mounted in any position and are ideal for custom motorcycle applications. *Courtesy Yuasa Battery, Inc.*

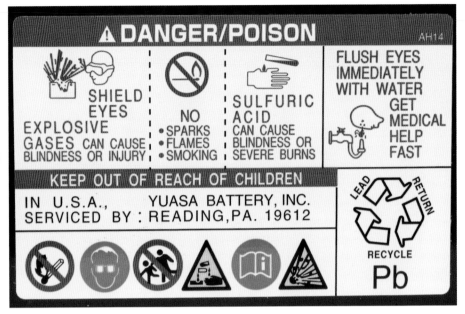

Because all batteries contain sulfuric acid and lead, they are required to have a warning label similar to the one here. Not only will battery acid burn your skin and eyes, it can create explosive gases when being charged or discharged. Lead is a "no-no" for the environment, and dead batteries should be recycled and not thrown into the trash, where they will end up in a landfill. *Courtesy Yuasa Battery, Inc.*

Thru-Partition Construction
provides shorter current path with less resistance than "over the partition" construction to get more cranking power when you need it

Patented Sealed Post
prevents acid seepage, reduces corrosion, extends battery life

Safety Valve/ Flame Arrestor
relieves excess pressure

Heat Sealed Case To Cover
bonded unit provides greater strength; protects against seepage and corrosion

Special Active Material
compounded to withstand vibration, prolong battery life and dependability

Polypropolyene Cover and Container
assures reserve electrolyte capacity for cooler operating temperatures; provides greater resistance to gas and oil; withstands higher impact in extreme weather conditions

Special Grid Design
withstands severe vibration, assures maximum conductivity

Special Separator
makes the battery spill-proof. Valve regulated design eliminates water loss and the need to refill with acid

Yuasa's VRLA (valve regulated lead acid) AGM batteries are maintenance free and do not require the addition of water. This type of battery is ideal for motorcycles that only see occasional use because they hold a charge longer than conventional batteries. *Courtesy Yuasa Battery, Inc.*

TYPES OF BATTERIES

There are two basic designs of batteries available for motorcycles and power sports equipment, conventional and absorbent glass mat (AGM). One difference between the two designs is the amount of maintenance required for each. AGM batteries are also known as "maintenance free" and do not have caps on the top of the battery case because they do not require the addition of water during their service life. Conventional batteries do have caps and must have their electrolyte level checked and will need to be topped off with distilled water. The up and down sides of each design is covered in this chapter. A general word of caution is in order when purchasing a new battery. Because a battery can potentially leave you and your motorcycle stranded, you should always buy only high-quality brands such as Yuasa. Rebuilt or "bargain basement" batteries may start your bike for a while but are sure to leave you by the side of the road sooner, rather than later.

CONVENTIONAL BATTERIES

Conventional batteries have filler caps on top of the cover, allowing each cell's electrolyte level to be checked. The individual cells need to be topped off with distilled water periodically due to inevitable water loss as a result of the charging and discharging process. When charging a conventional battery, always remove the caps to let the hydrogen gas escape.

AGM BATTERIES

Unlike conventional batteries, absorbent glass mat (AGM) batteries are designed so there is no free unabsorbed electrolyte solution to spill or evaporate. Also, they never need water added to them. Hence, these batteries are commonly referred to as "maintenance-free." The electrolyte "soup" is fully absorbed by fiberglass mat separators between the lead plates or grids. This design gives antivibrational support to the battery plates, keeping them from short-circuiting between negative and positive grids. AGM batteries will hold a charge longer than a conventional battery when not in use—winter storage for instance. In addition, AGM batteries can be physically smaller, yet provide the same or more cranking power than conventional designs. AGM batteries require charging systems that produce a regulated output of 14.0 to 14.8 volts to fully charge. Older motorcycle-charging systems produce slightly less voltage (around 13.5) and are not suited for use with AGM designs.

This Yuasa Yumicron battery is rated at 20 amp/hours and will start a large motorcycle like a Harley Davidson. Upper and lower electrolyte levels are indicated on the battery case. The translucent case allows the level to be check without removing the caps. *Courtesy Yuasa Battery, Inc.*

This Yuasa High Performance AGM battery has the most cranking power for its size and is ideal for use on high-performance engines. The battery is permanently sealed after it is activated. It never needs the water level checked or any additional water added during its service life. *Courtesy Yuasa Battery, Inc.*

BATTERY RATINGS

Because a battery's basic job is to power the starter motor while maintaining sufficient voltage to also run the ignition and fuel systems, there has to be some way to rate their ability to perform this job. Motorcycle batteries are rated in amp/hours (Ah) or cold cranking amps (CCA). Amp hour ratings are the most common and are usually found on the battery case. A battery's ability to discharge a given amount of current over a specific length of time is its Ah rating. The other method to rate a battery is cold cranking amps. CCA represents how much current, or energy at battery can produce.

BATTERY TESTING

While it may seem obvious that testing a battery before replacing it would be a good idea, often a battery is unnecessarily replaced only to find that the charging system or a loose battery cable connection is the reason for the discharged or dead battery. For example, a motorcycle's battery is discharged or dead. The owner (or dealer) replaces the battery and the engine easily starts. The battery must have been the problem as the bike starts consistently for a week. Eventually the battery becomes discharged again and the owner is facing the same problem. If the charging system on the motorcycle is weak, or there is a loose connection in the electrical system, the new battery only temporarily solved the discharge problem. Batteries should be tested to avoid unnecessary replacement.

There are several methods used to test a battery. For AGM and conventional batteries, measuring state-of-charge after charging a battery can determine if the battery is good. For conventional batteries, a hydrometer can be used to measure specific gravity and thus state-of-charge. Load testing is another method to determine if a battery is good. All of these tests require that the battery be fully charged before testing with one exception. The Yuasa Digital Powersports Battery Tester does not require a fully charged battery to perform testing. This tool will be covered later in this section.

INSPECTING A BATTERY

Battery testing should begin with an inspection of the battery using the following steps:

1. **Make sure the top of the battery case is clean and dry.** If the battery case is dirty it can cause the battery to discharge through the grime on top of the case. Use a soft brush, water and soap, or a solution of baking soda and water to clean the battery case or terminals. On a conventional battery, make sure filler cap plugs are finger tight so cleaning materials will not enter the cells and neutralize the acid.

2. **Inspect battery terminals, screws, clamps, and cables for problems, including breakage, corrosion, or loose connections.** Clean the terminals and clamps with a wire brush.

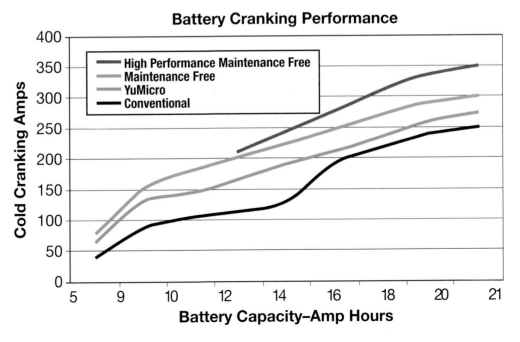

Figure 1-1: This chart illustrates a comparison between amp/hours (Ah) and cold cranking amps (CCA) for different types of batteries. To ensure consistent engine-starting performance, always consult a battery application chart before you replace the battery in your motorcycle. *Courtesy Yuasa Battery, Inc.*

JUMP STARTING

When a battery is discharged, explosive gases may be present. Connecting jumper cables from a fully charged battery to a dead battery may create a spark that could ignite these gases causing an explosion. Figure 1-2 illustrates the correct method for connecting jumper cables from a motorcycle with a dead battery to one with a good battery. Always follow these four steps when jump starting a motorcycle:

1. Connect the red jumper cable to the dead battery's positive terminal.
2. Attach the other end of this same cable to the charged battery's positive terminal.
3. Connect the black jumper cable to the good battery's negative terminal.
4. Connect the other end of the negative black jumper cable to the "dead" motorcycle engine, transmission, or engine mounting bolt.

The last connection (Step 4) is the one that has the potential to spark. This method will keep all sparks away from both batteries. Because motorcycle frames are painted or powder coated, don't connect battery jumper cables directly to the frame. Find something metal like an engine mounting bolt or engine/transmission case to make the connection. Start the bike that you're jump starting from and run the engine at 3,000 to 4,000 rpm. Now start the "dead" bike and let the engine run for a few minutes before disconnecting the cables from the two motorcycles. Remove the jumper cable connected to the frame of the "dead" bike first. The steps for connecting a dead motorcycle battery to a car or truck are the same. However, *don't* start the car's engine. The charging system in an automobile can overwhelm your motorcycle's dead battery and may cause damage.

Designed for jump starting motorcycles, these Yuasa 8-foot jumper cables are easy to take along when you ride. The 8-gauge-diameter cable has enough capacity to jump start even the largest motorcycle. A nylon storage bag is included. *Courtesy Yuasa Battery, Inc.*

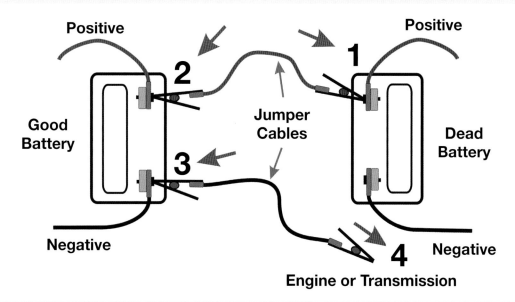

Figure 1-2: For safety when attempting to jump start your motorcycle, always make the last jumper cable connection (Step 4) is attached to the engine or transmission of the bike with the "dead" battery. This will prevent a spark from occurring at the negative terminal of the battery and possible explosion.

Battery Open Circuit Voltage

Figure 1-3: Measuring open-circuit voltage is an accurate method for determining if a battery is capable of accepting a charge. This chart shows percent of charge vs. open-circuit voltage for AGM, conventional, and 6-volt batteries. *Courtesy Yuasa Battery, Inc.*

State of Charge	Type of Battery		
	AGM (Maint. free)	Conventional	6-Volt
100%	12.8v–13.0v +	12.6v +	6.32v
75%–100%	12.5v–12.8v	12.4–12.6v	6.21v
50%–75%	12.0v–12.5v	12.1v–12.4v	6.12v
25%–50%	11.5v–12.0v	12.0v–12.2v	6.02v
0%–25%	11.5 or less	11.5 or less	5.93 or less

Once battery cables are installed, dielectric grease (available at most auto parts stores) or clear lacquer from a spray can help prevent oxygen from causing corrosion on the battery terminals.

3. **Inspect the battery case for obvious damage such as cracks or leaks.** Look for discoloration, warping, or a raised battery case top, which may indicate that battery has overheated or been overcharged.

4. **For conventional batteries, check electrolyte level and add distilled water if necessary.** Don't add acid—only distilled water. Before any testing, charge the battery so the water and acid mix.

TESTING USING A VOLTMETER (OPEN-CIRCUIT VOLTAGE)

A digital voltmeter can be used to perform an open-circuit voltage test. The test can be used for both conventional and AGM batteries. The test is used to determine the following: battery state-of-charge, ability to hold a charge, and shorted or open battery cells. It is possible that a battery can pass the open-circuit voltage test and still be unable to start a motorcycle. Battery load testing will be required to determine if the battery needs replacement. *Before performing an open-circuit voltage test the battery must be fully charged.*

Charging a battery using the vehicle's charging system or a battery charger creates a "surface" charge across the battery's cells. The surface charge needs to be removed before an accurate test for open-circuit voltage can be performed. To remove the surface charge, turn on the ignition key for about three minutes, then turn it off. Now let the battery sit for about 10 minutes. Turning on the ignition is not necessary if the battery has been

sitting for one hour after charging is complete. Connect a digital voltmeter to the battery, red lead to positive and black lead to the negative battery terminals. Open-circuit voltage indicates what percent of charge the battery has reached after charging. Open-circuit voltage for a 100 percent charged AGM battery is 12.8 to 13.0 volts. AGM batteries that are 75 to 100 percent charged will measure 12.5 to 12.8 volts. Conventional batteries have slightly lower open-circuit voltages: 12.6 volts for 100 percent charge and 12.4 for 75 percent charge.

If after charging, the open-circuit voltage indicates that the battery is less than 75 percent charged, the battery is probably no good and should be replaced. Before the battery is condemned, try charging it again. If the battery is still not close to 100 percent charged,

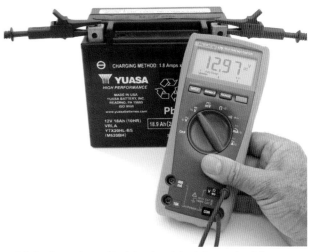

A digital voltmeter is used to determine state of charge of maintenance-free batteries. At 13 volts this battery is 100 percent charged. Less than 12.5 volts is only 75 percent charged and below 11.5 volts is between 25 and 0 percent charged. *Courtesy Fluke Corporation*

BATTERIES

it needs to be replaced. The open-circuit voltage test is not conclusive. It is possible to have a 100 percent charged battery, as indicated by the open-circuit voltage test that will not start a power sport vehicle reliably. A load test must be performed to determine actual battery performance after charging.

This hydrometer is specifically designed for testing the state of charge on conventional powersports batteries. Instead of reading specific gravity it uses colored balls to indicate state of charge. After sucking up enough electrolyte to cover the balls, the number that float are counted. One floating ball equals 25 percent charge, two balls, 50 percent; three balls, 75 percent; and four balls indicate 100 percent state of charge.

With the caps removed, each of the six cells can be tested using a hydrometer. Each individual cell is tested and compared to each other. Any cells that are not the same as the others indicate a open connection within the battery and battery replacement is the only option. *Courtesy Yuasa Battery, Inc.*

BATTERY TESTING USING A HYDROMETER

Because conventional batteries have filler caps, their state-of-charge can be checked using a hydrometer to measure the specific gravity (SG) of the battery acid, or electrolyte. If after charging, the battery's specific gravity does not increase in all the cells to indicate a full charge, the battery should be replaced.

There are two types of hydrometers used to measure SG: calibrated float and floating ball. The calibrated float provides an exact SG reading; however, due to the amount of electrolyte needed to cause the float to rise inside the hydrometer, they are impractical for use on small powersports batteries. The floating ball–type hydrometer is much smaller and easy to use on small batteries. Instead of reading specific gravity directly, it uses colored balls to indicate state-of-charge. After drawing in enough electrolyte to cover the balls inside

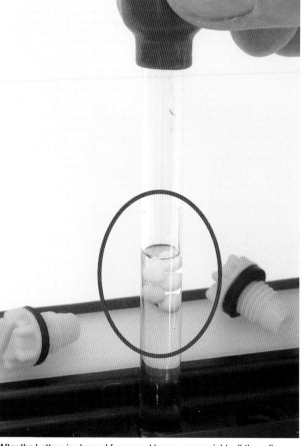

After the battery is charged for several hours, or overnight, all the cells should be at 100 percent charged. The cell being tested shows five colored balls floating within the hydrometer, indicating that the cell is 100 percent charged. The other five cells should be the same, indicating that the battery has no open or shorted cells and it is capable of accepting a charge.

OPTIMATE BATTERY AND CHARGING SYSTEM ANALYZER

As an alternative to using a digital voltmeter for battery load testing, the OptiMate Battery Analyzer is a lot more user-friendly, easier to use, and produces the same results. The tester will read voltage between 7 and 15 volts and display the results via a series of 18 LED lights. This tool really has an advantage over many digital voltmeters when it comes to capturing cranking voltage because it can record and display instant voltage drop during engine cranking. There is no need to disable the ignition or fuel-injection systems to prevent the engine from starting.

The battery must be fully charged before testing. When the tester is first connected to the battery open-circuit voltage is displayed, indicating the battery's state of charge. If the battery has been on a charger for several hours, and the LED is below 12.5 volts (red LED), that battery may be defective. When the start button is pressed, the LEDs indicate cranking voltage and this reading is displayed for 20 seconds, even if the engine starts and runs. If the LED drops into the yellow zone, and then rises into the green zone (9, 10, or 11 volts) the battery passes the cranking voltage test. If LED initially drops into the red/yellow (7 and 8 volts) zone and stays there, the battery is marginal and may have trouble starting the engine in cold weather. If the LED remains in the red zone (7 volts) the battery does not pass the cranking voltage test.

With the engine running after 20 seconds the voltage will increase. With the engine at idle, the LED should be green, or above 12.5 volts, indicating that the charging system is operating correctly. Some charging systems may not come up to charging voltage unless the engine is running above 2,000 rpm. Normal charging voltage for late-model motorcycles should be 14 to 14.5 volts. Check a service manual for specific charging voltages.

Colored LEDs, an easy-to-interrupt gauge face, and instructions make this tool easy to use, even for electrically challenged motorcyclists. In addition to testing motorcycles, the OptiMate Battery Analyzer works on any 12-volt electrical system, including cars and trucks with batteries of any size. In fact, it can be mounted on motorcycle handlebars for continuous voltage monitoring with the cable straps and Velcro strips that are included with the tester. The tester comes with an SAE connector and battery terminal clips.

The tester's face is divided into two sections: engine starting to measure battery cranking voltage and engine running to display charging system voltage. LEDs are colored red or green to indicate correct voltage or not. Instructions are located on the back of the tester.

The OptiMate Battery Tester comes with an SAE connector or battery clips. If an SAE connector is already installed on the motorcycle the tester can be left connected during a ride for continuous voltage monitoring.

This motorcycle has no SAE connector, so the battery terminal clips are connected directly to the battery for testing.

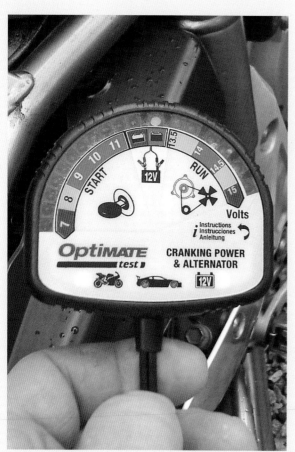

Open-circuit voltage is displayed, indicating that battery's state of charge. If the battery had been on a charger overnight and the LED was red (below 12.5 volts), it should probably be replaced.

After pressing the start button, battery cranking voltage is displayed for 20 seconds, even if the engine starts. The reading shown indicates that the battery passes the test.

the hydrometer, the number that float are counted. One floating ball equals 25 percent charge; two balls, 50 percent; three balls, 75 percent; and four balls indicate 100 percent state-of-charge. Again, if after charging, the battery's specific gravity does not increase to indicate a full charge, the battery should be replaced as it may have an open or shorted cell or excessive sulfation.

BATTERY LOAD TESTING USING A VOLTMETER

Once the battery is charged and passes the open-circuit voltage test, it's time to determine if it can really perform its main job: starting the engine. It might seem obvious that if the starter button is pressed and the engine starts, the battery must be okay. While a marginal battery might start an engine a few times, it may not reliably start it in the future, especially in cold weather.

The best way to test a battery is to make it perform its most difficult job: starting an engine. The motorcycle's starter motor can be used to provide the load to test the battery. While the engine is cranking, battery voltage is measured to determine the health of the battery. Low cranking voltage indicates the battery is getting tired and should be replaced. Higher cranking voltage readings demonstrate that the battery will start the engine reliably. Following are the steps for performing a battery load test using a digital voltmeter and the vehicle's starter motor.

1. Connect a digital voltmeter directly to the battery—red lead to the positive terminal and black lead to negative.
2. While watching the voltmeter, press the start button and crank the engine's starter (it's okay if the engine starts). Just before the engine starts, note the voltmeter reading. As the starter motor places an electrical load on the battery, cranking voltage will normally drop.
3. If cranking voltage is above 9.5 volts *while the engine is cranking* the battery is good.
4. If battery voltage drops below 9.5 volts (at 70 degrees F) while the engine is cranking, the battery needs to be replaced. Usually a bad battery will cause the cranking voltage to drop way below 9.5 volts rapidly.

If the engine starts too quickly to read cranking voltage, the ignition or fuel-injection computer fuse can be removed. This will allow the starter motor to operate (without the engine starting) and cranking voltage can be measured.

OPTIMATE BATTERY SAE CONNECTOR

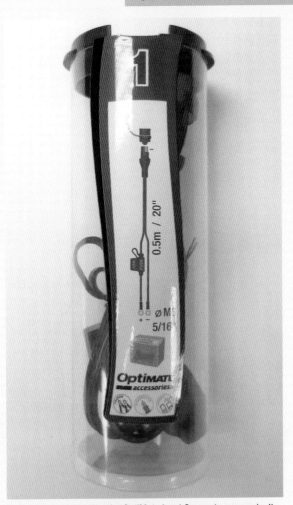

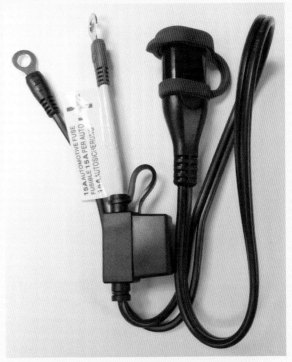

Here is the package that the OptiMate Lead Connector comes in. It makes a great gift for motorcyclists.

Heavy-duty battery terminal eyelets, inline fuse, and leads that are 20 inches long make the OptiMate Lead Connector ideal for motorcycle of all sizes.

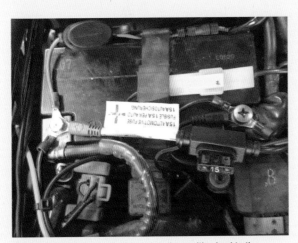

The inline fuse holder is positioned on the positive lead to the battery. A 15-amp fuse is supplied with the connector and protects the entire circuit.

Here the OptiMate Connector is installed. It comes with a heavy-duty rubber cap to cover the connector when not in use. The connector is perfect for connections to heated clothing or after riding, plugging it into a battery charger.

Having a permanent connection directly to your motorcycle's battery provides a convenient way to plug all sorts of items, including heated riding gear, battery charger, cell phone, or laptop connection, and more. The OptiMate WeatherProof Permanent Lead connector comes with an inline fuse and crimped eyelet terminals that attach directly to battery terminals. The connector is rated at 15 amps and the SAE connector's rubber sealing shroud prevents moisture from getting inside the connector. The heavy-duty connector is 20 inches long.

HAND-HELD BATTERY TESTERS

Hand-held battery load testers are becoming more widely available and can now be found in most auto parts stores. Even the largest motorcycle battery is generally smaller than the smallest automotive battery. Because the hand-held battery load tester was designed for the automotive market, some limitations and common sense should be applied before using one to test a motorcycle battery. These types of battery testers can electrically load a battery to 100 amps or more— more than enough to "fry" even a large motorcycle battery if applied for too long. Only use these load testers on motorcycle batteries that have an amp/hour rating of 14 Ah or greater (more than 200 cold cranking amps). When you perform the test, place the load on the battery for 3 to 5 seconds, and *no longer*.

To use the "Stinger" battery tester, connect the red and black cable clamps to the positive and negative battery terminals. Determine the cold cranking amps, or amp/hour rating, of the battery being tested. The switch located on the tester triggers a relay that connects an internal resistor to the battery's terminals. This places a 100-amp load across the battery. While watching the meter, depress the load switch on the tester for no more

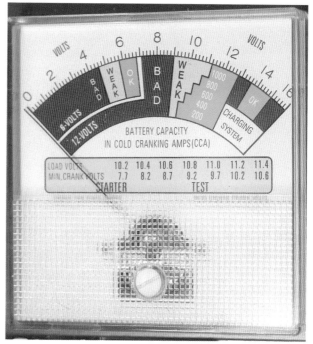

Depending on "CCA," loaded voltage in the range of 9.4 to 10.2 indicates a good 12-volt battery. *Courtesy SPX/OTC Service Solutions*

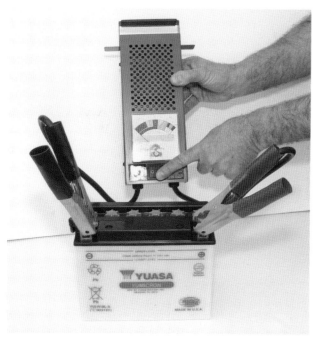

Automotive, hand-held battery testers will work for testing motorcycle batteries, but you have to use caution. Press the load button on this OTC Stinger Battery Tester (Part number 3180) for no more than 5 seconds to keep from "cooking" the battery. Also, don't try to test batteries with an amp/hour rating of less than 14 Ah. *Courtesy SPX/OTC Service Solutions*

than 5 seconds; 3 seconds is probably enough. Be sure to release the test button, and read the voltage on the tester. If the needle is in the green area, the battery is good. A steady needle reading in the yellow area means the battery may need to be charged or it is getting tired and could cause starting problems in the future, especially in cold weather. If the needle drops like a rock, the battery is bad and needs to be replaced.

YUASA POWERSPORTS BATTERY TESTER

The previous battery-testing methods required that a battery be fully charged before testing; however, there is a professional grade battery tester that will test a battery even if it's dead. These digital testers measure a battery's internal resistance regardless of its state-of-charge. Internal resistance is an indication of a battery's ability to deliver current. The more capacity a battery has to produce amperage, the lower its internal resistance. A digital capacitance battery tester uses single-load dynamic resistance technology to calculate battery performance. These testers use a modified DC load test to apply a small, momentary load to the battery while measuring instantaneous voltage drop across all of its cells. The load is then removed and voltage across the cells is measured again after a recovery period. These analog measurements are converted into digital

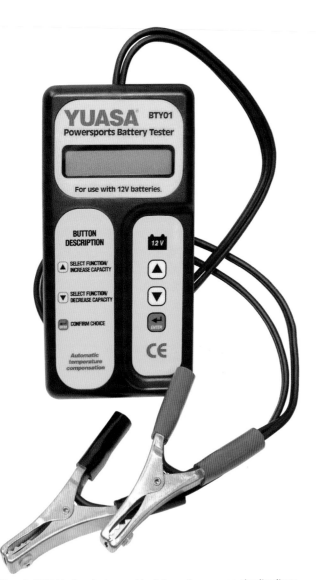

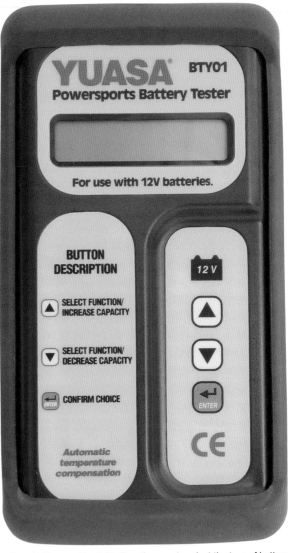

Yuasa's BTY01 battery tester provides information on open-circuit voltage, state of charge, and battery health and condition. The unit can test a partially charged or discharged battery. *Courtesy Yuasa Battery, Inc.*

The three buttons on the right allow the user to select the type of battery and its capacity. Testing is all automatic and results are displayed in seconds. *Courtesy Yuasa Battery, Inc.*

information; the tester calculates the dynamic internal resistance in order to evaluate overall condition. The entire process takes about two seconds and current drain on the battery is minimized. The tester provides information on open circuit voltage, state-of-charge, and battery health and condition. This tester can also test a partially charged or fully discharged battery whether on or off the vehicle. The only drawback is the price. These testers are not inexpensive and are mostly used by professional technicians.

To use the BTY01 tester, connect it to the battery. Battery voltage will be displayed when the connection is made. The next step is to program what type of battery you are testing—VRLA/MF/AGM/SLA (valve-regulated lead acid/maintenance free/absorbed glass mat)/sealed lead acid) or SLI (starting, lighting, and ignition) conventional batteries. "Set Capacity" is displayed and arrow keys are used to select the amp/hour rating of the battery being tested. Testing begins when you press, "Enter" and takes less than two seconds. Open-circuit voltage is displayed with each test result that include Good & Pass, Good & Recharge, Recharge & Retest, Bad & Replace, and Bad Cell & Replace. After testing, pressing the up and down arrow keys displays State-of-Charge and Battery Health, both listed as a percentage.

SELECTING A BATTERY

Selecting the right battery is an important decision as it will ultimately affect how reliably your motorcycle starts, especially on a cold morning. Often battery problems can be caused by the wrong battery for a specific application. Be careful just matching a new battery with what's installed in the vehicle—make sure that it is the correct battery or the same problem may be repeated, causing the battery to be replaced over again.

Yuasa may list more than one battery for a specific vehicle. For example, the page used as an example from the Yuasa Battery Specifications and Applications guide shows battery replacement information for a 1983 to 1986 Honda, V65 Magna. Here is how to read the chart: First find the Motorcycle Applications section and then Honda. Find the engine size (1,100cc). Look through the list until the VF1100C V65 Magna '83–'86 is located. There are three battery selections for this motorcycle:

- High Performance AGM—YTX20H-BS*
- AGM—YTX20-BS*
- YuMicron—YB18-A

There is no conventional battery for this application. Two of these batteries have an asterisk (*) at the end of the part number. In the guide, this refers to the Battery Supplier Cross Reference charts where other branded batteries may be substituted for the Yuasa battery part number. Which battery is best for this application? Any of these batteries are a good choice for the Magna; however, here are some things to consider: If the engine has been modified for higher compression or larger displacement, a battery with more starting capacity like the High Performance AGM would work well. If the bike will not be operated for long periods of time, the AGM or YuMicron batteries are a good choice. If there is any question about which battery is best for a specific application consult the Yuasa website (www.yuasabatteries.com) or contact Yuasa toll-free at 800-431-4784.

BATTERY CHARGERS

Quality battery chargers available today for motorcycles are sometimes known as "smart chargers" because they use a microprocessor to control multiple charging functions. Smart chargers monitor the battery's state of charge and will automatically start charging when the battery falls below a specific voltage.

This "smart" technology also is used to keep batteries from being overcharged, causing water loss in conventional batteries. Some chargers have diagnostic

MOTORCYCLE APPLICATIONS

CC	Model	Year	High Performance Maintenance Free	Maintenance Free VRLA AGM	YuMicron	Conventional
HONDA						
1100	CB1100F Super Sport	'83	YTX14AHL-BS*	–	YB14L-A2*	–
	CB1100	'10-'12	YTZ14S	–	–	–
	CBR1100XX	'01-'04	YTZ12S	–	–	–
	CBR1100XX	'97-'00	–	YTX12-BS	–	–
	GL1100 Gold Wing	'80-'83	YTX24HL-BS*	–	Y50-N18L-A-CX*	Y50-N18L-A
	ST1100, ABS-TCS, 1100A	'91-'02	YTX14H-BS*	YTX14-BS	–	–
	VF1100C V65 Magna	'83-'86	YTX20H-BS*	YTX20-BS*	YB18-A	–
	VF1100S V65 Sabre	'84-'85	YTX20HL-BS*	YTX20L-BS*	YB18L-A	–
	VT1100C2 Shadow Sabre	'00-'07	YTX14H-BS*	YTX14-BS	–	–
	VT1100C, C3, T Shadow (Spirit, Aero, A. C. E. Tourer)	'01-'07	YTX14H-BS*	YTX14-BS	–	–

Figure 1-4: One of the best sources for selecting the correct battery for your motorcycle is the Yuasa Battery Specifications & Applications Guide, which can be found online at www.yuasabatteries.com. *Courtesy Yuasa Battery, Inc.*

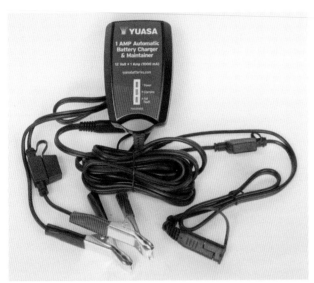

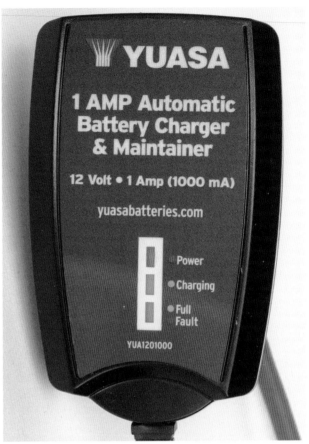

Designed for long-term use, Yuasa's 1-amp Automatic Battery Charger and Maintainer battery charger will not overcharge motorcycle batteries. The charging cycle reaches 14.4 volts then switches to maintenance float mode (indicated by a green LED). If a load is applied to the battery (by turning on the key and so on) while charging, the charger automatically switches back to charge mode then back again to a maintenance float charge. The charger plugs directly into a wall outlet and comes with a 12-foot output cord. The charger comes with a three-year warranty and is part number: YUA1201000. *Courtesy Yuasa Battery, Inc.*

Yuasa's 1-amp charger uses three LEDs to indicate charging status. Power LED (top) is on when the charger is plugged into an AC outlet. Red and yellow LEDs indicate charging and red and green indicate that the battery is at full charge. If the battery is connected backwards (reverse polarity), the power (red) LED and the red fault LED (bottom) will light. *Courtesy Yuasa Battery, Inc.*

features and indicate if a battery is worn out and needs replacing. In addition to these features, many smart chargers will not spark when connected to a battery and will tell you if they are connected backward. (Something you never want to do with an older charger or when jump starting a battery.) Battery chargers used to provide a maintenance charge for motorcycle-sized batteries should not exceed 2.5 amps. Be careful using automotive chargers, as they can overcharge and damage motorcycle batteries.

Least effective for charging a motorcycle battery are the "trickle" and automatic taper types of battery chargers. Both are similar in that their voltage is fixed. The taper charger reduces charging current, while the trickle charger keeps both voltage and current constant. These types of chargers are slow in charging even moderately discharged batteries. Another problem is that they are not safe to leave connected to a battery for long periods of time; they can over or under charge a battery.

Constant-current types of battery chargers are a better choice for battery charging. Constant-current chargers continuously increase voltage and can charge twice as fast as the constant-voltages or taper types of

chargers. The best chargers combine both these designs. The strong charging characteristics of a constant-current charger are used to initially charge the battery; then the charger automatically switches to a constant-voltage mode to float-charge or maintain the battery. This type of charger is also know as a "smart" battery charger because they use a microchip (computer) in their circuits to determine when to switch from charging mode to maintenance, or "float" modes of charging.

Most motorcycle battery chargers come with clips to connect the charger leads to the battery, and some have an additional SAE quick-disconnect plug that allows permanent connection to your bike's battery. When you want to charge the battery, just plug in the lead. This is especially helpful if your battery is hard to get to. Others are available with BMW-type sockets that can plug into BMW, Triumph, and some Ducati motorcycles.

The Yuasa 1-amp charger is connected to a Powerlet plug (left of charger). This is an easy way to connect the charger to a motorcycle when each ride is over. Charging powersports batteries with a smart charger whenever the vehicle is not in use will prolong battery life dramatically. It can also keep the battery from freezing if the vehicle is stored in cold weather. *Courtesy Yuasa Battery, Inc.*

The OptiMate4 "smart" battery charger is specifically designed for BMW CAN Bus electrical systems as well as standard electrical systems on other motorcycles. The charger can be connected to late model BMW without shutting down the CAN BUS connection between the bike's computer and the battery. The OptiMate4 Dual Program can be switched to a standard motorcycle. Both programs will test for the following: dead or shorted battery cells, voltage-retention tests (battery state of health), and de-sulphation and recovery. The charger can be left connected to any battery for extended periods of time without causing damage. In fact, it can even recover a dead battery that has as little as 2 volts. *Courtesy TechMate*

BATTERY DISCHARGE

Left unattended, batteries lose up to 1 percent of their charge each day at 70 degrees and more if the ambient temperature drops. Electronic fuel injection, computers, clocks, and radios also drain batteries, even when the ignition is off. Even if a motorcycle is ridden often, charging the battery between rides will keep the number of discharge cycles to a minimum. In addition to keeping a bike ready to start, using a battery charger has an additional benefit—prolonged useful battery life. Many owners of large displacement bikes only get one

or two years before they have to replace their batteries. I have no "scientific" evidence, and this theory may be at odds with some battery manufacturers' supplied technical information, but over the years, I (and others) have found that connecting a "smart" battery charger to the battery every time you park your motorcycle causes the battery to last longer. I typically get five years of life for all the batteries in my motorcycle using a smart charger.

Battery Charging Time in Hours

State of Charge	Battery Amp-Hours								Hours
	10AH		14AH		18AH		20AH		
75%	3	6	4	8	6	10	6	11	"
50%	6	11	9	14	11	18	13	20	"
25%	9	15	13	20	17	26	19	28	"
0%	13	20	18	27	23	34	25	37	"

1 amp taper charger
1 amp constant current charger

Figure 1-5: Battery charging time is determined by battery amp/hours and the current state of charge. Taper or "trickle" chargers charge at about half the rate of constant-current types of battery chargers. Many "smart" battery chargers use a combination of taper and constant-current charging, so their charge time will be somewhere in the middle. *Courtesy Yuasa Battery, Inc.*

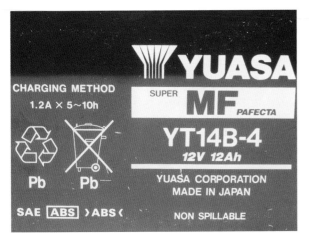

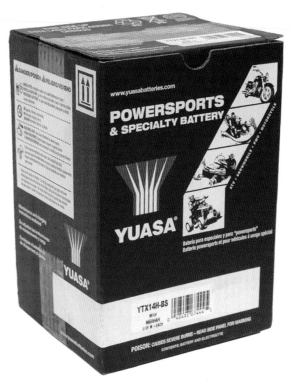

The case on this AGM, maintenance-free battery states the charging method as "1.2AX5~10h. That means 1.2 amps for 5 to 10 hours of charging time. The capacity of the battery is 12 Ah. "Nonspillable" is also printed on the case, as this AGM-type of battery can be mounted on its side. *Courtesy Yuasa Battery, Inc.*

What's in the box? This AGM battery comes complete with the acid pack, terminal nuts, and instructions. The shelf life is indefinite because the battery has no acid in it. *Courtesy Yuasa Battery, Inc.*

This Yuasa AGM battery will only be around 80 percent charged after it is filled with acid. The battery must receive an initial charge *before* it is installed on a motorcycle. If it is not charged, it will never charge more than 80 percent no matter how long the bike is ridden. In addition, its life expectancy will be shortened. *Courtesy Yuasa Battery, Inc.*

BATTERY ACTIVATION

New batteries require an initial charge before they are put into use. When a motorcycle dealer fills a conventional battery with acid it's only about 80 percent charged. This is also true for AGM (sealed) batteries that you can purchase via the Internet or through the mail. Both types of batteries when new must be charged to reach their full life expectancy as well as a 100 percent charge. Failure to charge a new battery can prevent it from ever becoming more than 80 percent charged. Many motorcyclists prefer to fill (with acid) and install their own batteries to make sure that they are charged before being put into service. If you don't do this yourself, ask your dealer to make sure the battery is charged for several hours before you pick up your bike.

This initial charge your new battery should have is called bulk or initialization charging and not all chargers are capable of performing this function. The charger used to initialize a new battery must be capable of reaching 12.8 volts. Yuasa and OptiMate battery chargers are all capable of performing this job. A battery is properly initialized if the open-circuit voltage reaches a minimum of 12.8 volts and does not exceed 13.8 volts. This range will work for conventional and AGM types of batteries. Open-circuit voltage should be checked after the battery has been disconnected from the charger for about an hour. This will avoid a false reading of the battery's surface charge.

BATTERIES

24

ACTIVATING AGM BATTERIES

Activating an AGM battery is a simple process and differs from activating a conventional battery (covered later in this section). Inactivated, AGM batteries (dry without acid) can be stored for long periods of time as long as they are kept in a cool, dry location and out of direct sunlight. Also the foil sealing strip covering the filler ports should not be removed until the battery is ready to be filled and activated. Use only the electrolyte container that comes with the battery for filling the cells as it has a higher concentration of sulfuric acid than the acid used for conventional batteries.

All AGM battery electrolyte containers are not the same. Each contains the proper amount of electrolyte for its specific battery. Before filling, read the electrolyte handling instructions and precautions on the label. Do not smoke when activating a battery or handling battery acid. Always wear plastic gloves and protective eyewear and do not smoke during this process. The following steps should be used to activate an AGM battery:

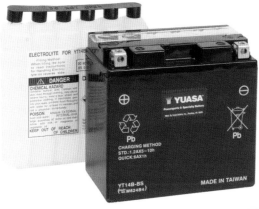

1. The battery must be out of the vehicle and placed on a level surface. Remove the electrolyte container from the plastic storage bag. To fill the battery use only the dedicated acid container that comes with the battery as it contains the proper amount of electrolyte for that specific battery. This is important for service life and battery performance. Do not pierce or otherwise open the foil seals on the electrolyte container. Do not attempt to separate the individual electrolyte containers. *Courtesy Yuasa Battery, Inc.*

2. Remove the strip of caps from the acid container. Put the strip aside as you will use it later to seal the battery cells. *Courtesy Yuasa Battery, Inc.*

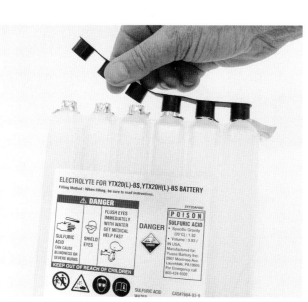

3. Remove the sealing strip from the top of the battery. *Courtesy Yuasa Battery, Inc.*

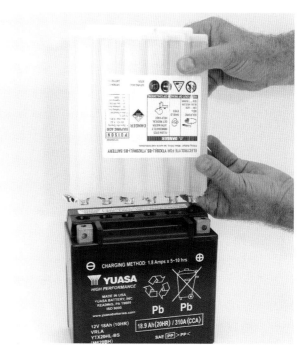

4. Place the electrolyte container with the foil seals facing down into the cell filler ports on the battery. Hold the container level and push down to break the foil seals. The electrolyte will start to flow into the battery and air bubbles will be seen inside the container. Do not tilt the electrolyte container. *Courtesy Yuasa Battery, Inc.*

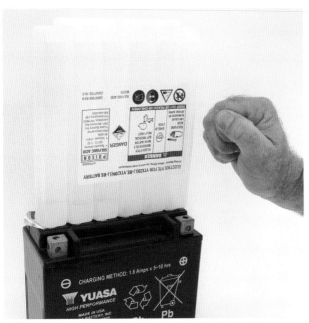

5. Check the electrolyte flow. Keep the container in place for 20 minutes or longer until it empties completely. If no air bubbles are coming up from the filler ports, or if container cells haven't emptied completely after 20 minutes, tap the container or battery case a few times to cause the electrolyte to flow into the battery. Do not remove the acid container from the battery until it is completely empty. The battery requires all of the electrolyte from the container for proper operation. *Courtesy Yuasa Battery, Inc.*

6. Remove the electrolyte container from the battery. Fully insert the strip of sealing caps (previously removed from the electrolyte container) into the battery filling ports. Make sure the strip of caps is fully inserted and flush with the top of the battery. Inset the caps by hand, do not use a hammer or excessive force. Never remove the strip of caps or add water or electrolyte to the battery during its service life. *Courtesy Yuasa Battery, Inc.*

7. For batteries with ratings of less than 18 Ah, let the battery stand for 20 to 60 minutes. For batteries with higher Ah ratings, or that have the High Performance rating (designated by an "H" in the part number or name) allow the battery to stand for one to two hours. The stand, or rest period, allows the electrolyte to permeate into the plates for optimum performance. Yuasa AGM batteries have the amp/hour printed on the front of the battery case.

ACTIVATING CONVENTIONAL BATTERIES

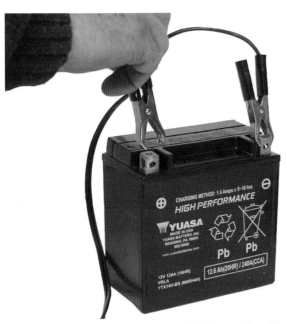

8. Newly activated AGM batteries require an initial charge. After adding electrolyte, a new battery is approximately 75-80 percent charged. After the "stand" period (Step 7), charge the battery to bring it to a full state-of-charge. The battery charger used for initial charging should be able to charge at 12.8, or more volts for an AGM battery. *Courtesy Yuasa Battery, Inc.*

Just like the AGM battery, this Yuasa Yumicron battery must be filled and charged before being put into use. *Courtesy Yuasa Battery, Inc.*

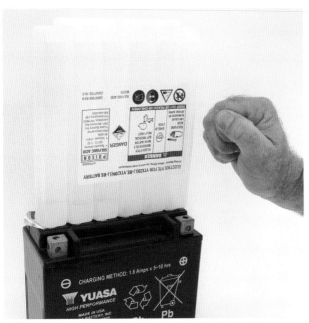

BATTERIES

Sealed at the factory, a new Yuasa conventional battery has an indefinite shelf life as long as it remains sealed (filler caps and red vent cap installed) and is stored at room temperature. Once the battery is unsealed, it should be activated and put into service. The cell plates on an unsealed, uncharged battery will oxidize, making charging difficult and reducing the service life of the battery. The following steps explain the process of activating Yuasa's conventional YuMicron and YuMicron CX batteries.

1. The battery must be out of the vehicle and placed on a level surface. Remove filling caps (red, yellow, or green battery caps). *Courtesy Yuasa Battery, Inc.*

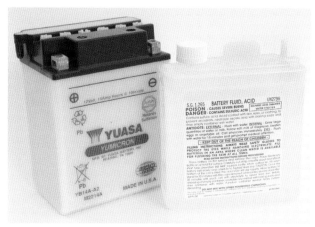

3. If using the acid bottle supplied with the battery, place the container upright on a flat surface. Carefully cut off the tip of the bottle's spout and attach the short tube provided. Caution: Do not squeeze the bottle when cutting the fill tip. *Courtesy Yuasa Battery, Inc.*

2. *Remove the red sealing cap from the vent elbow.* If the battery has a red cap on the vent elbow remove it and throw it away. Never put this cap back on the battery after it is filled with acid as the buildup of internal gas pressure can cause the battery case to rupture. *Courtesy Yuasa Battery, Inc.*

4. Fill the battery with electrolyte supplied with the battery or from a bulk container. Do not use water or any other liquid to activate a battery. Electrolyte should be between 60 and 86 degrees F before filling. If electrolyte is stored in a cold area, it should be warmed to room temperature before filling. Fill to the *upper level*, as indicated on the battery. *Note*: Never fill or activate a battery installed in a vehicle as electrolyte spillage can cause damage. Fill each battery cell slowly and carefully to the highest level line. *Courtesy Yuasa Battery, Inc.*

5. Let the battery stand for at least 30 minutes after filling. Move or gently tap the battery so that any air bubbles between the plates will be expelled. If the acid level has fallen, refill with acid to upper level.

6. Filling a conventional battery with electrolyte will bring it to 75 to 80 percent of a full charge. A battery must be charged to 100 percent before putting it into service. To find recommended charging current requirements in amps for a specific battery, divide battery ampere-hour capacity rating by 10. For example, a 14 Ah battery should be charged at 1.4 amps (14 Ah ÷ 10 = 1.4 amps).

7. During initial charging, check to see if the electrolyte level has fallen, and if so, fill with acid to the *upper level*. After adding acid, charge for another hour at the same rate as above to mix the water and acid together. Note: This is the last time electrolyte should be added to the battery. If the level is low during use, distilled water should be added as required.

8. When charging is complete, replace filler cap plugs and tighten by hand—do not use a screwdriver or pliers. Wash off spilled acid with a water-and-baking soda solution, paying particular attention that any acid is washed off the terminals. Dry the battery case and install the battery. *Courtesy Yuasa Battery, Inc.*

not used for more than two weeks or if the starter turns slower than usual when starting the engine. A conventional battery requires the periodic addition of distilled water when the electrolyte level becomes low. Water loss is normal in these batteries through the

This Yuasa YTZ12S is "factory" activated using an extensive activation process that ensures complete absorption of the electrolyte so no liquid acid is contained within the battery. This process allows these batteries to be shipped ready to install from the factory. *Courtesy Yuasa Battery, Inc.*

BATTERY MAINTENANCE
AGM Batteries

AGM batteries do not have to be checked as often as conventional batteries, about every three months or three months from the date of battery activation at the factory. Higher storage temperatures cause faster self-discharge and require checking more often. The battery will last longer if it is 100 percent charged most of the time and any of the smart chargers will maintain this type of battery for optimum performance and long service life.

The single most important aspect to maintaining an AGM battery is not to let it sit discharged for long periods of time. Keep it fully charged for peak performance. AGM batteries have a predetermined quantity of electrolyte added at the factory or in the field specified for the battery. Once activated, the battery is permanently sealed and must never be opened. The addition of water is never required for an AGM battery.

Conventional Batteries

Conventional batteries should be checked for state-of-charge about once per month if not used on a regular basis. Recharging may be required if the vehicle is

Touring bikes, watercraft, snowmobiles, and ATVs can use Yuasa's Yumicron conventional type of battery. It features special, thin separator packs and extra cell plates that provide 30 percent more cranking power than a plain conventional battery. It also uses Sulfate Stop, which reduces cell sulfation, providing longer battery life. *Courtesy Yuasa Battery, Inc.*

process of electrolysis and evaporation. Low electrolyte levels ... ... r will result ... ... aintain the ... ll lines on ... ine. Clean ... make sure ... ays replace

... lisconnect ... rain from ... y month ... onths for ... tes a low ... es below ... ire more

... ies can ...damaged are sulfation and freezing. These are not a problem if the battery is properly charged and, for conventional batteries, the water level is maintained. Battery sulfation takes place for two reasons: continuous discharging or low electrolyte levels. When a battery discharges, the lead in the plates turn into lead sulfate. The lead sulfate is actually a crystal that grows larger when the discharge is continuous and uninterrupted. In a conventional battery, low electrolyte levels expose the cell plates to air, causing the lead material to oxidize

and form sulfates. In either case it doesn't take long before the battery won't hold a charge. Low electrolyte levels cause another problem because the acid in the electrolyte becomes more concentrated, causing the active material to corrode and fall to the bottom of the battery case. If this condition takes place over a long enough time period the process will internally short out the battery.

Freezing is not a problem for a fully charged battery; however, if the battery becomes discharged (and the acid in the electrolyte turns into mostly water) the electrolyte will freeze. Freezing can cause a condition called "mossing," which is indicated by small red lines on the battery plates. Freezing can also crack the battery case and buckle the plates, permanently damaging the battery. A fully charged battery can be stored at subfreezing temperatures with no damage. As the chart on this page indicates, a fully charged battery will not freeze unless the temperature drops past minus 75 degrees F. By contrast, a discharged (dead) battery will freeze at only 27 degrees F. That's a difference of more than 100 degrees between the low temperatures a charged and discharged battery can withstand.

BATTERY TERMINAL CLEANING

Press the start button and instead of the engine cranking and starting, a clicking sound is heard. Time to spend $100 on a new battery? Not so fast. When was the last time the battery was actually inspected? Motorcycles in which the battery is located under the seat make it easy to do a visual inspection. On other motorcycles the battery is hidden under body panels or the fairing and a visual inspection could be an hour-long project. Easy to get to, or not, before assuming that battery is the reason that the engine won't turn over, it's worth inspecting the condition of the battery terminals and cables.

Battery terminals are subject to the natural process of corrosion. As the battery is used to start the engine, over many miles it produces gases that contain sulfuric acid and hydrogen. These will react with oxygen in the air and stick to the lead terminals, forming corrosion.

Electroylyte Freezing Points	
State of Charge	**Temperature**
100%	–75° F
75%	–25° F
50%	5° F
25%	16° F
0%	27° F

Figure 1-6: As long as a battery is charged it can withstand very low temperatures, but when it becomes discharged it can freeze solid at 27 degrees F—a common temperature in much of the United States in winter time. A frozen battery even when thawed out will have to be replaced—usually because the case cracks, spilling battery acid all over whatever motorcycle it was installed in. *Courtesy Yuasa Battery, Inc.*

This usually appears as a white, yellow, or even greenish crusty substance that causes high resistance between the battery terminals and the battery cables. When the starter motor tries to operate, not enough current from the battery makes its way to the starter and the result is that it cranks the engine over slowly or not at all. Loose battery cables are another common cause for the same symptoms. Removing the cables from the battery terminals and cleaning them will solve both of these problems and most likely save the cost of a new battery. The tools required are simple: a wrench or screwdriver to remove the battery cables, a wire brush and either baking soda or a can of Coca-Cola. Here are the steps for cleaning a motorcycle battery's terminals and cables.

The condition of the battery terminals and cables shown is typical of a battery that has seen a lot of use. This doesn't necessarily mean that the battery needs replacement, just terminal cleaning.

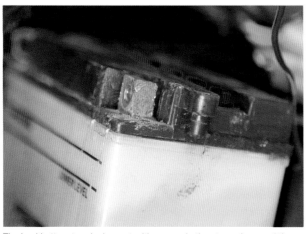

The lead battery terminals react with oxygen in the atmosphere and the battery's outgassing to form corrosion. All powersports and automobile batteries have the same corrosion problems to varying degrees.

Two household chemicals can be used to a clean battery terminal and cable corrosion—baking soda and water, or Coca-Cola (yes, Pepsi works as well). Battery-cleaning chemicals are available at auto parts stores but are unnecessary. Notice that the battery-cleaning person is wearing rubber gloves—a good idea when handling sulfuric acid or its residue.

The corroded battery cable is dipped into the Coke for a few minutes to start the process of removing the corrosion. Coke can also be poured on the battery terminal directly.

After a few minutes, the cable is pulled out of the Coke. Most of the corrosion has dissolved. A quick rinse with some water will finish the process.

BATTERIES

Once the cable is cleaned with Coke, it's a good idea to use pliers to hold the cable and a wire brush to finish the job.

Make sure that eye protection is worn whenever using a wire brush to clean battery terminals or cables. The small particles of corrosion get thrown everywhere and if some lands in an eye it can be quite painful.

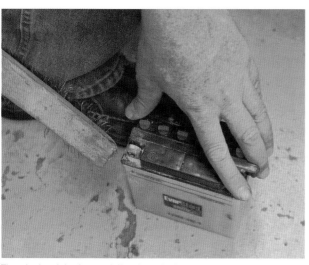

The wire brush is also used directly on the battery terminals. Wear eye protection to avoid a trip to the emergency room.

Once the terminals and cables are clean, they should be reassembled. Just doing this step takes care of a loose battery cable, a common cause for slow cranking or not starting. Make sure to dip all the tools used for removing the cables (wrenches, screwdriver, pliers, and so on) into the Coke to remove any battery corrosion. The next step is to use petroleum jelly to keep the terminals and cables from being exposed to the atmosphere.

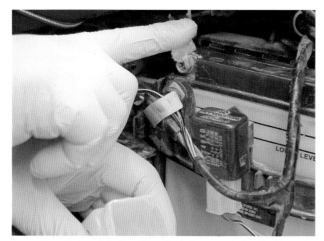

Smear the petroleum jelly liberally on the battery terminal and cable and between them and the battery case. The idea is to prevent their exposure to the atmosphere.

When no oxygen can get to the lead battery terminals, corrosion will be slowed down, if not completely stopped. An alternative to using petroleum jelly is spray paint. The paint does the same thing as the petroleum jelly in preventing oxygen from reaching the lead terminal. Clear lacquer is better than colored spray paint as overspray will not show on the surrounding areas.

BATTERIES

Chapter 2
Charging Systems

In the early part of the 1900s, before batteries were used in motorcycles, or cars, only ignition systems required electricity in order to operate. These early vehicles used a magneto, a small generator capable of producing only enough energy to charge an ignition coil. Once electric lights and eventually starters were

The components that make up charging and starting systems can be expensive when purchased from a dealer, especially for an older motorcycle. Rick's Motorsport Electrics, Inc., remanufactures both starters and charging systems for most Japanese motorcycles. *Courtesy Rick's Motorsport Electrics, Inc.*

Honda Gold Wings and Valkyries and some BMWs use an alternator (left) similar to those used on automobiles. The diodes used to convert AC to DC volts and regulator is contained inside. On the right are a stator and rectifier. This style of AC charging system can't produce the power that the single alternator can, but they are smaller and more compact. The stator fits inside the engine cases and the rectifier can be mounted almost anywhere on the frame. *Courtesy Twigg Cycles*

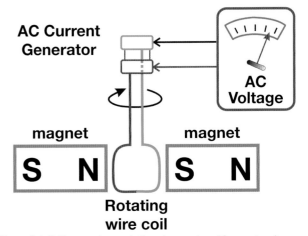

Figure 2-1: Both generators and alternators produce AC current and work in a similar manner. A coil of wire is rotated between two magnets. As the invisible lines of magnetic force are cut, voltage and current are induced into the coil of wire. The rotating coil of wire is connected to the motorcycle electrical system via slip rings (shown at top with voltmeter connected).

introduced for use on motorcycles, storage batteries were added as well. With the addition of a battery, there had to be some way to keep it charged.

The last chapter focused on the storage battery and battery chargers in general. In this chapter, the focus shifts to the motorcycle's "onboard battery charger," more commonly known as the charging system. The charging system is the heart and soul of a motorcycle's electrical system. Without a reliable charging system, anything on your bike requiring electricity will not work for long.

Pictured is an alternator from a Honda Gold Wing. Unlike three-piece separate charging systems that use a stator, rotor, and separate rectifier, this alternator uses internal diodes and a voltage regulator, forming a complete charging system. Alternators are far superior to three-piece charging systems because they can produce more electrical power and are more reliable; the downside is they're heavy, take up lots of space, and if you ever have to replace one, bring your wallet. *Courtesy Twigg Cycles*

Early motorcycles used direct current (DC) generators in their charging systems. Later these were replaced with alternating current (AC) charging systems. Introduced in the early 1960s, AC charging systems represented new technology—solid-state electronics, that is, the transistor and diode. Since their inception, cars and motorcycles can only use DC voltage to charge their batteries and power ignition systems. Both types of charging systems (AC and DC) produce AC voltage, which must be converted into direct current for use in a vehicle. Old-fashioned DC generators make this conversion mechanically, while modern alternators (including those used on motorcycles) use diodes.

The charging system has only two purposes: (1) to charge the battery and (2) to power all the electrical components used on a motorcycle once the engine has started. The charging system must have enough capacity to meet all the electrical demands of the bike, including any accessories added by the owner, and still charge the battery at the same time. The charging system's output and electrical requirements of the motorcycle must be matched and work together. For reliability, motorcycle manufacturers don't design charging systems to operate at their maximum rated power output for long periods of time. Most motorcycle-charging systems will have some excess current-producing capacity. This isn't always the case and some factory charging systems are close to being overloaded even without the addition of any electrical accessories.

Older motorcycles use DC generators instead of alternators. These can be found on Harley-Davidson, BMW, Moto Guzzi, and others. This generator on a Harley FL is made by Cycle Electrics, which manufactures new generators and voltage regulators for Harleys, including solid-state voltage regulators that replace mechanical designs. *Courtesy Iron Mike, Vietnam Vets MC*

This Cycle Electric solid-state voltage regulator introduces modern technology to a generator type of charging system on this vintage Harley-Davidson. The regulator senses the temperature of the armature, and when cold (after cold engine startup) it allows more current to be produced by the generator to help charge the battery. After the generator has been operating for a while, current is limited to keep from overworking the generator. *Courtesy Iron Mike, Vietnam Vets MC, and Cycle Electric Inc.*

Unlike automobile charging systems that are rated in amps, a motorcycle's charging system output is rated in watts. In addition, motorcycle electrical accessories, lights, and heated riding gear are also rated in watts. Using watts as a common denominator makes it easy to figure out if nonfactory electrical accessories can be added to a motorcycle without taxing the charging system.

For example, a stock motorcycle, with a total electrical power requirement of 400 watts, would typically have a charging system capable of producing 525 watts. This provides an excess of 125 watts (525–400 = 125) that could be used for adding electrical accessories. If a 100-watt heated jacket liner is connected to the motorcycle, the charging system will still have 25 watts left over. However, if two 30-watt auxiliary driving lights are added, the charging system cannot power all the factory electronics, charge the battery, and run the heated liner and extra lights all at the same time. In this scenario, the motorcycle would still run because the battery will take over powering up the added electrical demand—until it runs out of current and goes dead. When that happens, the engine will stop running as there will be no power for the ignition and fuel systems.

THREE-PIECE CHARGING SYSTEMS

By far the most common style of motorcycle-charging system consists of three components: rotor (that is

These Glenda driving lights use LED technology and only require 12 watts of power for each light. They are five times brighter than a standard halogen bulb that uses 50 watts (100 watts for a pair of lights). Because they are so bright and can blind oncoming drivers, the lights come with a dimmer controller that is connected to the motorcycle's high-beam circuit. When the high beams are activated, the Glenda lights go to full power. *Courtesy Clearwater Company*

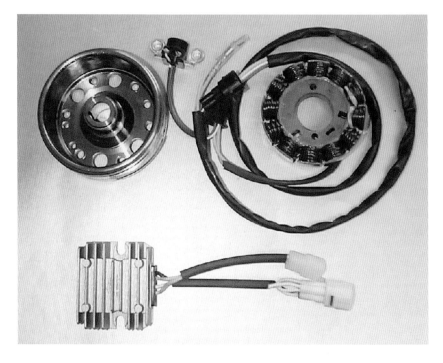

The most common type of motorcycle-charging system consists of three components: rotor (left), stator (right), and rectifier (bottom). In general, these systems are highly reliable and require no maintenance. *Courtesy Rick's Motorsport Electrics, Inc.*

Every time winter comes around, it's time to take a look at ways to extend the riding season. Heated jackets and vests have been around for some time and the technology used to deliver heat to riders has always been a series of small wires imbedded within heated garments. These designs usually work pretty well but do have some drawbacks; hot spots (from where the wires are too close to the rider's skin) and long warm-up times. Powerlet Products has come up with a unique, new heat-delivery system that overcomes the disadvantages of standard heated clothing: the RapidFIRe ProForm Heated Jacket and Glove Liners.

Here's how this new technology works. Far infrared is a form of light that is transmitted through a carbon nanocore material within the liner. This type of light is part of the electromagnetic spectrum that is not visible to our eyes and is felt as heat. The Powerlet liners use nanocore material instead of small wires to transfer warmth to the rider. Because the heat source is the material itself, there are no hot spots. The end result is that the heat produced is almost instantaneous, and more penetrating, because more of the heated surface area is in contact with the rider than with traditional (wired) types of liners.

The jacket liner has some unique features: dual heat ranges (100 or 60 watts for small motorcycle-charging systems), glove connectors at the ends of the sleeves (glove liners draw 28 watts for the pair), wind- and water-resistant polyurethane-coated nylon outer shell, ProForm stretch panels for a snug fit, and an ultra-thin design that provides ease of wear under a riding jacket and small storage space when not in use. Because both jacket and glove liners provide so much heat, a variable temperature controller should be used. Powerlet makes a dual, wireless temperature controller that is designed for the jacket and glove liners, but can be used with any type of heated clothing. The receiver is kept in a zippered pouch within the jacket liner and the transmitter can be mounted anywhere on the bike. The controller-transmitter has two knobs (one for the jacket liner and the other for the gloves) and two LEDs to indicate the heat setting.

With the use of wireless technology, the jacket, glove liners, controller-transmitter, and receiver all require only one connection to the motorcycle. The jacket and glove liners use coax cable connectors and Powerlet sells adaptors for SAE- and BMW-style connections to the bike's electrical system. We tried the liners in temperatures as low as 20 degrees F for two-hour rides and only had to turn the controller up to around 50 percent. The major difference felt with these liners is the evenness of the warmth distributed to torso and hands—no hot or cold areas and a deeper heat than wired liners. In fact, the jacket liner heats up in as little as 20 seconds. The nanocore technology is more effective in heat transfer than older designs of heated clothing. Powerlet's Proform heated clothing is available in a variety of sizes and comes with a lifetime warranty. *Courtesy* RoadBike Magazine *and Powerlet Products*

The Powerlet RapidFIRe jacket liner features dual heat ranges, 60 watts for smaller motorcycles that have limited charging system capacity or 100 watts for large touring bikes. Depending on what is worn for a jacket, the liner can keep a rider comfortable in temperatures down to 20 degrees F. *Courtesy Powerlet Products*

Glove liners feature molded female connectors to attach to the sleeves of the jacket. Because both the jacket and glove liners can get very hot, they require the use of a variable heat controller. The wireless controller has two knobs, one for the jacket and the other for the gloves, plus LEDs to indicate heat settings. *Courtesy Powerlet Products*

turned by the engine's rotation), stator (is fixed within the rotor), and rectifier. The stator is made up of a laminated steel core stack each with a copper coil of wire surrounding it. These stacks are placed inside the circumference of the stator. The stator and rotor are usually located at the end of the engine's crankshaft. The rotor is a metal drum that has magnets cast into it. As the magnets spin around the stator, AC current and voltage are produced within the coils of wire that make up the stator.

The development of a solid-state device called a diode led to the wide use of alternators in automobiles in the early 1960s. By the 1970s, most motorcycles used either a single alternator or three-piece alternator charging system. Diodes are the key to these systems' ability to convert AC to DC voltage and current. A diode is an electrical one-way valve that allows current to pass in one direction but not the other. The diodes are used in motorcycle rectifiers (and alternators) to convert AC current and voltage into DC current by means of a process called rectification. The diodes for a three-piece motorcycle-charging system are located inside the rectifier and are connected to the stator via three wires. The diodes block negative current from the stator and only allow positive current to reach the battery.

The rectifier is also responsible for regulating both current and voltage from the stator. Inside the rectifier

The rectifier used on a motorcycle-charging system is basically an aluminum box that contains one-way electrical valves called diodes. In the process of converting AC voltage and current to DC voltage and current the diodes get hot. Heat fins are cast into the rectifier to help remove this heat. *Courtesy Twigg Cycles*

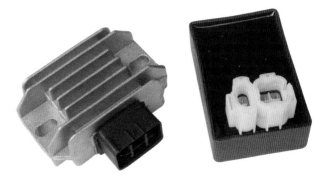

These voltage rectifiers are aftermarket replacements for Yamaha all-terrain powersports vehicles. While most rectifiers work in a similar manner, a service manual should be check for specific testing procedures. *Courtesy Rick's Motorsport Electric*

You can see the three wires coming from the stator (right). These connect all the coils on the stator to the rectifier. The rectifier's job is to convert AC current or voltage to DC and regulate both current and voltage output from the stator. *Courtesy Twigg Cycle*

KOSO SUPER SLIM VOLTMETER INSTALLATION

Unlike automobiles, motorcycles don't come with instrumentation that tells the rider that the charging system is operating correctly or even at all. Even the most basic car or truck has at least a charge indicator light that glows red if the charging system stops working. Many cars have a voltmeter gauge that gives the driver a general idea if the charging system is operating as it should, or not. If the charging system on a motorcycle stops working, the engine will eventually shut off leaving rider and bike by the side of the road.

Installing a digital voltmeter provides the rider with some piece of mind as to the status of the bike's charging system. By monitoring the charging voltage, a rider that uses heated clothing or extra lighting will know if all of their electrical accessories can be turned on all at once, or separately if charging voltage drops too low. Koso North America makes the Super Slim Voltmeter that we installed on a Suzuki GSX-R. Here are the steps:

The Koso Super Slim Voltmeter is small enough to fit on many bikes. The meter is approximately 2¼ inches long × 1 inch tall and is a little less than ½ inch in height. It comes with two splice connectors and two-sided tape for mounting. *Courtesy Koso North America*

These 3M Scotch Lock splice connectors require no soldering and are ideal for tapping into an existing wire without cutting it. The connector is placed over the wire and the wire that is to be connected is placed in the plastic holder. The plastic cover pushes down on the metal strip and is locked in place for a clean splice. *Courtesy Koso North America*

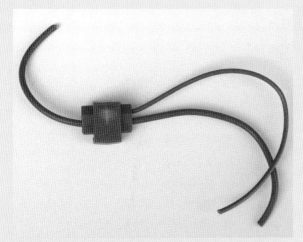

Here is what the Scotch Lock connector looks like with the wires connected. The red wire was not cut and the blue wire was spliced into the red wire. These connectors make a quick connection without cutting wires. *Courtesy Koso North America*

Mounting is easy using the two-sided tape that is included with the meter. The voltmeter is water proof so riding in the rain will not cause it to stop working. *Courtesy Koso North America*

(continued)

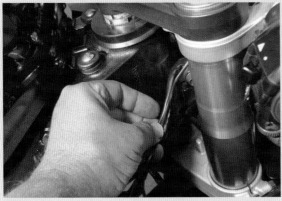

When routing the wires from the meter to the motorcycle's ground and key-on power source make sure that they do not interfere with steering or suspension movement. *Courtesy Koso North America*

The best way to find a ground wire is by using a 12-volt test light connected to battery positive. When a ground wire is stabbed with the pointy end of the test light, it will light up. *Courtesy Koso North America*

Here the test light is being used to find a key-on power wire. The test light is connected to ground. The voltmeter should only come on when the key is turned to the RUN position. If the meter was on all the time it could drain the battery. *Courtesy Koso North America*

Here is the meter installed with the engine running. Charging system voltage is 14.0. The meter has a great built-in feature: If charging voltage drops below 11.5 volts, the meter will flash, warning the rider of a problem. The blue backlighting is easy to see, even in sunlight. All in all it's a very clean installation. *Courtesy Koso North America*

Rather than just stabbing a lot of wires to find the ground and key-on power wire, a wiring diagram can make this exercise a lot quicker. This service manual shows the location and color of the wires on the GSX-R. *Courtesy Koso North America*

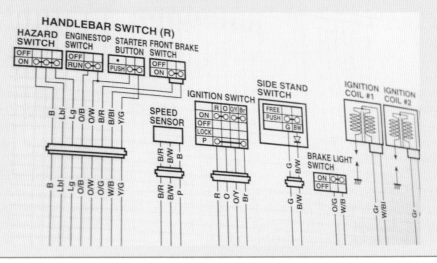

is a voltage-sensing circuit that limits the rectifier's output voltage. When DC voltage reaches a preset level (usually between 13.5 and 14.5 volts DC) the voltage sensor sends a signal to "disconnect" the stator from the rectifier. When DC voltage drops below 13.5, the sensing circuit reconnects the stator and the process begins again. This switching process takes place thousands of times per second. The effect of turning the charging circuit on and then off this rapidly creates a lot of heat. That's why motorcycle rectifiers are made from aluminum and have heat fins—just like an air-cooled motorcycle engine.

CHARGING SYSTEM TESTING

If your battery goes dead after riding several miles or the acid gets "cooked" out of it, the bike's charging system is probably at fault. Charging systems are usually reliable on modern motorcycles. In fact, charging system problems are more often than not caused by something "stupid," rather than as a result of a component malfunction. To eliminate needless hours of electrical testing, the following common problems need to be eliminated first as the most likely source of a charging system malfunction. They are listed in order of the most common problem first: (1) tired or bad battery, (2) loose or poor electrical connections, (3) burned fuses or open-circuit breakers, (4) a bad stator, and (5) a bad rectifier.

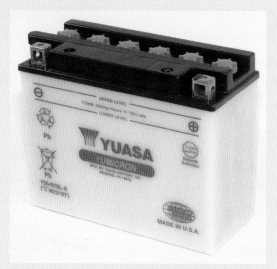

Before blaming the charging system for a dead battery, make sure that the battery is good. A shorted battery cell or an old, tired battery that can't take a charge may damage the charging system by overloading the stator or rectifier, or both. Always test the battery before attempting to diagnose charging system problems. *Courtesy Yuasa Batteries, Inc.*

BATTERY CONDITION

If a motorcycle's battery keeps going dead overnight, or even after only several hours, replacing charging system components won't necessarily fix the problem. This may seem obvious at first glance, but *not* testing the battery first has been the cause of numerous wasted charging system component replacements. Even if the battery is fairly new, it doesn't necessarily mean it's good. Test it to make sure, and don't forget to check for loose battery cable connections. (See Chapter 1 for battery-testing procedures.) Two basic rules will help out with charging system problems: (1) The battery should be fully charged *before* testing or installing charging system components, and (2) do *not* disconnect the battery on any motorcycle while the engine is running. Disconnecting the battery with the engine running was a questionable charging system test even for older motorcycles with DC generators, but those bikes didn't have solid-state electronics, which are easily damaged by such a procedure.

CHARGING VOLTAGE TEST

It's more efficient to do the simplest test first that provides the most information. The charging voltage test will test for basic charging system operation. Here are the steps for testing charging system output voltage:

1. Connect a digital voltmeter directly to the battery—red meter lead to battery positive (+) and black lead to battery negative (-).
2. Read and remember the open-circuit voltage displayed on the voltmeter.
3. Start the engine and run it at around 4,000 rpm or whatever the service manual recommends for charging system testing.
4. The charging system output voltage should be at least 1 volt above the open-circuit voltage in Step 2. This will be 13.5 to 14.5 volts for most motorcycles. Check the service manual for exact output voltage.

As long as the charging system voltage, in Step 4 above, is higher than open-circuit battery voltage, the charging system is producing amperage, or current. The limitation of this test is that it cannot measure how much current is being produced. A reading with an ammeter is required to know for certain if the charging system is producing its maximum current output. If charging system voltage is higher than battery open-circuit voltage, but the battery keeps doing dead, the

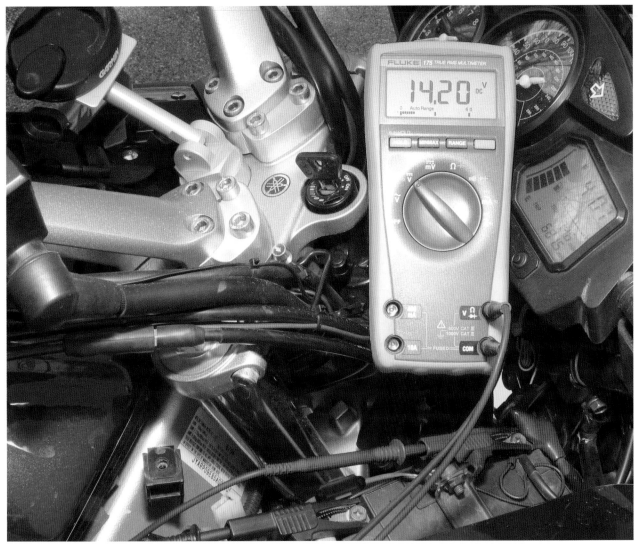

Charging system voltage should be at least 1 volt over open-circuit battery voltage. With the engine running, the charging system voltage is 14.2 volts, indicating that the system is operating correctly provided that the battery is not going dead after riding. The test is not 100 percent conclusive and further testing may be required. On most motorcycles it should be between 13.5 and 14.5 volts. Engine rpm has a substantial effect on charging system voltage. Engine speeds above 4,000 rpm may be required for maximum charging system output. See a service manual to find out what charging voltage should be at any given engine rpm for your motorcycle. *Courtesy Fluke Corporation*

other components of the charging system will still have to be tested.

If charging system voltage does not go higher than battery voltage with the engine running at high rpm, then something is wrong with the charging system. Listed in the order of what goes wrong the most are: loose or poor connections, burned fuses or open-circuit breaker, faulty stator or a bad rectifier. Don't forget the battery. More charging system components have been unnecessarily replaced because of a bad battery. Test the battery *before* testing the charging system.

WIRES, FUSES, AND CONNECTORS

Always make sure to check for loose wires or connectors at the alternator, stator, voltage rectifier, and battery before assuming that the charging system is faulty. Take a close look at the three-wire connector from the stator (coming out of the engine case) to the rectifier. A loose or poor stator connection is a common problem. Even though a connector may appear tight, and might not feel loose, that doesn't mean it's actually working electrically. A voltage drop test is the fastest way to determine the strength and solidity of the connection between the wires coming from the stator, voltage rectifier, and

VOLTAGE DROP TESTING

Voltage drop testing does not test the charging system, only the connections between the system and the battery. The test electrically tests if a connection is sound and making good contact. The advantage of this test is that nothing has to be dissembled to perform the test. Once the charging system's connections are verified, testing of individual components can be performed. Keep in mind that loose or poor electrical connections are far more common than components that are faulty. If you are new to electrical diagnosis, the voltage drop test should be practiced on a charging system that is not having problems. When you're faced with voltage drop testing a "problem" charging system, the voltmeter readings will make more sense if you've had some practice beforehand.

Here are eight steps that will voltage drop test a typical motorcycle-charging system. Some manufacturers have this procedure in their service manuals, but not all of them do.

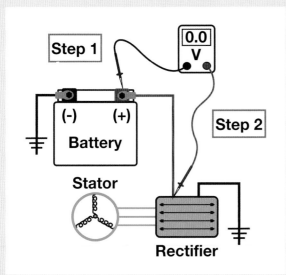

Step 1: Connect the black voltmeter lead to the positive battery terminal. Step 2: Connect the red meter lead to the battery wire at the rectifier.

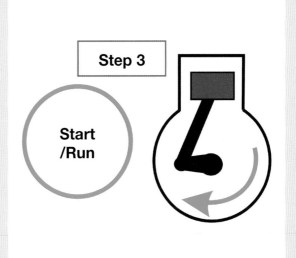

Step 3: Start the engine and run it at around 4,000 rpm (check the service manual for specific engine rpm). This will allow the charging system to produce full output.

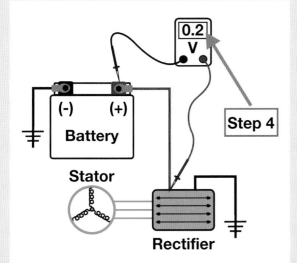

Step 4: With the engine running at high rpm, check the voltmeter reading. Two-tenths (0.02) is about normal for most motorcycles. If the reading is much higher, the connection at the battery or rectifier is either loose or not making good electrical contact.

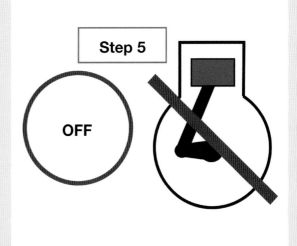

Step 5: Stop the engine.

(continued)

CHARGING SYSTEMS

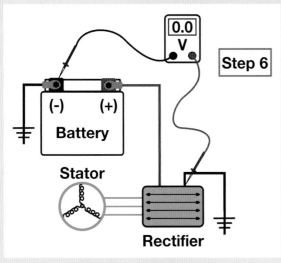

Step 6: Connect the voltmeter as shown; black lead to the battery negative terminal, red lead to the case of the rectifier.

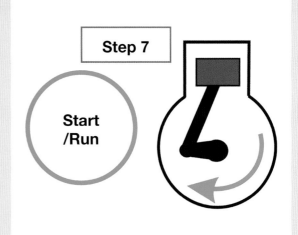

Step 7: Start the engine and run it at around 4,000 rpm (check the service manual for specific engine rpm, same as Step 3).

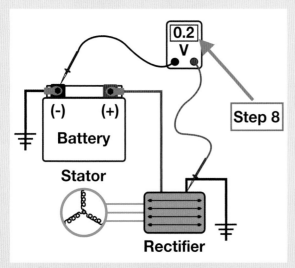

Step 8: With the engine running at high rpm, check the voltmeter reading. Two-tenths (0.02) is about normal for most motorcycles. If the reading is much higher, the connection at the battery negative cable, rectifier, or rectifier mounting bolts is either loose or not making good electrical contact.

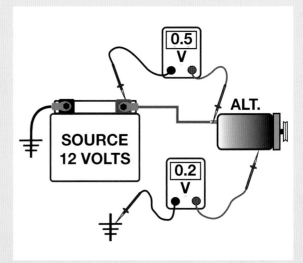

Voltage drop testing on motorcycles that have alternators (some BMWs and Honda Gold Wings) is a similar procedure to the tests for the rectifier. Both the positive and negative connections are shown and can be performed separately. The engine must be running at high rpm to perform the test. See a service manual for details.

the positive battery terminal. Basically, a "voltage drop test" will help you determine if the voltage produced at the alternator is actually getting to the battery.

STATOR TESTING

Most stators are simple in construction and easy to test. They have two common problems: the stator

windings can become shorted together (or to ground) or open (not connected to anything). Many service manuals recommend using an ohmmeter to check stator windings. This is not the best way to test stator windings. While the theory of checking for opens and shorts using an ohmmeter is good, the reality is the stator may "pass" an ohmmeter test but not produce

Generally reliable, motorcycle-charging system stators can sometimes malfunction. The coils of wire that make up the stator can short together or to ground, or become open. Motorcycles with lots of extra electrical accessories can also wear or burn out a stator. This stator has been "cooked" as evidence by the two melted coils (top right). *Courtesy Twigg Cycles*

This stator has overheated and does not pass the AC voltage output test. It even smells bad—burnt plastic. *Courtesy Rick's Motorsport Electric*

Here is a close view of the burned stator windings. The varnish is melted and some of it has tuned to charcoal. *Courtesy Rick's Motorsport Electric*

Here is a rewound stator from Rick's Motorsport Electrics (www. Rick'smotorsportelectrics.com). The original iron core is used and new copper wires, or windings, are applied. This stator costs less than half of what a dealer will charge for a factory part. *Courtesy Rick's Motorsport Electric*

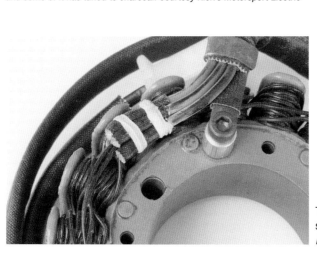

This is the back of the rewound stator. The three stator wires are shown where they connect to the stator windings. *Courtesy Rick's Motorsport Electric*

enough AC voltage to charge the motorcycle's battery. Dynamic testing with the engine running and the stator operating is the best way to determine if a stator is working correctly.

Shorts between windings can be tested with a digital voltmeter and shorts to ground can be tested using a test light. To test the stator, unplug its connector from the rectifier and start the engine. All three wires from the stator should produce AC voltage. A service manual will tell you how much AC voltage the stator should make and at what engine rpm. If you don't have a service manual, look for increased AC voltage as engine rpm rises. A rule of thumb is to take the system charging output in watts and divide it by four. The result is what the three stator wires should collectively produce in AC volts. For example, if a charging system is rated at 400 watts, then the AC voltage output from the stator should be 100 volts AC (400, 4 = 100 volts). Each of the three stator wires should output 100 volts AC. An open, shorted stator winding may output low or no AC voltage.

In addition to the stator AC voltage output test, the stator windings should be tested for a short to ground. If any of the windings are touching the engine case, the stator will not produce enough AC voltage and will have to be replaced. This test can be done using an ohmmeter, but a test light is a better method to check for shorts to ground.

RECTIFIER TESTING

The rectifier has three jobs: to convert or rectify AC to DC volts, to control charging system voltage, and to prevent the battery from discharging through the stator when the engine is off. With this basic knowledge of what a rectifier is supposed to do, it's easier to understand how testing procedures can determine if a stator is good or bad. There are two methods that can test for a bad rectifier: (1) the process of elimination and (2) using a diode tester.

Using the process of elimination is straightforward. If the stator's AC voltage output is good (on all three wires), the battery checks out, and all the connectors and wires are in good condition, the only component left in the charging system that could be causing a problem is the rectifier. The Charging Voltage Test, outlined earlier in this chapter, tests the rectifier's ability to control or regulate charging voltage. With the engine running, voltage at the battery should be above 13.5 volts and below 15.0 volts. If charging voltage is outside that range, *and* there are no excessive electrical loads on the charging system, the rectifier is probably bad.

A multimeter with a diode-testing function can be used to confirm that a stator has a bad diode. An ohmmeter can also be used as well; however, the ohmmeter test is not as accurate as a diode test. The diode test function on a multimeter sends a small

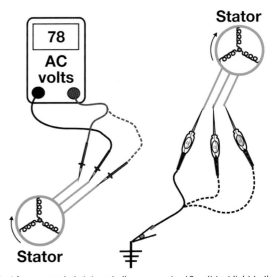

Stator–Engine Running

Unplug the stator from the rectifier and connect a voltmeter to two of the stator wires. With the engine running at high rpm (see a service manual for specific testing rpm) voltage should increase as engine rpm rises. Each of the three combinations of the stator wire pairs should produce the same AC voltage within 5 percent of each other. If one of the pairs of wires produces low, or no AC voltage, the stator will have to be replaced.

Stator

To test for a grounded stator winding, connect a 12-volt test light to the engine case (ground). Start and run the engine at high rpm while touching the pointy end of the test light to each of the three wires. The test light should *not* light or flicker when touched to any of the stator wires. In this example, the stator wire to the far right is shorted to ground, causing the test light to glow. The stator needs to be replaced.

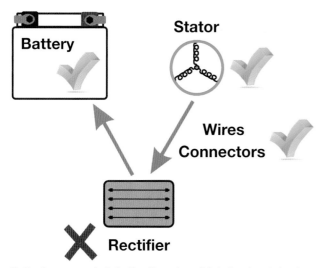

Testing by process of elimination: If a motorcycle's battery is not charging and the battery, stator, and wires and connectors are all good, the only charging system component that's left is the rectifier. Battery testing is covered in Chapter 1 and stator test is discussed in this chapter. Wires and connectors can be tested using voltage drop testing, which is covered in this chapter.

Many quality digital multimeters have a diode-testing function (yellow circle). When switched to the diode test, the meter will send enough current (provided by the meter's battery) to the diode to turn it on for testing. Using the ohm function will sometimes work, but many meters will not trigger diode operation using the ohm function. *Courtesy Fluke Corporation*

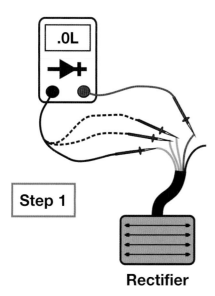

Step 1: To test the three positive rectifier diodes, connect the red meter lead to the red wire from the rectifier. The red wire goes directly to the battery. Touch the black meter to all three stator wires (they are usually the same color). The meter should read nothing or ".OL."

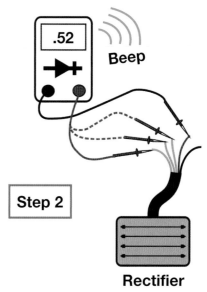

Step 2: Reverse the meter leads—black lead to the rectifier red wire. Touch the red meter lead to all the stator wires. The meter should sound a "beep" and display voltage each time the lead is touched to the stator wires. This indicates that all the positive diodes are good. If any of the stator wires caused different results during this test the rectifier has a bad diode and should be replaced.

amount of current from the meter's battery through the diode. When the meter is connected in one direction, the diode blocks the current. When the meter leads are reversed, the current is allowed to pass through the

diode and the meter either beeps or indicates diode operation on its display. Using the ohmmeter function on a multimeter will not reliably test a diode because the meter may not send enough current through the

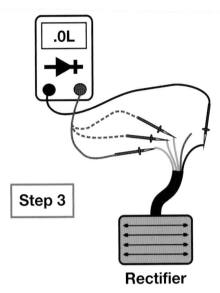

Rectifier

Step 3: Testing the negative diodes within the rectifier is similar to the positive diode test. Connect the black meter lead to the rectifier's ground wire (usually black). Touch the read meter lead to each of the stator wires. The meter should read nothing or ".0L."

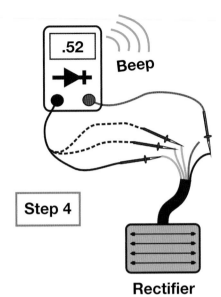

Rectifier

Step 4: Reverse the meter leads—red lead to the rectifier black wire. Touch the red meter lead to all the stator wires. The meter should sound a "beep" and display voltage each time the lead is touched to the stator wires. This indicates that all the negative diodes are good. If any of the stator wires caused different results during this test the rectifier has a bad diode and should be replaced.

diode to trigger its operation. Within the rectifier are three positive and three negative diodes. All six must be tested. Turn the function knob to the diode test on the multimeter and follow these steps for diode testing.

Another diode test uses a voltmeter to measure AC voltage that is "leaking" past a diode about to go bad. To perform the test, connect the voltmeter leads directly to the battery. Set the scale on the voltmeter to read AC millivolts. AC voltage should not exceed 55mV AC with the engine running and several accessories turned on. If AC voltage is greater than 55mV, one or more diodes could be about to malfunction.

FLYWHEEL CHARGING SYSTEMS FOR SMALL MOTORCYCLES

Off-road and smaller motorcycles use a variation of the three-piece charging system often called a flywheel alternator charging system. These systems have been

Off-road motorcycles and some older, smaller street bikes use a variation of the three-piece charging system: the flywheel alternator. As the flywheel rotates, current is generated in the charging coil. For daytime operation the battery is charged using the B terminal of the charging coil. At night when more current is required to operate the lights, the A terminal is used. The A and B terminals provide different amounts of current due to the length of wire in each— more wire or coils in A and less in B. A simple diode serves as a rectifier to convert AC current to DC before it's used to charge the battery.

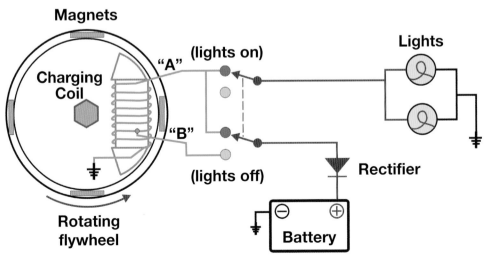

around for years and have some variations but basically operate on the same principles. The engine's flywheel has magnets cast into it just like the typical three-piece charging system. Instead of a stator, a laminated pole shoe is used and a coil of wire is wound around it. As the rotating magnets pass in over the coil of wire on the pole shoe AC voltage is generated.

Many of these charging coils have three wires. One end of the coil is grounded and the other two are voltage outputs. The two outputs are for operation with and without the running lights. With the running lights off, only battery charging takes place and less current is needed. Terminal B is used for daytime operation as it is only about half of the charging coil's length of wire and therefore only produces enough current to charge the battery. At night when the lighting system is on, Terminal A is used because it uses the entire charging coil to produce more power. The ignition system uses a separate charging coil for power that is not shown.

The AC voltage and current must still be converted to DC for use in the bike's electrical system. The same type of voltage rectifier used for the three-piece charging system is used with the flywheel alternator. Modern systems use a solid-state integrated circuit (diodes) for rectification and voltage regulation.

FLYWHEEL CHARGING SYSTEM TESTING

Testing flywheel charging systems can be done using an ohmmeter or AC voltmeter. For specific ohm values for the charging coil see a service manual. In general, one terminal will have more resistance (high ohm reading).

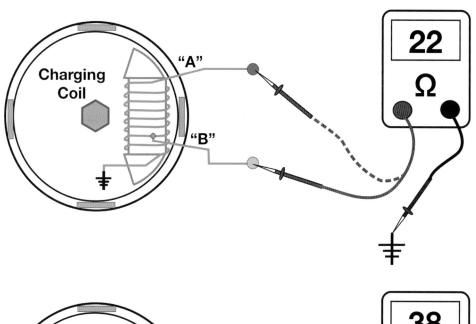

A service manual will provide resistance (ohm) specifications for the charging coil. Both coil terminals should have resistance with the lighting coil terminal having more than the run coil terminal. Neither terminal should show an open (infinite resistance) or short to ground (no resistance).

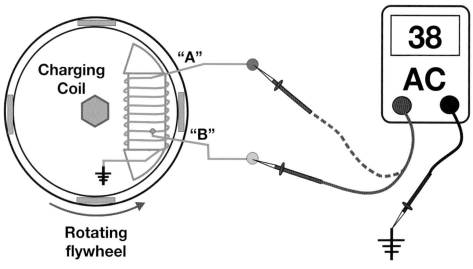

The same test points are used for measuring AC voltage. With the engine running, both charging coil terminals should produce AC voltage. As engine rpm increase, AC voltage should rise. See a service manual for exact AC voltage numbers.

Both the A and B terminals should not be open or shorted to ground. Measuring AC voltage with the engine running is a better test. Again, reference a service manual for specific AC voltage values. Both terminals should produce AC volts that should increase with engine rpm. The lighting coil terminal should produce more voltage than the run terminal.

ONE PIECE ALTERNATORS

Alternators used on motorcycles are similar to the stator or rectifier charging systems in that both use diodes to convert AC current or voltage to DC. In general, large touring bikes use alternators because they produce more power. One disadvantage is that alternators take up more space and are more difficult to mount to the

Honda Gold Wings and Valkyries and some BMWs use an alternator similar to those used on automobiles. The diodes used to convert AC to DC volts and regulator can be located internally or mounted remotely. Late-model Honda Gold Wing alternators put out 1,300 watts, enough to light up several motorcycles. *Courtesy Twigg Cycles*

The diodes on the Honda alternator are located under the black plastic cover with the bolts protruding through it. The slip rings and brushes can be seen at the end of the alternator shaft. *Courtesy Twigg Cycles*

This BMW alternator is located under the front engine cover. The diodes are not part of the alternator and can be seen at the far right. A mechanical voltage regulator is used in this older system. *Courtesy Bob's BMW*

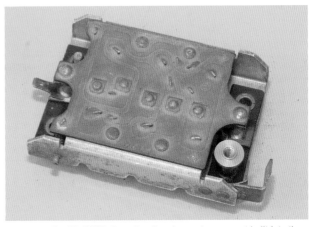

The diodes for this BMW alternator charging system are not built into the alternator. Instead they are housed in a metal box that is located inside the front engine cover. *Courtesy Bob's BMW*

engine because they either use a gear set or belt to turn them.

Alternators differ from three-piece charging systems in that they do not use permanent magnets that rotate around a stator coil. Instead they use a rotor that is an electro magnet. When the ignition is turned on, current is sent to the rotor. The rotor is connected to the battery via two slip rings and carbon brushes. With the engine running the rotor turns within a fixed stator, which is similar to the stators used in three-piece systems. The diodes can be located inside the alternator (Honda Gold Wing) or mounted externally like those on some BMW motorcycles.

With the rotor removed on this Gold Wing alternator the brushes can be seen. They are made from carbon and are spring-loaded so they will make contact with the rotating slip rings when the alternator operates. An internal voltage regulator (fined box at bottom) is used to control voltage output. *Courtesy Twigg Cycles*

A coil-type spring exerts pressure on the alternator slip ring brushes in this BMW alternator. In general, slip ring brushes won't wear out before other alternator components such as bearings and diodes fail. *Courtesy Bob's BMW*

The alternator's stator is made up of three separate coils. The rotor spins inside the stator, inducing voltage and current into the stator windings. *Courtesy Twigg Cycles*

An alternator's rotor consists of a coil of wire and two iron pole pieces. The slip rings that transfer power to the rotor coil are located at the end of the rotor shaft next to the bearing. An internal cooling fan is mounted between the slip rings and rotor in this alternator. *Courtesy Twigg Cycles*

Chapter 3
Starters

STARTER MOTORS

Electric starters have not always been used on motorcycles. Older riders remember, if not fondly, kick starting their bikes to get the engine started—not a particularly fun task on a cold morning. With no camshafts or valves, two-stroke engines were relatively easy to kick start. The same cannot be said of four-stroke. Triumph, BSA, and Harley-Davidson motorcycles with their long engine strokes and heavy flywheels were "fun" to kick start. Stories of being

This is a typical starter motor from a Japanese motorcycle. The only electrical connection is a large terminal that connects to the starter solenoid. The starter's drive gear turns an over-running clutch that drives the engine's crankshaft when the starter motor operates. *Courtesy Twigg Cycles*

Looking very much like it really belongs in a car, this BMW starter uses the starter solenoid to push the starter's pinion gear into the engine's flywheel to start the engine. On modern motorcycles the solenoid is mounted remotely from the starter. *Courtesy Bob's BMW*

This drawing shows how a starter motor operates. When current from the battery is applied to the field poles (coils of wire) they become electromagnets. The commutator has battery current applied to it via the starter brush, and it too becomes an electromagnet with poles that are opposite to the field coils. The magnets repel each other, causing the starter to rotate. The spinning starter motor engages the engine's flywheel via a gear set, the engine turns, and it eventually starts. Modern starters use permanent magnets instead of field pole coils.

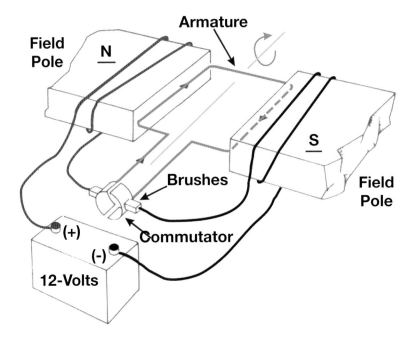

This 1971 Suzuki T-500R Titan, owned by Adrian Eichhorn, was introduced by Suzuki as the Cobra in 1968. Suzuki manufactured T500 two-stroke models like the Cobra until 1975. The Titan's two-stroke engine made 47 horsepower at 7,000 rpm, and because it was a two-stroke, it was fairly easy to kick start (the kick start lever is highlighted in the yellow circle). *Courtesy Vintage Japanese Motorcycle Club*

Pictured is an armature and commutator bars (lower right). At top left are the drive splines that connect the starter to the engine when it's rotating. Wear (black area) can be seen on the commutator bars. It's generally not a good idea to try to rebuild a starter, and a professional rebuilder is a better investment both in time and money. *Courtesy Twigg Cycles*

This armature has been rebuilt. New windings and a reconditioned commutator make this old part good as new again. The armature will be used to rebuild the starter motor. *Courtesy Rick's Motorsport Electric*

thrown over the handlebars or breaking an ankle when the engine backfired and the kick start lever was still engaged with the engine's flywheel did actually happen, though not as frequently as old-timers will tell you. Starting in the late 1960s a few motorcycles were offered with electric starters. They also had 12-volt batteries replacing 6-volt electrical systems that did not have enough power to operate a starter motor.

A starter motor uses field coils to create a magnetic field around a rotating armature. Most modern motorcycle starters use permanent magnets instead of field coils because they are lightweight and more compact. At the end of the armature is a gear that engages with the engine's flywheel. When the start button on the handlebars is pressed, a starter solenoid is energized, sending current directly from the battery to the starter. Current from the battery energizes the field coils (if applicable), causing them to have a strong magnetic field. At the same time, battery current is also applied to the commutator brushes that carry current

Pictured is the commutator and four starter brushes. With four starter brushes, each pair of brushes will energize armature coils opposite each other or 180 degrees apart. The brushes are spring loaded against the commutator and will eventually wear out—usually the motorcycle wears out first. *Courtesy Twigg Cycles*

Instead of field coils this starter uses four permanent magnets that surround the armature. This design allows all the battery's current to go to the armature. Permanent magnets take up less room than field coils and allow the starter overall dimensions to be more compact. *Courtesy Twigg Cycles*

Because of the expense of purchasing a new starter for a used motorcycle, starter rebuild kits are sometimes more practical. New starter brushes can add new life to a tired starter and cost a fraction of a new replacement. Brushes are not the only components that wear out, however. The commutator and bearings should be replaced along with the brushes. *Courtesy Bob's BMW*

from the battery to the armature. The armature rotates because the opposing magnetic lines of force between the field coils or permanent magnets and the armature repel each other, and since the armature has multiple wire loops, it continues to rotate. Starter motors may use as many as four commutator brushes, and older models may have from two to four field coils.

Under a "no-load" condition, during starter bench-testing, or when a starter's pinion gear doesn't engage the engine's drive gear or flywheel, starter speed will continue to increase until centrifugal force destroys the starter. It then makes a big loud noise, like a bang, followed by a shower of sparks.

STARTER SOLENOIDS

The starter motor on any motorcycle requires by far the most amperage of any electrical component. For example, on a typical fuel-injected motorcycle the fuel and ignition system would use about 135 watts, lighting would need around 90 watts, and the cooling fan (if the bike is liquid cooled) would need another 60 watts—a grand total of 285 watts, or 20 amps. The starter motor alone on a Harley Davidson uses 180 amps or 2,500 watts. Even a 750cc cruiser, or 600cc sport bike starter requires around 1,400 watts or about 100 amps. Because of the high amperage need to power the starter motor, additional hardware needs to be added to connect the battery to the starter—the starter solenoid.

Starter solenoids perform only one function, connecting the battery positive terminal directly to the starter motor. Solenoids can be mounted either directly on the starter case (older BMWs) or more commonly in a remote location. The solenoid allows the starter to be activated by the small start button on the handlebars. All the electrical power from the battery goes to the solenoid and on to the starter. The start button only controls a small control coil inside the solenoid that takes only a few amps to operate.

Starter solenoids are really just overgrown relays that use a small amount of current to energize a coil of wire, producing a magnetic field. The strength of the magnetic field pulls the solenoid's plunger into contact with two terminals—one from battery positive and the other to the starter. Positive engagement starters use a shift fork or lever connected to the solenoid that is mounted directly onto the starter. When the starter receives battery voltage, the solenoid moves the lever, causing the starter to engage the engine's flywheel.

When the start button is pressed, the low-amperage solenoid coil is energized and pushes up a plunger that contacts both high-amperage terminals of the solenoid. This provides a direct connection from battery positive to the starter motor. In general, only two things usually go wrong with a solenoid: The high-amperage contacts become corroded or dirty and not enough amps flow to the starter, or the solenoid coil opens or shorts out and the solenoid won't operate.

STARTER TESTING

Depending on its location, replacing a starter on a motorcycle can either be a 15-minute job or take many hours. Most motorcycle owners reason that if the engine is cranking or turning over slowly, the battery must be at fault and must be either charged or replaced. If that doesn't solve the problem then the starter motor is probably bad and it's replaced as well. If the motorcycle is still having starting issues, the owner has already spent as much as $400 for a new starter and another $100 for a battery. With $500 missing from their wallet or purse, they probably wish that they had actually tested both the battery and starter before spending all that money.

A starter solenoid (left) is just an overgrown relay and its job is to connect the battery directly to the starter when the start button is pressed on the handlebars. The two large copper terminals on top of the solenoid go to the battery's positive cable and the starter motor. One of the smaller wires is ground and the other will eventually end up at the start button. When the start button is pressed, the solenoid's low amperage coil electro-magnetically moves a plunger that connects the two large terminals connecting the battery to the starter and starting the engine. *Courtesy Twigg Cycles*

These starter solenoids are aftermarket replacements from Rick's Motorsport Electric. They cost far less than the same parts purchased from a dealer and are a good choice for economical repairs. *Courtesy Rick's Motorsport Electric*

Bench testing a starter solenoid is easy. Just connect 12 volts to one of the small wires (in the connector) and a ground to the other. The solenoid should sound a "click." As long as power and ground are connected to the small wires, the two large terminals should have continuity as tested with an ohmmeter. *Courtesy Twigg Cycles*

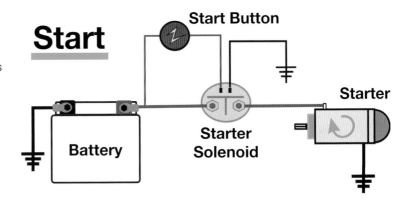

This drawing shows the starter circuit. Battery power is connected to the start button and the starter solenoid. Pressing the start button will activate the solenoid connection between the two large terminals. The handlebar mounted start button can be small because it only has to control a small amount of current—just enough to activate the starter solenoid.

OFF

Start Button

Starter

Starter Solenoid

Battery

Start

Start Button

Starter

Starter Solenoid

Battery

With the start button pressed, the starter solenoid connects the two large terminals (and battery cables)—causing the starter motor to operate. On a motorcycle there are other components that keep the starter motor from operating unless the transmission is in neutral or the clutch lever is pulled in.

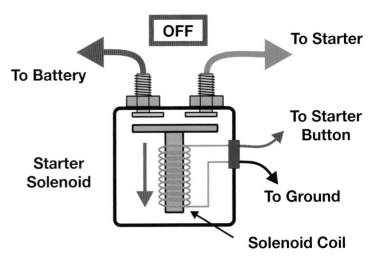

This cutaway shows how the starter solenoid operates. When the starter button is not being pressed the solenoid coil is not energized and the high-amperage contacts are spring-loaded in the downward position.

OFF

To Starter

To Battery

To Starter Button

Starter Solenoid

To Ground

Solenoid Coil

STARTERS

When a motorcycle's engine is not cranking over fast enough to start, this is the list of things that typically go wrong, starting with the most common:

1. Problems with the battery: Don't just charge it—test it to make sure it's not the problem. There's simply no point in trying to figure out which part of the starter circuit is bad if the battery doesn't have enough energy to crank the engine. See Chapter 1 for battery-testing procedures.

2. Loose battery cables. Both the positive and negative cables at the battery terminals should be clean and tight. Also, the connections for the positive cable at the starter solenoid and at the starter motor need to be inspected. Voltage drop testing can check cable connections without taking anything apart. See the sidebar in this section.

3. The starter motor may be the problem. An inductive ammeter can diagnose a fault with the starter. See this chapter for details.

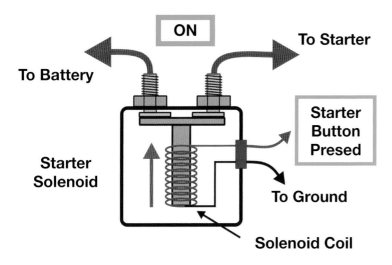

ON

To Starter

To Battery

Starter Solenoid

| Starter Button Presed |

To Ground

Solenoid Coil

When the starter button is pressed the solenoid coil is energized, causing the contact plunger to move upward. This connects the positive cable from the battery directly to the starter motor. While as much as 100 amps are flowing through the starter solenoid, only about 2 amps are required to operate the solenoid coil—easily controlled by the small start button.

This new starter motor has two connections to the motorcycle's electrical system. The large terminal (top) goes to the positive battery cable from the starter solenoid and the other connection is the starter case that is bolted to the engine. This connection goes directly back to the battery negative terminal. *Courtesy Rick's Motorsport Electric*

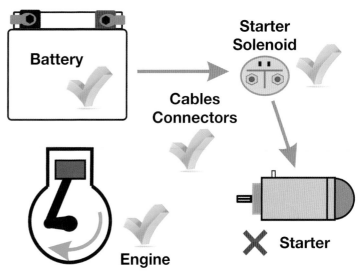

Battery

Cables Connectors

Starter Solenoid

Engine

Starter

Without an ammeter it's difficult to directly test the starter. By eliminating the battery, starter solenoid, cables that connect everything together, and mechanical issues with the engine, the starter is the only reason that the engine won't turn over fast enough to start.

4. A mechanical problem with the engine: If something is causing excessive friction within the engine even a good battery, cables, and starter motor will not turn it over fast enough to start. A partially seized piston or fuel system problem that has leaked gallons of fuel into the engine's crankcase will make the motor difficult, if not impossible to turn over. This is easy to check. Get the back tire off the ground, put the transmission in fourth gear, and try to turn the back tire. If you can't, neither can the starter motor and the engine "friction" issues will have to be fixed.

With starters for motorcycles costing from $200 to more than $500, it's a good idea to make sure that the starter is actually having a problem. Motorcycle starters can be tested in one of two ways: using an inductive ammeter or by the process of elimination. Not everyone has an inductive ammeter so the process of elimination is an economical way to test a starter.

STARTER AMPERAGE DRAW

A few years ago, an inductive ammeter used to be expensive; however, one can now be found on the Internet for around $50. It's a great tool for testing starting and charging systems on motorcycles, cars, and light trucks. Here are the steps for testing a starter motor using an inductive amp probe.

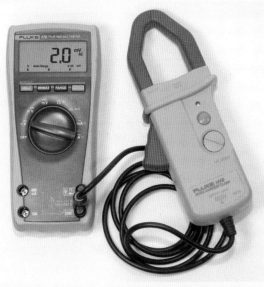

The Fluke i410 AC/DC Current Clamp can be used with any digital multimeter capable of reading in millivolts. This current clamp will measure up to 400 DC amps and is useful for checking starting and charging systems. *Courtesy Fluke Corporation*

1. Connect an inductive ammeter to the positive battery cable. Turn the headlights on, and read the ammeter. If it reads negative, the probe is connected correctly; if it reads positive, turn the amp probe 180 degrees. The meter is now ready to test the starter. Don't forget that the battery has to be fully charged.
2. Disable the ignition system so the engine won't start. The engine needs to crank long enough to use the ammeter to test the starter. On some bikes, where the ignition coil(s) are accessible they can simply be unplugged to prevent an ignition spark. If you can get to the spark plugs remove the spark plug wire(s) and use a jumper wire to ground the plug wire. This will prevent the engine from starting because the spark from the coil will bypass the spark plugs and go directly to ground. Don't just remove the spark plug wires and leave them dangling in the air. The high-energy spark from the coil has to go somewhere and since it can't get to the spark plug it may find its way to ground through the ignition box or module or the ECM on a fuel-injected bike. Some EFI motorcycles have an ignition fuse or ECM fuse that will disable the ignition system without affecting starter motor operation.
3. Press the start button and read the ammeter. Do not operate the starter for more than five seconds. That should be more than enough time for the ammeter to display the current used

by the starter. The meter reading should indicate one of the following: normal starter amperage, slow turning starter, low amperage, and slow turning starter, high amperage.

NORMAL STARTER AMPERAGE DRAW

Before you can recognize abnormal starter amp draw, you need to know what "normal" looks like. Small motorcycle engines between 250 and 500cc should draw between 40 and 80 amps, 600 to 800cc around 80 to 120, and large displacement engines between 1,000 and 2,000cc could be as high as 200 amps. Some service manuals will give you more specific numbers, but these will work most of the time for the purposes of testing. Gear-reduction and permanent magnet type starters yield slightly different results. Be sure to check out service manuals for starter draw specifications for these starters.

SLOW TURNING STARTER, LOW AMPERAGE

A slow-turning starter with a low-amperage draw is the most common result of the starter amperage test. The engine will crank over slowly, or even not at all, because the start circuit has high resistance. High resistance is, by far, the most common reason for low starter circuit amperage. The resistance could be caused by poor battery cable connections or a bad solenoid. Battery connections at the battery, starter solenoid, and starter should be checked. If the connections are not too difficult to get to, just take them apart and clean with a file or sandpaper, reassemble, and run the amperage draw test again. A voltage drop test can be used to tell which connections have the high resistance. See (on page 58) the sidebar in this chapter for starter circuit voltage drop testing. The low amperage can't possibly be a battery problem since the battery has already been tested and charged before the test was run—right?

SLOW TURNING STARTER, HIGH AMPERAGE

If the amp reading is excessively high and the engine is turning slowly, or not at all, there could be a problem with the starter motor or engine.

To eliminate the engine as the reason for a slow-turning starter, place the transmission in fourth or fifth gear and use the rear wheel to turn the engine. Even with spark plugs installed, the engine should rotate with relatively little force. If the engine won't turn by rotating the rear wheel with the bike on its center stand, or pushing it with the transmission in gear (if your bike doesn't have a center stand), there is a mechanical problem with the engine and a bad starter is the least of the problem.

Both high-voltage coil wires from this dual-plug coil have been grounded by connecting them using a jumper wire. This prevents the engine from starting and provides enough time to take an amp meter reading when cranking the starter motor. *Courtesy Iron Mike, Vietnam Vets MC*

An inductive ammeter is clamped around the battery cable going to the starter motor on this Moto Guzzi. With the ignition disabled and the starter cranking, amperage can be measured. The most common problem is low amperage and is usually due to poor connections at the starter or battery. *Courtesy Bob's BMW*

Engine mechanical problems could include high-viscosity oil in cold weather (colder than 20 degrees F), carbon buildup in the cylinders, crankcase could be full of fuel from a leaking petcock, or the engine was run with low or no oil and the crankshaft has welded itself to the connecting rods or has overheated, causing other mechanical problems.

If the engine can be rotated easily the starter motor has a problem and should be replaced. The presence of high amperage flowing into the starter circuit indicates a "shorted" starter armature or field coil and not an engine problem. The high amperage also indicates that the battery cable connections and battery are good.

STARTER CIRCUIT VOLTAGE DROP TESTING

Cleaning or tightening a bad connection is often all that is required to get the starter to spin faster. The poor connection is caused by high resistance somewhere in the starter circuit. The point of high resistance could be on either the positive or negative sides of the starter circuit so both need to be tested. Performing a voltage drop test is generally easier than cleaning all the connections, especially the ones that are hard to get to. With starter motors costing upward of $400, it's worth the time to eliminate a bad connection before wrongly blaming the starter for hard or no starter operation. Here are the steps for performing a voltage drop test on the starter circuit.

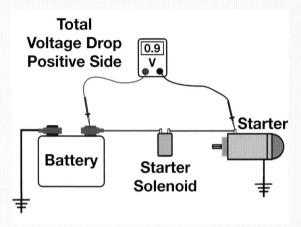

1. The positive side of the starter circuit should be tested first, as it is the most likely place to find a problem. Connect the red lead of a voltmeter to the positive battery terminal (not the battery cable). Connect the black meter lead to the starter terminal, where the battery cable is attached to the starter. Crank the engine while watching the voltmeter. If the total voltage drop is less than 0.5 volts (less than 0.2 for smaller engine sizes), the positive side of the starter circuit doesn't have high resistance and is not the problem. If voltage is higher perform Steps 2 and 3.

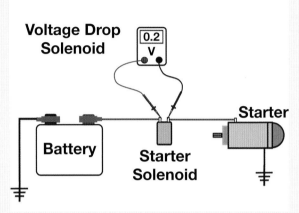

The next most likely place for high resistance is the starter solenoid. Connect the meter leads as shown and crank the engine. Voltage drop should not be more than 0.2 (two-tenths) of a volt. If voltage is higher, the high-amperage contacts within the starter solenoid are dirty or worn out. Some solenoids can be dissembled for cleaning but not all of them.

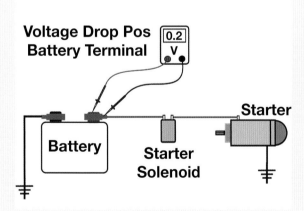

If the starter solenoid is okay, then the dirty connection may be the positive battery cable's connection to the battery terminal. Connect the voltmeter as shown and crank the starter. Voltage should not be higher than 0.2, indicating that the connection is clean and tight. If voltage is higher, clean the cable to battery terminal connection and retest.

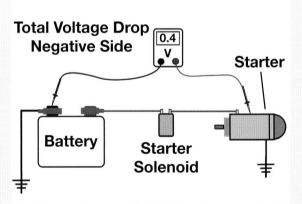

The voltage drop on the negative side of the starter circuit should be tested last. Usually high resistance would be caused by a loose or dirty connection at the negative battery terminal. The drawing shows the voltage drop across the entire negative side of the circuit. If voltage is less than 0.4, then the negative side is not the problem.

Chapter 4
Ignition Systems

Ignition-related problems, whether real or only perceived, are the cause of more needless parts replacement than on any other motorcycle electrical system. In the past, ignition malfunctions were often fixed by simple replacement of points, condenser, ignition coils, wires, and spark plugs. In early 1970, that repair method changed with the introduction of electronic-ignition systems. These parts were far more costly to replace as a method of diagnosis in the hope of fixing ignition-related problems.

Today ignitions systems used on motorcycles are all solid-state with no moving parts and can come in the form of a dedicated ignition system only or as part of a motorcycle's electronic engine-management (fuel-injection) system. Consequently, it's much more cost-effective to test ignition components before simply throwing them in the trash and replacing them with new parts that can cost hundreds of dollars. Modern ignition systems are not as difficult to diagnose as you might think,

This single plug coil is for an off-road motorcycle that doesn't use a battery. A magneto powers the capacitive discharge ignition (CDI) box and the ignition coil. *Courtesy Rick's Motorsport Electric*

Old and new ignition coils from BMW motorcycles. The conventional coil (left) can only produce about 20,000 volts at the spark plug, which may seem like a lot, but it's not enough to be compatible with a modern fuel-injected motorcycle. By contrast, the late-model coil-over-plug (right) weighs about one quarter the weight of the conventional coil and can put out more than 60,000 volts. The design also eliminates spark plug wires as the coil is connected directly to the spark plug. *Courtesy Bob's BMW*

High Output Single Fire Coil from Daytona Twin Tec produces more voltage than the stock Harley-Davidson coil. This coil (part number 2005) will work with most aftermarket or stock single-fire ignition systems. *Courtesy Daytona Twin Tec LLC*

This ignition coil fits all Harley-Davidson Twin-Cam 2001–2006 models with Delphi electronic fuel-injection systems. The fuel-injection computer in these motorcycles also controls the ignition system. *Courtesy Daytona Twin Tec LLC*

ignition systems and to as much as 60,000 volts in electronic systems. These high voltages are required to bridge the air gap on the spark plugs. With today's high-compression engines and lean fuel mixtures, it takes a great deal of electrical energy to overcome the spark plug air gap.

Both conventional and electronic-ignition systems have two circuits: primary and secondary. The primary circuit is the first step in the process causing voltage to step up or increase in the ignition system. Charging system voltage is around 14 volts and the primary circuit increases this to more than 300 volts. The primary ignition circuit is made up of half of the ignition coil, points, and a condenser (in older motorcycles), or an electronic-ignition module or computer (in newer bikes). The secondary circuit raises voltage a step further to as much as 60,000 volts. The secondary circuit consists of the other half of the ignition coil, plug wires, and spark plugs. Thus, every ignition coil contains both primary and secondary circuits and operates in a similar manner on both points-type and electronic-ignition systems.

as there are a great number of similarities between old-style, conventional points-type ignition systems and electronic ignition. A basic understanding of how primary and secondary ignition circuits operate goes a long way toward figuring out if you have a bad pickup coil, Hall-effect switch, or electronic-ignition module. We'll start out by taking a look back at conventional ignition systems, which haven't changed much in the past 100 years.

HOW TO GET FROM 12 VOLTS TO 100,000 VOLTS

An ignition system has two jobs: spark production and spark distribution. Spark distribution consists of several designs of ignition coils that provide a spark to single or pairs of spark plugs. Spark production on both points-type and electronic systems is basically the same; the only difference is the manner in which the ignition coils are controlled. Ignition coils on both types of systems operate in the same manner by simply "stepping-up" electrical voltage within the systems from 14.5 volts (charging voltage) to 20,000 volts in points-type

High Output Twin-Cam Coil works with most 1999 and later carbureted Twin-Cam 88 Harley-Davidson ignition systems. *Courtesy Daytona Twin Tec LLC*

IGNITION COILS

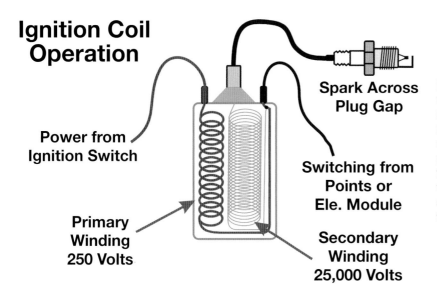

Ignition Coil Operation

Spark Across Plug Gap

Power from Ignition Switch

Switching from Points or Ele. Module

Primary Winding 250 Volts

Secondary Winding 25,000 Volts

In this conventional ignition coil the primary windings actually surround the secondary windings (the drawing separates the two in order to illustrate how they're internally connected). An ignition module, computer, or points switch the coil's ground circuit on and off. Each time the coil is turned off, the secondary windings produce high voltage that travels along the plug wire, to the spark plug, across the plug's air gap, and back to ground.

This conventional ignition coil is used by a Kawasaki GPZ. The red wire (left of coil) is powered from the ignition switch. The green wire is from the electronic module and switches the coil on and off, creating a spark. The secondary spark plug wire can be seen exiting the coil at right. *Courtesy Twigg Cycles*

CONVENTIONAL IGNITION COILS

There are two basic designs of ignition coils: conventional coils that fire a single spark plug and dual spark plug coils. Both types produce a spark but have different circuit designs. Conventional coils can be used on a single-cylinder engine or sometimes on multi-cylinders with one coil per cylinder. Some late-model bikes use coil-over-plug systems that have individual coils for each cylinder and don't have spark plug wires. Conventional coils have three terminals: a power source for the primary circuit, a ground for the primary circuit, and a high-voltage terminal connected to the spark plug via a high-voltage plug wire. Power for the primary circuit is supplied from the ignition switch. A set of mechanical points, on older motorcycles, or an ignition module or computer on later models controls the coil's primary circuit by switching the ground side of the circuit on and off. When the primary circuit is switched off, a spark will be produced in the secondary coil winding inside the coil.

The coil's primary circuit is connected internally to the secondary circuit at the negative coil terminal. Power for the secondary circuit comes from the primary circuit's collapsing magnetic field, which produces about 300 to 500 volts. Voltage is stepped up to thousands of volts in the secondary circuit, causing current to pass through the high voltage tower in the center of the coil, then onto the spark plug, across the plug's air gap, and then return to battery ground.

DUAL SPARK PLUG IGNITION COIL

The two high-voltage terminals on a dual-plug coil are connected to two spark plugs and they are fired in pairs. Two cylinder engines like Harley-Davidson use one coil, and four cylinder engine use two coils. The primary circuit is powered and controlled in the same manner as on a conventional coil, but the major difference between the two types is that the secondary windings are not connected to the primary circuit inside a dual-plug coil.

The dual coil fires the spark plugs in two cylinders simultaneously. One cylinder is on its compression stroke and the spark ignites the air/fuel mixture. The other "companion" cylinder is at the end of its exhaust stroke and the second spark has no effect because there is nothing to burn inside the combustion chamber.

There is no internal connection between the primary and secondary windings on a dual spark plug coil. The high-voltage path starts at one end of the secondary windings, onto plug number 1, through the cylinder head and plug number 2, and back to the other end of the coil's secondary winding.

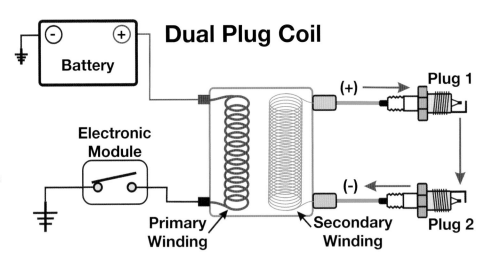

The dual coil (left) fires two spark plugs simultaneously, but only one of the spark plugs is used to ignite air and fuel. The other spark doesn't do anything, as it is "wasted" on the cylinder with no fuel mixture. Hence, the name "waste spark ignition." The coil at right fires a single spark plug. *Courtesy Bob's BMW*

Dual spark plug ignition coils, like the one used on this 1969 Harley-Davidson FL Shovelhead, are common even today. These types of ignition systems were introduced in the mid-1980s for use on automobiles, and they were confusing to many technicians who were used to working with only a single-ignition coil and distributor. *Courtesy Iron Mike, Vietnam Vets MC*

The cylinder that is on its compression stroke has high resistance across the plug's air gap and most of the coil's energy goes to that spark plug. The companion cylinder is on the exhaust stroke and because the exhaust valve is open there is no compression in that cylinder. Without the high-pressure air surrounding the air gap it takes relatively little voltage to overcome its resistance.

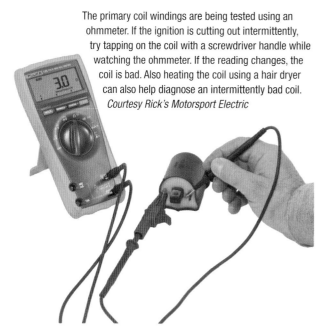

This dual-style coil from a 1955 BMW/2 uses screw-type terminals for connection to the spark plug wires. Dual coils found on a Harley-Davidson motorcycle are similar and have been used for more than a few years. *Courtesy Bob's BMW*

Because one of the two cylinders gets a spark that is not used for ignition, dual-coil ignition is sometimes called "waste spark ignition."

OHMS TESTING

Because both dual- and single-ignition coils are just varying length of wire, a simple ohmmeter test can often determine if a coil is bad. The ohmmeter test is not 100 percent conclusive, as a coil could pass the test but still not be able to produce a spark, and other methods of testing should be used. Both dual- and single-types of coils can be checked for opens or shorts using an ohmmeter. To check resistance on a conventional coil, connect one ohmmeter lead to the negative side of the coil and the other to the positive. Primary resistance should read between 1.5 to 3.5 ohms. Resistance in the secondary circuit can be measured by connecting one ohmmeter lead to the negative coil terminal and the other to the high-voltage tower. Resistance should be between 7,000 to 25,000 ohms.

Testing a dual-plug coil is a little different because the primary and secondary windings are not connected. Primary resistance should measure between 0.5 to 3.0 ohms, while secondary resistance should be from 5,000 to 10,000 ohms. A service manual will provide specific resistance values, but the numbers provided here are close enough to determine if there is a problem

GENERIC COIL TESTING

The primary coil windings are being tested using an ohmmeter. If the ignition is cutting out intermittently, try tapping on the coil with a screwdriver handle while watching the ohmmeter. If the reading changes, the coil is bad. Also heating the coil using a hair dryer can also help diagnose an intermittently bad coil. *Courtesy Rick's Motorsport Electric*

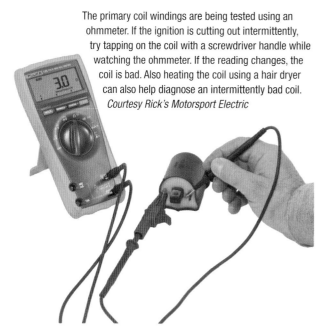

Using an ohmmeter to check secondary coil resistance: This reading is 5,600 ohms, which is typical for this type of coil.

Coil Primary Ohms Testing

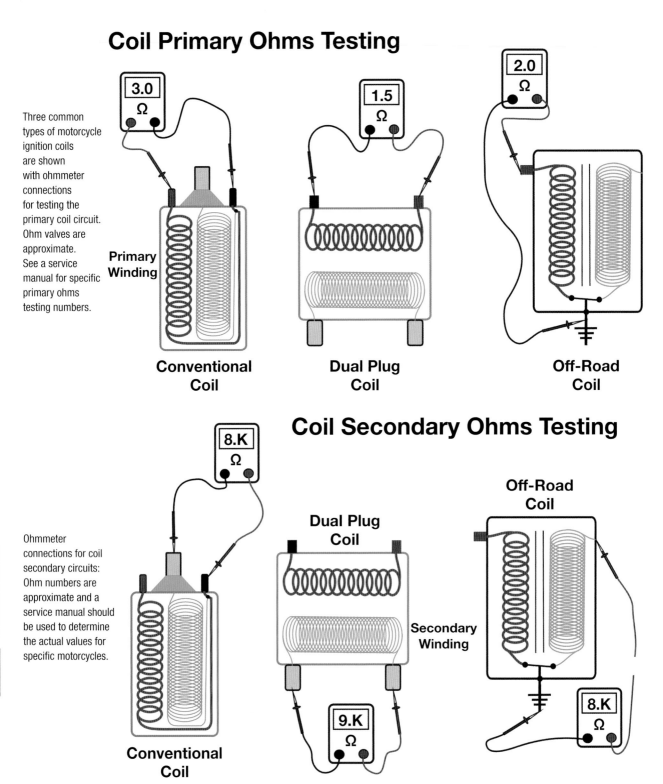

Three common types of motorcycle ignition coils are shown with ohmmeter connections for testing the primary coil circuit. Ohm valves are approximate. See a service manual for specific primary ohms testing numbers.

3.0 Ω

Primary Winding

Conventional Coil

1.5 Ω

Dual Plug Coil

2.0 Ω

Off-Road Coil

Coil Secondary Ohms Testing

8.K Ω

Ohmmeter connections for coil secondary circuits: Ohm numbers are approximate and a service manual should be used to determine the actual values for specific motorcycles.

Conventional Coil

Dual Plug Coil

9.K Ω

Off-Road Coil

Secondary Winding

8.K Ω

with the coil's windings. If the coil passes the initial ohmmeter test, but still causes a misfire with the engine running, another test can be used to diagnose the problem. With the ohmmeter connected to the coil's primary or secondary windings, try tapping on the coil with a screwdriver handle or heat it using a hair dryer. If the ohmmeter's readings change while doing this, the coil windings are broken and it needs to be replaced.

DYNAMIC COIL TESTING

Testing an ignition coil can be problematic. If you use an ohmmeter and measure the coil's primary and secondary winding resistance and they check out okay, does it mean the coil is okay? Not necessarily. Sometimes an ignition coil with internal resistance that meets specifications won't produce a spark when connected to the vehicle's ignition system. A better way to test a coil to determine if it can produce a spark is by using a universal coil tester. A universal ignition coil tester can be simply made using a condenser and some jumper wires. A coil tester basically functions like a set of ignition points and can be used to fire any type of ignition coil. This dynamic test is a more effective tool for discovering a bad coil winding that may break down when under an electrical load.

Automotive condensers can be purchased at most auto parts stores. To use the tester, disconnect the negative side of the coil. Connect the condenser wire to the negative coil terminal and ground the condenser's mount tab using a jumper wire. Connect a second jumper wire to ground and turn the ignition on. Now tap the grounded jumper wire to the negative side of the coil. It should produce a spark between the high-voltage terminal and ground on a conventional coil, or between high-voltage terminals on a dual-plug coil. If there is no spark, check for battery voltage at the coil and good connections on all jumper wires. Be careful doing this on a dual-plug or stick-type coil. The spark produced can really "zap" you if you get your hands or fingers in the way.

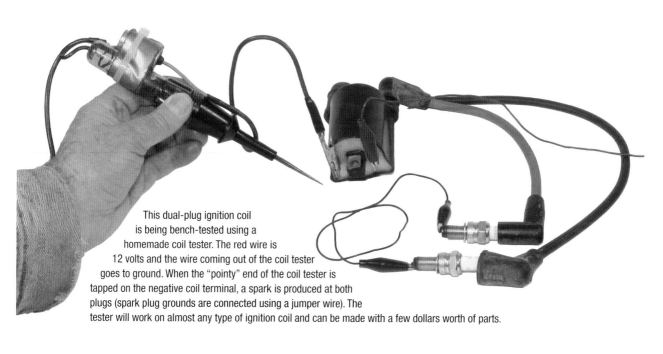

This dual-plug ignition coil is being bench-tested using a homemade coil tester. The red wire is 12 volts and the wire coming out of the coil tester goes to ground. When the "pointy" end of the coil tester is tapped on the negative coil terminal, a spark is produced at both plugs (spark plug grounds are connected using a jumper wire). The tester will work on almost any type of ignition coil and can be made with a few dollars worth of parts.

An automotive condenser and some jumper wires can make an effective coil tester. It can dynamically test almost any type of ignition coil, causing it to produce a high-voltage spark during the test. The test light is only used as a way to hold the condenser and wires together; the test light bulb has been removed.

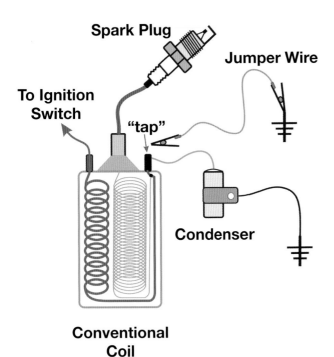

Spark Plug

Jumper Wire

To Ignition Switch

"tap"

Condenser

Conventional Coil

Using an automotive condenser and a jumper wire is a great way to dynamically test a conventional ignition coil. When the clip on the jumper wire is tapped to the negative side of the coil, a spark should be produced at the spark plug. Make sure the ignition and kill switch are both on for the tap test.

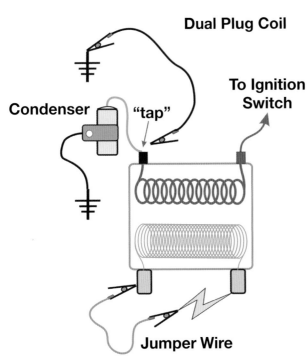

Dual Plug Coil

Condenser   "tap"

To Ignition Switch

Jumper Wire

Here are the connections for the coil tester when testing a dual-plug ignition coil. The spark will jump between the end of the jumper wire (alligator clip) and the secondary terminal on the coil. Keep fingers out of the way as these types of coils can produce enough spark to really zap you.

Motorcycles that use points and condenser and some early electronic ignitions use a mechanical system to provide ignition timing advance. These units consist of weights and springs that rotate along with the crank or camshaft. As rotational speed increases, the weights are thrown to the outside by centrifugal force and a cam advances the ignition timing by moving the breaker points or speed pick up. Solid-state electronics have replaced these troublesome mechanisms and calculate ignition advance using engine rpm and, on some models, throttle position. *Courtesy Bob's BMW*

Contact points (red circle) have been in used for nearly 80 years in motorcycles. These simple mechanical switches are subject to wear and had to be adjusted every 3,000 miles or so. The condenser (yellow circle) keeps the points from arcing during operation. Motorcycles fitted with points ignition systems were hard to start when cold or sometimes impossible when it rained. *Courtesy Bob's BMW*

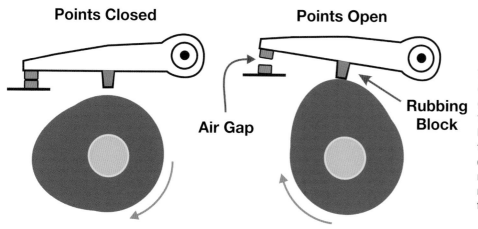

Points Closed   **Points Open**

Air Gap

Rubbing Block

The rubbing block wears as the engine is running. This causes the air gap to become smaller over several thousand miles. Points are adjusted by changing the air gap between the contacts when the points are open. This distance varies among manufacturers and model years of motorcycles. See a service manual for the correct adjustment.

Ignition cam mounted to end of camshaft

CONTROLLING THE IGNITION SYSTEM— IGNITION POINTS

Mechanical means of coil switching have been used for more than 80 years on motorcycles. They are simple to diagnose and repair but do not provide consistent or reliable performance and are not used on modern motorcycles. The contact or ignition points are a mechanical switch that control conventional ignition systems. When the points are closed, ground is supplied to the coil's primary circuit, causing the coil to charge. When the points are open, the primary circuit loses its ground and the magnetic field inside the coil collapses, causing the secondary windings to produce a spark. The points open and close according to engine rpm and are timed via a cam on the end of the camshaft. Ignition points wear out in normal use and must be adjusted periodically, usually about every 3,000 miles.

All points-type ignition systems use a condenser as part of the primary circuit. The condenser (or capacitor) is connected across the points and reduces arcing between the contact points as they open and close. Without the condenser, an electric arc would occur at the points instead of at the spark plugs, causing the points to quickly burn out.

CONTROLLING THE IGNITION SYSTEM— ELECTRONIC IGNITION

In the 1980s, automotive manufacturers were forced to modernize fuel and ignition systems to meet stricter exhaust emissions. The motorcycle industry, while not subject to these early clean air standards,

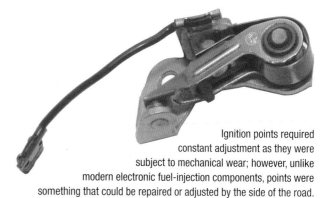

Ignition points required constant adjustment as they were subject to mechanical wear; however, unlike modern electronic fuel-injection components, points were something that could be repaired or adjusted by the side of the road.

did follow to some extent by providing more reliable solid-state ignition system designs. It is often said that before the 1980s, if you wanted to own a motorcycle, you had better be able (and willing) to repair it yourself. The introduction of solid-state electronics—including ignition, charging, and eventually fuel injection—would provide a machine that mechanically challenged riders could own and not have to pick up a wrench (or voltmeter) to keep on the road.

Contact point-type ignition systems on motorcycles usually had to be adjusted every 3,000 miles or sooner. If a condenser went bad, the points would promptly burn out, leaving rider and motorcycle by the side of the road. Many owners carried an extra set of points in a jacket pocket along with the spare spark plugs and master-link for the drive chain. By contrast, electronic-ignition systems contain no moving parts, are quite

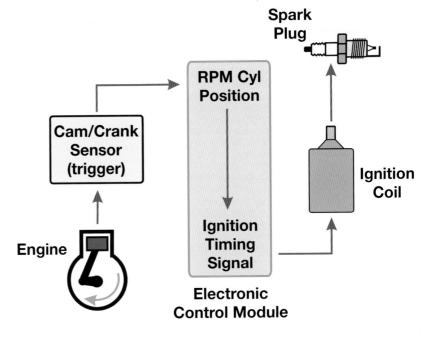

Spark Plug

RPM Cyl Position

Cam/Crank Sensor (trigger)

Ignition Coil

Engine

Ignition Timing Signal

Electronic Control Module

Motorcycles with electronic ignition, or fuel injection, control the ignition system in a similar manner to conventional type systems. As the engine rotates, cam and crank sensors register engine rpm and cylinder position. These signals are sent to the engine-management system that converts them into the ignition timing data. Timing information is used to switch the ignition coil on and off and the coil fires the spark plug.

This ThunderMax fuel-injection computer is a complete replacement for the stock Harley-Davidson engine-management system. The ThunderMax controls both fuel-injection and ignition systems and both are adjustable by the user. Aftermarket products like ThunderMax allow the installation of all manner of custom engine parts—camshafts, exhaust systems, performance air filters, and more. Without the limitation of the stock engine-management system, the fuel-injection and ignition mapping can be matched to the performance parts installed on the engine. *Courtesy Zippers Performance Products*

reliable, and consequently don't wear out before the engine and motorcycle does. The only ignition related maintenance items are spark plugs and on some bikes, ignition wires. In fact, maintenance intervals on late model coil-over-plug systems (with no spark-plug wires) are often as high as 16,000 miles, and the maintenance usually amounts to nothing more than spark-plug changes. As more manufacturers continue to expand their use of electronic fuel injection, the stand-alone electronic-ignition systems are going by the wayside as they are replaced with onboard computer-controlled EFI ignition systems. Both stand-alone and computer-controlled ignitions systems operate in a similar manner.

Both street and some off-road motorcycles today have an ignition module or engine-management systems that are quite sophisticated. Information about engine rpm, cylinder identification, and crankshaft position and throttle position are sent to the module or ECM (engine control module), where the ideal ignition timing is calculated. Some EFI systems use additional sensor information to calculate timing, including engine and intake air temperature, engine load, knock or ping, barometric pressure, and transmission gear selection. The onboard computer crunches the numbers from the various digital inputs and sends a modified timing signal to the module, which then fires the ignition coils. These systems still require a trigger signal for ignition coil switching, and points have been replaced with several trigger designs, and that's where we'll start our discussion of electronic-ignition systems.

ELECTRONIC IGNITION TRIGGERS

Both electronic and computer-controlled ignitions use a transistor to switch current to the ignition coil instead of a mechanical set of points. The transistor requires a signal, or trigger, in order to determine when to switch the ignition coil on and off. There are only three types of triggers currently in use in motorcycles: an AC pickup coil, a Hall-effect switch, and an optical sensor. Whatever trigger is used is mounted to the engine's crank, camshaft, or sometimes both, where it produces a signal indicating engine speed. This signal is sent to the ignition module. In addition, some triggers are capable of providing crankshaft or camshaft position and cylinder identification as well. Because these components are part of a motorcycle's engine-management system, they are expensive to replace. Motorcycle dealers won't let owners return electronic parts, so swapping them out to diagnose an ignition problem can be expensive. For this reason, it's better to test them before replacement. Following is an explanation of how each of the triggers can be tested.

This Daytona Twin Tec TC88A ignition module uses four rotary switches to set the ignition advance characteristics and engine rpm limit. Harley-Davidson Twin Cam engines use a nonadjustable crankshaft position sensor, and mechanical timing adjustments are no longer possible. The TC88A solves this problem with a switch for setting the initial timing. A second switch sets the slope of the advance curve. The combination of these two switches allows the user to optimize the timing advance for a wide range of applications from stock to highly modified engines. *Courtesy Daytona Twin Tec LLC*

AC PICKUP COIL

By far the most common trigger used on motorcycles is the AC pickup coil. Whenever a wiring diagram shows an engine "speed sensor" with only two wires coming going to it, it's an AC pickup coil. AC pickup coils operate in the same manner as an alternator to produce AC voltage. A rotating magnet passes across the pickup coil and produces an AC voltage pulse. As engine speed increases, the number of pulses per second increase as well. The ignition module or computer counts the number or frequency of the pulses and based on this information, calculates engine rpm, and in some cases, crank or camshaft position. In addition to the increase

This is a typical AC pickup coil that can be located next to the crank or camshaft. Each time a magnet, embedded in the crankshaft or camshaft, passes the pickup coil, an AC voltage pulse or signal is generated and sent to the ignition module where engine rpm is calculated. AC pickup coils are common on many motorcycles and are usually reliable and require no maintenance. *Courtesy Twigg Cycle*

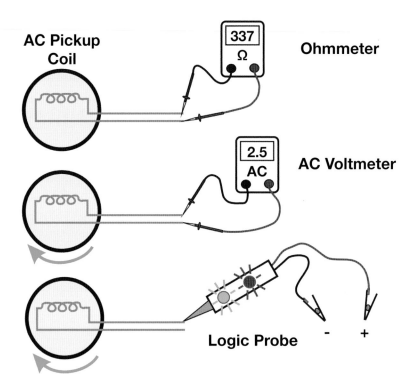

AC Pickup Coil

337 Ω Ohmmeter

2.5 AC AC Voltmeter

Logic Probe

− +

Here are three methods for testing an AC pickup coil speed sensor. The sensor is unplugged for all tests. An ohmmeter can be used to measure the coil's resistance. See a service manual for the correct ohms values. With the engine cranking, an AC voltmeter can be used to determine if the pickup coil is working. Voltage should be between .5 and 3 volts AC. A logic probe will detect an electronic pulse from an operating pickup coil. Most logic probes will flash LED or even "beep" when detecting a pulse.

in pulses per second as engine rpm increases, AC voltage output from the pickup coil also increases. The increase in AC voltage is ignored by the computer or module, but is a good way to verify whether an AC pickup coil is working or not.

AC pickup coils can be tested using a voltmeter, ohmmeter, or logic probe. To test one using a voltmeter, disconnect the AC pickup coil and connect the meter leads to the pickup wiring harness. Set the voltmeter to read AC voltage and crank the engine. As the engine turns, AC voltage should be produced, generally between 0.5 and 3 volts AC. A logic probe can also be used to test a pickup coil just as easily and effectively. Connect the logic probe to the vehicle's battery. Leave the AC pickup coil connected and back probe one of the two wires coming from the pickup coil with the logic probe. Crank the engine and watch for a pulse on the LED display of the logic probe. If no AC voltage is present, or if the logic probe doesn't show a pulse, you can always check a pickup coil's resistance using an ohmmeter. Resistance will vary depending on the manufacturer of the pickup coil, but a resistance reading somewhere in the 150 to 1,200 ohm range is generally okay. Also, always check for broken wires leading to the pickup coil, metal filings between the coil and magnet, a loose coil, or too large an air gap between

the coil and magnet. The service manual for your bike will provide you with the air gap measurement if applicable and pickup coil resistance.

HALL-EFFECT SWITCH

The Hall-effect switch, or sensor, consists of a sensor, magnet, rotating shutter blade, and three-wire connector (the latter will distinguish it from an AC pickup coil or other speed sensor on a wiring diagram). The three-wire connector has power, ground, and signal wire that goes to the computer or ignition module.

Hall-effect switches are powered by a "reference voltage" that is sent by the computer or module. Each Hall-effect switch is equipped with a magnet situated opposite the switch; between them is a series of rotating shutters or blades, one for each cylinder. As the blades rotate between the sensor and magnet, the magnet's magnetic field is interrupted and voltage at the sensor drops. The output signal from the Hall-effect switch is a square wave or series of "ON and OFF" pulses. These pulses are sent to the vehicle's computer or ignition module, which then uses them to calculate engine rpm and crankshaft position.

To test a Hall-effect switch, turn the ignition ON and back probe each of its three wires with a voltmeter. A process of elimination will help you identify what each wire is used for. The voltmeter display should indicate one wire is "reference voltage." It should have between 2.5 to 12 volts, depending on year, make, and model of the motorcycle being tested. If a wiring diagram is being used to identify the signal wire, locate all the wires going from the switch to the ECM. The more marked "REF" is the signal wire, though not all manufacturers use this identifier. Another wire is the ground wire and has no voltage. The third wire is a signal output wire from the Hall-effect switch, and it will show either "reference voltage" or something less than "reference voltage" depending upon whether or not a shutter blade has stopped rotating between the Hall-effect switch and magnet. Turn the engine over by hand and watch the signal wire. If the Hall switch is working, voltage will switch from "reference voltage" to a lower voltage (sometimes "0" volts) and back. If a signal is not present, try the other wire that had voltage on it, since you just might have been reading the "reference" wire by mistake.

Dual Hall-effect sensors from a BMW use a rotating metal disk with shutter blades that pass between the Hall sensor and permanent magnets. As the magnetic field is broken by the shutter blades, a square wave (on-and-off voltage signal) is generated and sent to the motorcycle's ignition computer to trigger the ignition coil. Hall-effect switches are very reliable and don't require any maintenance. *Courtesy Bob's BMW*

This logic probe can detect signals from AC pickup coils and Hall-effect switches. It can also sense a fuel-injector pulse from the vehicle's electronic control module (ECM). A search on the Internet for "logic probe" will locate numerous sources for this inexpensive but versatile tool (less than $20).

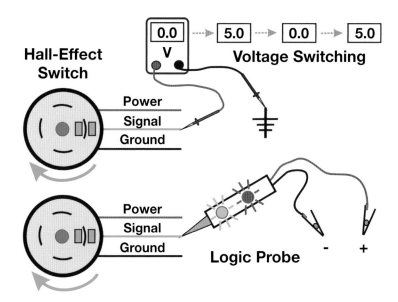

The Hall-effect switch should be plugged in for all testing. There are two methods for testing: digital voltmeter or a logic probe. Determine the signal wire from the Hall-effect switch using a wiring diagram or by process of elimination. With a voltmeter connected to the signal wire, turn the engine over by hand. The voltmeter reading should switch from low voltage to high. In this example, the voltage switches from 0 volts to 5 volts. Check a service manual for specific voltage values. The other test method is a logic probe that will detect a pulse on the signal wire as the engine is turning.

In addition to testing a Hall-effect switch with a voltmeter, a logic probe can also be used. Connect the logic probe's leads to the vehicle's battery: red lead to positive and black to negative. Leave the Hall-effect switch connected and back probe the signal wire. Crank the engine using the starter and watch the LEDs on the logic probe. They should indicate a pulse by flashing. Most logic probes use red and green LEDs—red for positive and green for negative. If the logic probe does not flash, check to make sure there are both power ("reference voltage") and ground sources to the Hall-effect switch, as well as for broken wires or loose connections. If the power and ground wires are good, the Hall-effect switch is bad and should be replaced. A logic probe can also be used to test AC pickup coils and optical sensors.

OPTICAL SENSORS

Optical sensors typically consists of an LED, a phototransistor, and a rotating metal or plastic disk. These sensors provide trigger signals for ignition switching that are similar to those produced by Hall-effect switches. When in use, a beam of light from the LED is projected through the holes in the disk onto the phototransistor. As the disk rotates, the spaces between the holes interrupt the light beam. Each time the light beam is interrupted a pulse is generated by the sensor's processor (computer). Some optical sensors are really two sensors in one: One measures crankshaft angle (position); the other measures camshaft position and identifies which cylinder is the number one cylinder in the engine's firing order.

The Daytona Twin Tec VT-I system is a dual-fire electronic-ignition system for most Harley-Davidson V-twin engines up to 1999. The VT-I uses a trigger rotor in conjunction with the stock mechanical advance mechanism. A Hall-effect sensor detects the teeth on this special trigger rotor and provides a spark timing signal. A rotary switch is used for a precise digitally set rpm limiter (200 rpm steps from 5,200 to 7,000 rpm) and a red status LED allows easy static timing. *Courtesy Daytona Twin Tec LLC*

Another form of logic probe comes in the form of a test light that uses LEDs to indicate the presence of an electronic pulse. Search "logic probe test light" on the Internet. Make sure that the logic probe test light has both red and black alligator clips. If the light has only a single alligator clip, it is a plain test light and does not have the logic probe function.

A logic probe is the best way to test an optical sensor. With the logic probe connected to the battery, back probe each signal wire and crank the engine. There should be a pulse on each wire. If there is no pulse, check for oil or dirt blocking the holes on the metal plate and make sure the sensor has both power and ground. See a service manual for specific procedures on checking optical triggers.

This Newtronic optical ignition kit is a good way for older motorcycles to use modern electronics. Pictured are two optical sensors and a sensor plate. As the plate rotates it breaks a beam of light and triggers the ignition module. These kits are available for a whole range of older bikes from Motorcycle-Ignition.com of Tasmania, Australia. Owner Shayn Harkness sent in this picture of his 1973 Suzuki T500K, a 500cc two-stroke twin cylinder—a wild ride to be sure. *Courtesy Motorcycle-Ignition.com*

Pictured is the Spyke Acculight Ignition System. It uses an optical trigger with phototransistor and LEDs (left) and a slotted disc that rotates with the crankshaft. This unit has four preset ignition advance curves, as well as programmable ignition advance. It also features a triple-spark ignition that fires the spark up to three times on the engine's compression stroke and can be set to dual- or single-fire modes. *Courtesy MCAdvantages*

Ignition Trigger Wave Forms

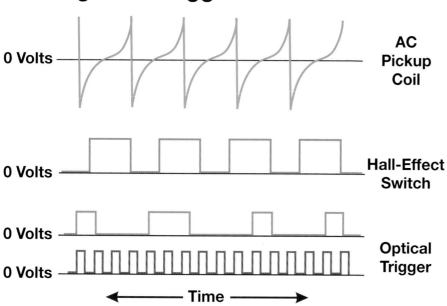

0 Volts — **AC Pickup Coil**

0 Volts — **Hall-Effect Switch**

0 Volts —

0 Volts — **Optical Trigger**

← **Time** →

This drawing shows what each of the three trigger signals look like on an oscilloscope. An oscilloscope is just a voltmeter with pictures. An AC pickup coil's wave form shows AC voltage transitioning between negative and positive as the sensor is rotated. Both the Hall-effect switch and optical sensor produce a square wave. The optical sensor has two signals, one for cylinder identification (upper wave form) and one for engine rpm (lower wave form).

IGNITION MODULES

In its most simplistic form, an electronic-ignition module is simply a modern replacement for a set of points. Points receive engine rotational speed information by direct mechanical means as a cam pushes them open and closed. An ignition module performs the exact same function, but it uses a trigger signal.

While ignition modules may look different, they all perform the same function: switching the coil on and off. All ignition modules require power, ground, and a trigger signal (engine rpm) to function. Some newer modules also receive throttle position and engine temperature inputs as well. *Courtesy Twigg Cycles*

Once a trigger signal (or wave form) is produced by the engine's speed sensor, the ignition module processes it and then fires the coil with an internal transistor. Later model vehicles use onboard computers instead of an ignition module to control coil switching. Either way, the basic operation of an ignition module is equivalent to a set of points.

GENERIC IGNITION MODULE TESTING

When facing a "no-spark" problem, pull the high-voltage wire off of a spark plug and insert a pocket screwdriver into the plug boot. Hold the metal shank of the screwdriver near ground. Crank the engine and watch for a spark to jump between the screwdriver and ground. If there is no spark, checking primary ignition switching is next.

When electronic ignitions were first introduced, and even today with modern electronic fuel-injected motorcycles, many technicians have trouble diagnosing "no-spark" problems. Without any moving parts to check, it was visually impossible to determine if primary coil switching is occurring. Fortunately, even though one can't see a transistor operating, there is a way to see the results of primary ignition switching. The first step in the process of determining if an ignition module is operational is a testing procedure originally used on points-type ignition systems—"looping" a test light across the ignition coil and cranking over the engine. Here's how: Connect the alligator clip of the test light

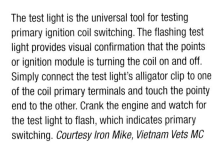

The test light is the universal tool for testing primary ignition coil switching. The flashing test light provides visual confirmation that the points or ignition module is turning the coil on and off. Simply connect the test light's alligator clip to one of the coil primary terminals and touch the pointy end to the other. Crank the engine and watch for the test light to flash, which indicates primary switching. *Courtesy Iron Mike, Vietnam Vets MC*

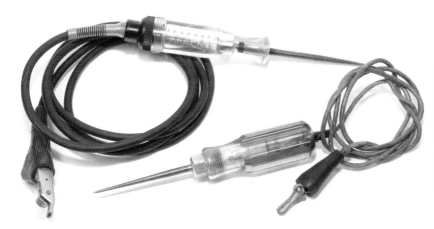

These are $25 and $5 test lights. In addition to using heavier gauge wire, a quality, $25 test light (upper left) has a strain relief (metal spring or rubber) shield located where the wire exits the test light's body. This guard prevents the wire from breaking, even after years of use. The $5 version will work as well for testing, but the metal tip is not hardened like the more expensive test light and will have to be sharpened a lot.

to the negative side of the coil and touch the test light's probe to the positive coil terminal. With the test light "looped" across the coil, crank the engine over. The test light should flash or flicker if primary switching is taking place.

A flashing or flickering test light provides the following information: (1) the ignition module is switching the coil ON and OFF, (2) the trigger is sending a signal to the module, and (3) the ignition coil has power. This test works regardless of the type of ignition box, module, or engine computer management system used. If the test light doesn't flash because no primary switching is occurring, however, the ignition module should be checked for power, ground, and trigger input. Because each year, make, and model of motorcycle is different, a wiring diagram should be consulted to determine module inputs and outputs and wire colors. Powers and grounds can be checked using a digital voltmeter. Make sure ground voltage is close to 0 volts and the power wires have battery voltage. Check for power and grounds with the ignition switch ON. Then be sure to recheck them with the engine cranking (especially the grounds), since some ground voltages that checked out okay with the ignition on may increase (indicating a bad ground) once the starter is turning. The trigger signal will either come directly from the trigger (Hall-effect switch or AC pickup coil), or on some vehicles, from the computer. If any of the module's wires don't have correct electrical values for voltage, grounds or trigger signals, you must repair them before further testing. If all the wires going to the ignition module have correct values, however, the module needs to be replaced.

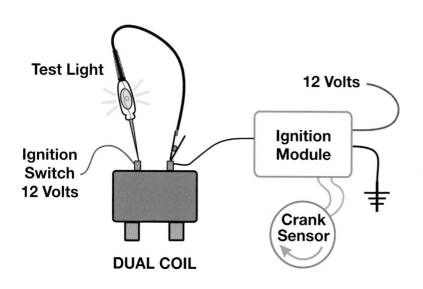

The test light provides visual confirmation that the module is sending a primary switching signal to the ignition coil. This test will work on both dual plug and single coils. The test will not work on bikes that only use a magneto and have no battery. Not enough current may be available at the coil primary terminals (even if everything's working) to light the test light.

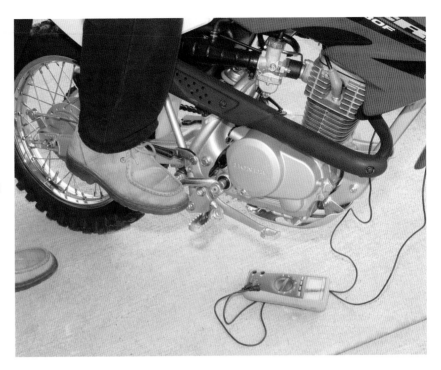

Because this small Honda off-road bike doesn't have a battery, using a test light to check for primary switching will not work. The energy produced when the engine is kicked over won't light the test light. Instead, a voltmeter set to read DC volts can indicate the presence of primary switching at the ignition coil. Around 0.2 volts are produced at the coil primary when the engine is kicked over. *Courtesy Twigg Cycles*

This generic ignition module requires the presence of three things in order to fire the ignition coil: (1) power, (2) ground, and (3) trigger input. On a specific motorcycle, a wiring diagram will identify what each of the wires at the ignition module is used for. If all the inputs are present, and the module will not fire the coil, the ignition module is probably bad and should be replaced. Motorcycles with electronic fuel injection do not have a separate ignition module but use the fuel-injection computer to perform the same function. Powers, grounds, and trigger inputs should be checked to determine if the computer is a fault for no primary coil switching.

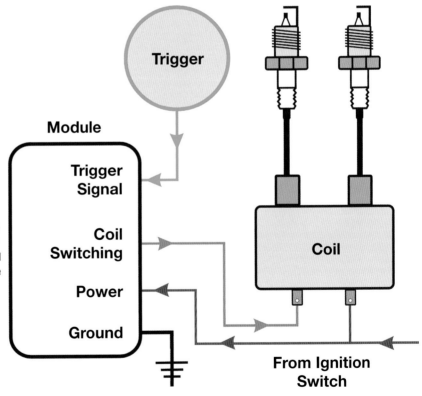

IGNITION MODULE "TAP" TESTING

Another useful method for testing an ignition module or fuel-injection computer is to provide a substitute trigger signal to determine if the coil can produce a spark. This method is called a "tap test" since a grounded (or powered) test light is used in place of a trigger to "tap" on the trigger inputs to the ignition module. If the module is okay and all the power and ground wires going to it are also good, it should fire the coil. If there is no spark after performing a "tap test," always check for the presence of power and a good ground at the module or computer or a bad ignition coil. Also, make sure the test light used to perform the tap test has a resistance value of less than 10 ohms since test lights with bulbs with more resistance may not pass enough current to make a tap test work. Never use a jumper wire to perform a tap test; you could "fry" the ignition module or computer.

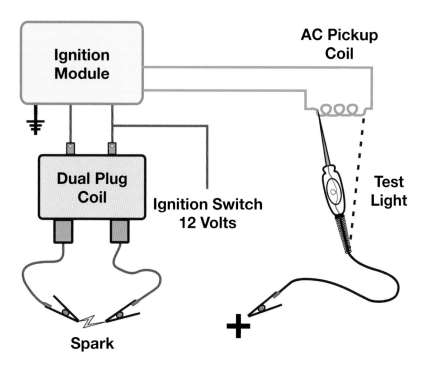

To perform a tap test on an ignition system using an AC pickup coil, leave all connectors plugged in. Use jumper wires connected to the high-voltage terminals of the ignition coil (this is where you'll look for a spark). Turn the ignition key on. Connect a test light to battery positive and tap the pointy end back and forth between the module terminals where the AC pickup coil is plugged in. The coil should produce a spark. If there is still no spark connect the test light to ground and repeat the test. Still no spark? Replace the ignition module.

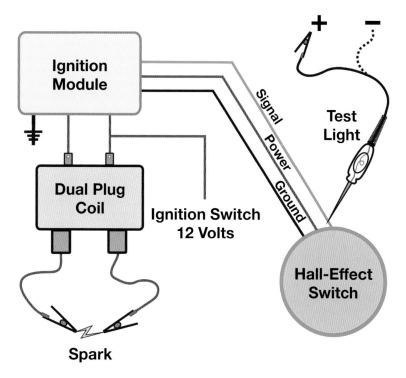

To perform a tap test for ignition systems that use a Hall-effect switch trigger, leave everything plugged in. Use jumper wires connected to the high-voltage terminals of the ignition coil (this is where you'll look for a spark). Turn the ignition key on. Using a test light connected to battery positive tap on the signal terminal from the hall switch to the ignition module. If a spark is produced at the ignition coil, the ignition module is good. If you don't get a spark try tapping using a test light connected to battery negative or ground. Use a voltmeter to make sure that the Hall-effect switch has power and ground. If it does, then the ignition module is bad and should be replaced.

SECONDARY IGNITION CIRCUIT

So far we've dealt only with primary ignition switching. The focus now shifts to the secondary ignition circuit. When a spark is produced at the ignition coil, it must travel from the coil, through the spark plug wire or cable and on to the spark plug. Motorcycles that use coil-over-plug designs do not use spark plug wires as the coils are connected directly to the spark plug. These systems are more reliable than ignition systems that use spark plug wires.

Voltage at the spark plugs must overcome the high resistance of the plug's air gap between the center and ground electrodes. When the engine's cylinder is on its compression stroke, the resistance of the air gap is increased; consequently, a great deal of voltage is required for the spark to jump the gap. Older motorcycles with points-type ignition systems require as much as 15,000 to 20,000 volts to fire a spark plug with the throttle open and about 7,000 volts at idle. On late-model bikes that use electronic fuel injection and three-way catalytic converters, the air/fuel mixtures are leaner, causing spark-plug firing voltage to be even higher. This combustion chamber environment increases the spark plug's air-gap resistance well beyond what older ignition systems could provide, and plug firing voltage may reach 50,000 or more on some late-model systems.

SECONDARY TESTING OHMMETER

Because of high ignition voltage requirements, secondary voltage will try to make its way to battery ground via a path of least resistance. The secondary plug wires eventually wear out with age and must be inspected periodically for damage or arcing caused by voltage leaks. Ignition coils should be checked for corrosion where the spark plug wires are connected. Secondary wires should be visually inspected for cracks, brittle insulation, or loose connections at the ignition coil or spark plug boots. High-voltage spark plug wires can also be checked using an ohmmeter, but resistance values vary widely between manufacturers, so be sure to consult a service manual for specific ohms per inch or foot values. Keep in mind that using an ohmmeter for resistance checking has limited value. When the throttle is twisted open engine compression increases to its maximum. The added resistance of high compression may cause a bad wire to "leak" voltage to ground without going to the spark-plug first.

SECONDARY TESTING TIMING LIGHT

There are several low-dollar methods for diagnosing secondary ignition misfires. An inductive timing light clamped on one of the spark plug wires can serve as a poor man's ignition scope. To check for ignition misfires, connect the timing light to the spark plug

Because of the high voltage produced (more than 20,000 volts) at the ignition coil, secondary ignition wires have to use high-resistance insulation to prevent the spark from taking the path of least resistance and going to ground before it reaches the spark plug's air gap. Secondary spark plug wires and spark plug boots should be inspected periodically for damage. *Courtesy Twigg Cycles*

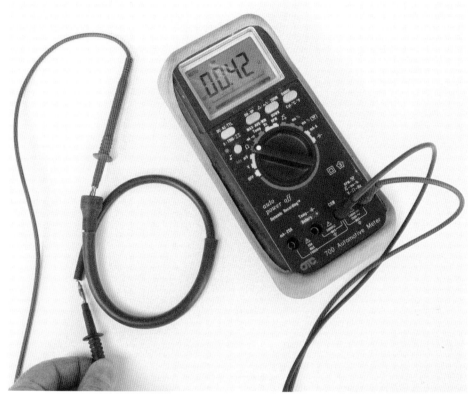

Spark plug wires can be checked using an ohmmeter. Most service manuals will provide a range of acceptable readings. Sometime plug wire resistance is given in ohms per foot. *Courtesy Rick's Motorsport Electric*

An inductive timing light clamped around the ignition coil's high-voltage wire going to a spark plug can serve as a "poor man's" ignition scope. The human eye is fast enough to detect an ignition misfire on this Moto Guzzi. *Courtesy Bob's BMW*

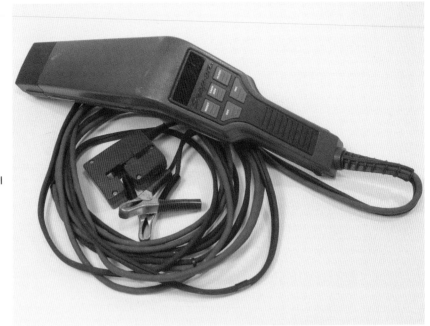

Any inductive timing light (one that uses a clamp over the ignition wire) can be used to determine if an engine misfire is ignition related. When connected to an ignition wire, the flashing light will "skip" a flash whenever a misfire is detected.

wire and start the engine. Point the timing light at your face and snap open the throttle. The human eye is quick enough to observe the results of an ignition misfire by watching the flashing timing light. If the flashing light skips a few flashes, the misfire could be caused by either a bad spark plug wire or primary switching problem. If no misfire is detected with a timing light, but the engine is obviously misfiring, move the inductive clamp of the timing light to each individual ignition wire and repeat the test. This will help isolate the bad spark-plug wire. On coil-over-plug systems, the coil must be removed and a temporary plug wire installed between the coil and spark plug in order to provide a place to connect the timing light for the test.

By observing the distance a spark jumps on the spark tester on the left, an approximation of spark-plug-firing voltage can be determined. The tester's air gap width can be set by the user to increase or decrease the firing voltage required to jump the gap. The spark tester on the right has a fixed air gap that requires about 25,000 volts from the ignition coil to jump its air gap. A spark at the tester is a good indication of coil strength on most electronic-ignition systems. These testers are available at most auto parts stores.

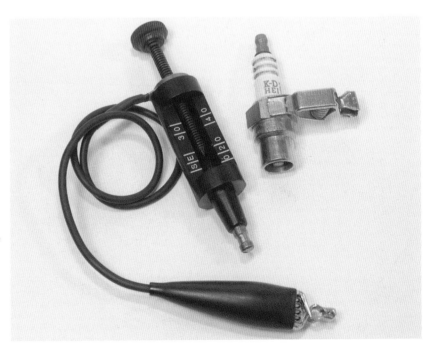

SECONDARY TESTING SPRAY BOTTLE AND TEST LIGHT

Another method for finding bad ignition wires requires a grounded test light and water. Using a spray bottle filled with water, get the ignition wires really wet. The water helps magnify a spark-plug boot or wire that's leaking high voltage. Connect a test light to ground and start the engine. Move the tip of the test light along all the ignition wires while listening to the engine. When the test light is placed close to a bad section of wire, secondary voltage will jump to the sharp tip of the test light, causing the engine to misfire. If it's dark outside when you do this test, you can see as well as hear where the problem is occurring.

After spraying secondary ignition wires with water, a grounded test light can be used to find bad wires or spark plug boots. With the engine running, the tip of the test light when placed close to the leaky wire will attract the high-voltage spark and the ignition for that cylinder will misfire.

SPARK PLUGS

Spark plugs have been in existence since 1860 and have been patented by Nikola Tesla, Robert Bosch, and others. While modern spark plugs use high-tech materials, the basic function of a spark plug—igniting the air/fuel mixture inside the combustion chamber of an internal combustion engine—has not changed in more than 150 years. Spark plugs provide a path and location for the discharge of electrical energy from the motorcycle's ignition coil. Voltage from the coil must be high enough to overcome the resistance created by the air gap of the spark plug. In general, spark plug firing voltage depends on engine throttle opening—around 12,000 volts at idle and 25,000 at full throttle. Modern motorcycle engines with high compression ratios and lean fuel mixtures may require upward of 45,000 volts. Another factor in spark plug design is its heat range, or plug firing temperature. The temperature of the spark plug's tip must be low

These spark plugs are an upgrade for a Yamaha FJR 1300. Stock plugs are NGK CR8E and need to be changed at 8,000 miles. These NGK Iridium IX plugs last longer and will only have to be changed every 30,000 miles. The small center electrode tip diameter slows the wear rate considerably. *Courtesy NGK Spark Plugs*

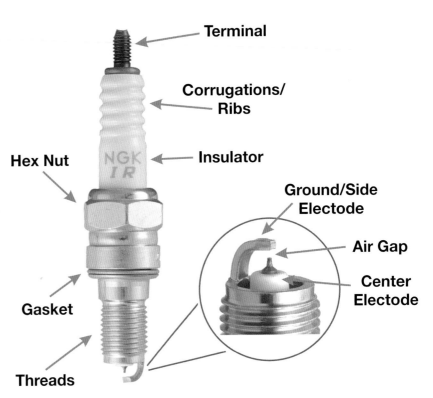

Terminal

Corrugations/ Ribs

Insulator

Hex Nut

Ground/Side Electode

Air Gap

Center Electode

Gasket

Threads

The function of spark plugs has not changed much in 150 years, but their designs and materials have evolved to produce 45,000 volts across the plug's air gap. This NGK spark plug uses an iridium center electrode and can last up to 100,000 miles before needing replacement. *Courtesy NGK Spark Plugs*

This standard NGK spark plug is OEM recommended and used on many brands of motorcycles. The spark plug uses a triple-gasket sealing process and is the workhorse for thousands of powersport and automotive vehicles. *Courtesy NGK Spark Plugs*

This NGK Iridium is designed for performance enthusiasts and offers an extremely long life and superior anti-fouling properties. Smaller in diameter than the standard plug, the Iridium tip has sharper edges and will not melt or corrode as easily as the standard plug electrode. In addition, the smaller electrode absorbs less heat from the combustion process and lasts longer. *Courtesy NGK Spark Plugs*

IGNITION SYSTEMS

enough to prevent pre-ignition (knock or ping) but high enough to prevent fuel fouling.

Motorcycle engines require periodic spark plug changes and there are several good sources of information for selecting the correct spark plug for each application. The owners' manual or factory service manual are good places to find out what type of spark plug to use. These sources will recommend a particular brand as well, such as NGK or others. The factory-recommended, stock spark plug is a no-brainer when choosing what

replacement plug to purchase; however, it is worth the effort to research an upgrade to the stock spark plug if one is available.

On many motorcycle applications the stock spark plugs can be upgraded to longer lasting plugs. Spark plugs wear out due to the metal transfer between the center and side electrodes. This wear is normal and as it progresses it takes higher voltages to bridge the air gap. At some point the engine may experience misfires due to an inconsistent spark across the plug gap. If a plug is available that has either a platinum alloy or iridium tip, they are worth the extra money (about two times what a standard plug costs). These types of plugs will last longer because there is less metal transfer between the electrodes. For example, a 2004 Honda GL1800 Gold Wing takes an NGK BKR6E-11 standard spark plug. An upgrade is NGK's BKR6EIX-11 iridium spark plug. Another factor to consider is how much time and trouble it is to change spark plugs on a particular motorcycle. A two-cylinder BMW offers easy access to spark plugs and changing them only takes a few minutes. By contrast some four-cylinder bikes that have lots of body panels may require hours of labor just to get to the spark plugs, let alone change them.

How often should spark plugs be changed? An owner's or service manual will recommend how many miles between plug changes for the stock, factory-equipped spark plugs. This could be anywhere from 8,000 miles or more. If a high-performance platinum

This is how a normal spark plug looks after many miles. The plug's tip is light brown or gray and the center electrode has slight wear. The color of the plug indicates that the heat range is correct and that the engine has no mechanical problems. *Courtesy NGK Spark Plugs*

This plug shows excessive carbon deposits on the plug's tip. This indicates an overly rich air/fuel mixture or weak ignition system. This plug would cause misfires and a hard start when the engine is cold. *Courtesy NGK Spark Plugs*

This plugs shows oil fouling caused by a mechanical problem with the engine. Worn piston rings, leaking valve seals, or worn valve guides all let oil enter the combustion process fouling the spark plug. This will cause hard starting and misfires. Time to rebuild the engine. *Courtesy NGK Spark Plugs*

or iridium plug is installed the maintenance interval between plug changes can easily be doubled. The reality is that modern electronic-ignition systems produce voltage high enough to overcome worn electrodes so frequent spark plug changes only serve to give owners peace of mind. Spark plug change intervals on many cars is at 100,000 miles, and as long as a motorcycle engine doesn't have any mechanical problems (burning oil or a coolant leak) spark plugs are not a frequent maintenance item. Older motorcycles that use points types of ignitions are altogether different and do require frequent spark plug changes due to the relative low-voltage output of their ignition systems. Following are the steps for changing spark plugs in a typical four-cylinder engine.

The fuel tank on this Yamaha FJR1300 has already been removed and a frame T-bar support has to be taken off as well to gain access to the spark plugs. Spark plug access on other motorcycles may be easier or more difficult.

When removing spark plug wires don't pull on the wire as it will cause damage. These spark plug wire removal pliers grab the spark plug boot and make it easier to remove the wire from the plug, especially if it has not been removed in a while.

Before removing the spark plug some compressed air is blasted into the spark plug recess. This will blow out any dirt that has become trapped. If the plug is removed without this step all the dirt will end up inside the engine's combustion chamber. Wear eye protection when using compressed air.

A speed handle is being used to loosen and twist the spark plugs out of the cylinder head.

Spark plugs that are recessed deep inside the cylinder head may be difficult to extract. A short piece of ⅜-inch rubber hose can grab the spark plug insulator so the plug can be pulled out. This same hose is a good way to install new spark plugs as it will not cross-thread the plugs when first screwing them into the cylinder head.

Here are the spark plugs when removed. This set of plugs has a little more than 30,000 miles on them and would probably go for even more miles. Looking at the center electrode insulator the general condition of the engine can be determined to some extent. All these plugs look about the same with clean center electrodes indicating that the engine is not burning oil and is in good mechanical shape. *Courtesy NGK Spark Plugs*

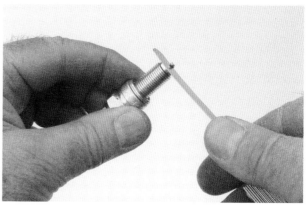

Spark plugs come pregapped, but their gap should be checked to make sure that they match the specifications for a particular year, make, or model of motorcycle. In general, iridium or platinum spark plugs do not have to be gapped. *Courtesy NGK Spark Plugs*

All NGK spark plugs feature Trivalent metal plating on the threads for anticorrosion and anti-seizing properties. It is unnecessary to use anti-seize compound on NGK spark plugs, but other plug manufacturers do not offer this type of plating and the anti-seize lubrication is a good idea. *Courtesy NGK Spark Plugs*

Dielectric grease should be used on the ceramic insulator. This will make spark plug wire removal easier next time a plug change is necessary. It will also keep out moisture and dirt. *Courtesy NGK Spark Plugs*

Each spark plug comes in a box with international instructions printed on it. Starting at the left, Step 1 is to hand tighten the spark plug. The "M10:½" in Step 2 means that the spark plug is a 10-millimeter thread size and should be tightened a half turn after the plug gasket contacts the cylinder head (Step 1). At right are a couple of cautions. The top image warns about using a screwdriver to change the plug gap, and the bottom image shows that these plugs should not be used in an ultra light or aircraft applications. *Courtesy NGK Spark Plugs*

Each spark plug is tightened an additional half turn after hand tightening. This will ensure the proper torque on the plug's threads and keep it from loosening up as miles accumulate on the engine. This is an important step as these plugs will not be looked at again for another 30,000 miles.

CONVERTING POINTS TO ELECTRONIC IGNITION

If you own an older motorcycle that has a points-type of ignition system, it can be upgraded to electronic ignition. The following article, written by Steve Lita, is reprinted with the permission of TAM Communications:

We at *RoadBike* are fans of vintage bikes, even though there are a few of us who were born after some of our bikes were built. Not trying to show my age here, but I'll say I've installed more than my share of points and condensers on cars and bikes over the years. Imagine my frustration when some staffers asked, "What's that?" when I said I was going to upgrade the points ignition to electronic on my 1970 Honda CB750.

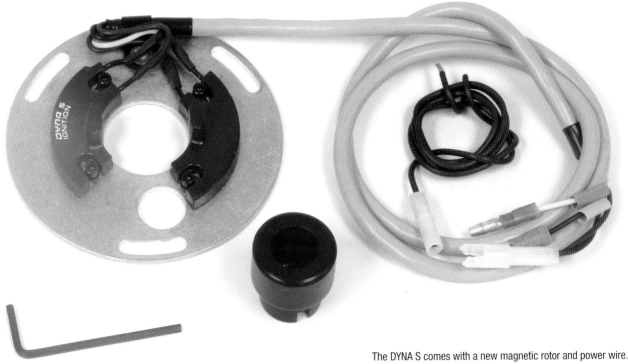

The DYNA S comes with a new magnetic rotor and power wire.

Remove the points cover on the right side of the engine to expose the points plate.

Remove the 10-millimeter nut (some bikes have a bolt) and hex washer holding the spark advance mechanism. Remove the three screws holding the points plate, and then remove the plate and advance mechanism from the engine.

The points plate wiring connects to the main wire harness behind the oil tank. Remove three bolts, and the tank will swing away for access.

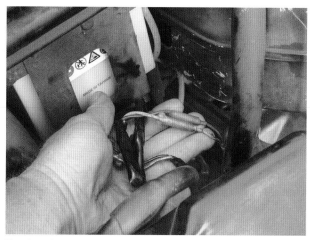

Turn the points cam to the right and pull to remove.

If there's a small pin on the spark advance mechanism (not all CBs have this pin), it will need to be removed. Gently tap on the side of the pin with a screwdriver and hammer.

Install the advance mechanism onto the advance plate.

Lubricate the shaft with oil and slip the DYNA S rotor onto the advance mechanism shaft until it engages the weights.

Install the advance mechanism onto the engine. Reinstall hex washer and 10-millimeter nut. Ensure that the rotor turns freely.

Install the DYNA S plate with the stock screws.

If you're scratching your head wondering what I'm referring to, I'll describe it in a nutshell: Points are what ignition systems once used as a trigger to fire the ignition coils at just the right time to send energy through the spark plug wire to the spark plugs. This allowed the spark plug to make a spark and burn the compressed fuel mixture in the engine's combustion chamber. To think about it now, ignition points are sort of a Rube Goldberg–like device containing springs and rubbing blocks that ride on a cam that's timed to the engine. There's friction, sparks, and crude adjustments involved that seem archaic when compared to the invisible magic of today's solid-state electronics in a bike's ignition system. If you are now asking who Rube Goldberg is, go look him up.

Luckily for me, the wizards at Dynatek have the conversion all figured out. The DYNA S ignition system is a complete, self-contained electronic-ignition system and has been used by top racers over the past two decades. The DYNA S is housed behind the stock ignition cover and uses a magnetic rotor with the engine's original spark advancer, so the factory ignition advance curve is maintained. The venerable DYNA S ignition system is a time proven solution for bringing a vintage muscle bike up to today's standards.

The DYNA S can be used with stock or aftermarket coils that have at least three ohm primary resistance. Dynatek offers several models to fit popular vintage bikes. For our needs, they offer the DS1-2, which fits 1969–78 Honda 500/550/750 four-cylinder CBs. There are some fine-tuning adjustments necessary to make sure that the DYNA S fires the coils at exactly the right moment. But the good news is that once the timing is set, there are no moving parts to wear out like on the original equipment points. While motorcycle restoration purists might not appreciate the upgrade, folks who ride their vintage bikes will. Tools required are minimal and include a Phillips screwdriver, 10-millimeter socket wrench, and a hex key (supplied with the DYNA S). For more information check out their website at www.dynaonline.com.

Unless you have owned and ridden a motorcycle with a points-type ignition system and then changed it to electronic ignition, it's hard to appreciate the difference in performance that this upgrade makes. If the motorcycle has a kick starter your right leg will thank you as the engine will start with less kicks—especially when in cold weather. No more points to adjust, ever. Throttle response will be quicker and the engine will run smoother under all throttle positions. An upgrade to electronic ignition is really worth the time and money—on any motorcycle.

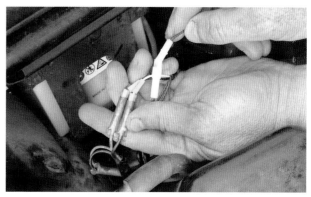

Route the cable and connect the blue and yellow wires to the bike's wire harness where the points were disconnected. Power the DYNA S with switched 12 volts to the red wire.

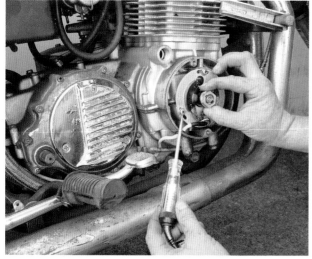

To static time the engine (cylinder 1 to 4), connect a test light from the blue wires to ground. Rotate the engine clockwise (with rotor in full advance, clockwise position) until the test light turns on and then adjust the plate as needed.

Replace the "points cover" on the engine, which now has no points.

Chapter 5
Electronic Fuel Injection

With a final gasp of breath, the use of carburetors for fuel delivery on medium- and large-sized motorcycles for U.S. sales died on or about 2010. First introduced by BMW, and then followed by Japanese manufacturers, Harley-Davidson, Ducati, and Moto Guzzi electronic fuel injection (EFI) is here to stay. Why electronic fuel injection? Just like automobiles and light trucks, motorcycles must face ever-tightening emissions standards. Three-way catalytic converters used on bikes to clean up the air must have precise fuel-delivery control to function and EFI is the only technology that accomplishes this task.

In addition to motorcycles, other powersports applications are currently experiencing a transition phase from carburetion to EFI, including watercraft, ATVs, scooters, and even lawn tractors. Today the professional technician or home mechanic working on an EFI-equipped motorcycle who doesn't have an understanding of how these systems work is severely limited in his or her ability to perform even basic electronics diagnostics and repair. In addition, many owners want to add aftermarket performance accessories to their EFI-controlled motorcycles. High-flow air filters, performance exhaust, or camshafts all require EFI computer tweaking to get them to work properly.

However, working on or modifying an EFI system does not have to be as complex as many people think. Just like electronic-ignition systems, different EFI designs share many similarities—once the basics of EFI operation are understood, most types are relatively easy to work on. Before we get into EFI, a review of just what a carburetor actually does will make EFI systems easier to digest.

This electronic control module (ECM) is out of a late-model BMW motorcycle. The combination of government-mandated emissions and inexpensive computers has caused motorcycle manufacturers to follow the automotive industry to make the switch from carburetors to electronic fuel-injection systems. *Courtesy Bob's BMW*

CV Carburetor Circuits

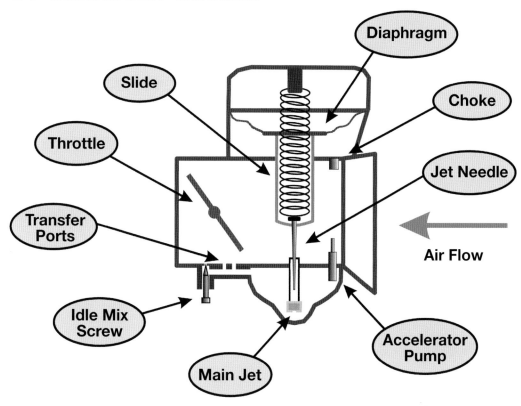

Diaphragm

Slide

Choke

Throttle

Jet Needle

Transfer Ports

Air Flow

Idle Mix Screw

Accelerator Pump

Main Jet

The fuel circuits within this constant-velocity (CV) carburetor provide the correct mixture of fuel and air for all engine speeds and loads. The idle mixture screw, main jet, jet needle, and accelerator pump are all duplicated in an electronic fuel-injection system. While the carburetor provides reasonable power and fuel economy, it can't lower emissions to a level to keep the federal government happy and is being phased out of use for motorcycles.

CV Carburetor Circuits

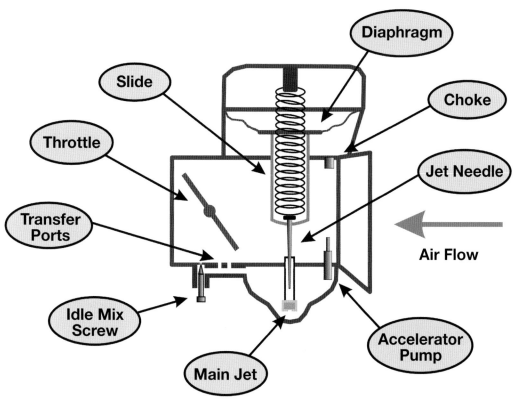

Diaphragm

Slide

Choke

Throttle

Jet Needle

Transfer Ports

Air Flow

Idle Mix Screw

Accelerator Pump

Main Jet

This pair of CV carburetors provides fuel and air for a two-cylinder engine. About the only thing they have in common with an EFI system are the throttle plates and butterfly valves (arrows). *Courtesy Twigg Cycles*

ABOVE: The main jet (upper left) controls fuel at maximum throttle opening. It can be removed and exchanged for one with a larger (more fuel) or smaller (less fuel) opening or hole. The pilot jet (lower left) controls fuel at part throttle. The emulsion tube (right) mixes air and fuel together before it enters the main carburetor body. *Courtesy Twigg Cycles*

CARBURETORS

All gasoline-powered engines need only two basic ingredients in order to run: the correct amount of air and fuel for any given rpm and throttle opening and a spark from the ignition coil at the right time. Motorcycles have used electronic-ignition systems for some time, but carburetors are still found on smaller, less expensive motorcycles. A carburetor's fuel-delivery system is made up of separate fuel circuits, each with a specific job to perform.

Let's take a look at how a stock CV carburetor's fuel-delivery circuits work. When the engine is cold the choke lever, or knob, is pulled out for cold starting. This opens several holes in the carburetor that add extra fuel and air. The additional fuel provides the engine with a rich mixture required for cold starting and the extra air flowing into the carburetor raises the idle speed to keep the engine from stalling until it's warmed up. Once the engine is hot, the choke is turned off and the choke circuit is closed. At idle, and just as the throttle is opened, the idle mixture circuit and transfer port circuits provide fuel to match the airflow for these operating conditions. As the throttle continues to open, the main jet and jet needle take over fuel delivery. Increased throttle opening causes the jet needle and slide to rise upward. This allows more air and fuel into the engine. The main circuit provides fuel delivery at throttle openings from one quarter to full throttle. If the throttle is opened suddenly, the accelerator pump circuit squirts fuel directly into the intake manifold. This is necessary because air is 400 times lighter than gasoline and without the accelerator pump the air would get to the intake valve and into the cylinder ahead of the fuel, causing a flat spot and possible backfire during acceleration.

Although carburetors have been providing fuel delivery services for more than 100 years and have worked pretty well, there are some things they just can't handle. A carburetor is basically a hunk of aluminum with a bunch of holes drilled in it. As air pressure within the carburetor changes, fuel and air flow through the various holes in the carburetor and into the engine.

However, a carburetor's ability to deal with constantly changing operating environments is limited with regard to reactions to changes in altitude, compensation for engine temperature, and lack of precise control of fuel for emissions purposes. In a word, carburetors are just too plain dumb to continue being able to provide accurate air/fuel mixtures for modern motorcycles. What is needed is a fuel-delivery system with some brains.

ELECTRONIC FUEL INJECTION

Electronic fuel-injection (EFI) systems perform all the functions that a carburetor does and also control engine idle speed and the ignition system. All the fuel circuits that are found in carburetors are programmed into the software that controls an EFI system. EFI systems regulate fuel delivery using electromagnetic valves (fuel injectors) that turn on electronically for varying lengths

This 2005 Yamaha FJR1300 EFI system provides better performance, more reliability, cleaner emissions, and increased fuel mileage than the carbureted motorcycles of the past. *Courtesy Twigg Cycles*

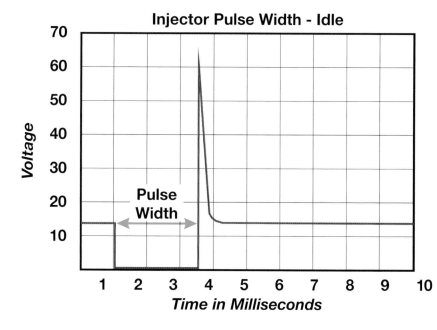

This graphic of voltage over time shows what takes place on the fuel injector's ground wire when the ECU turns on the fuel injector. Voltage at left is at 14 volts, indicating that the injector is off. When the computer turns the injector on, voltage drops to 0 and fuel is sprayed into the engine. With the engine at idle only a small amount of fuel is required and the pulse width is 2.5 milliseconds, or two and a half, one thousandths of a second. Electronic control of fuel delivery is more precise than the idle mixture screw that a carburetor uses for the same function.

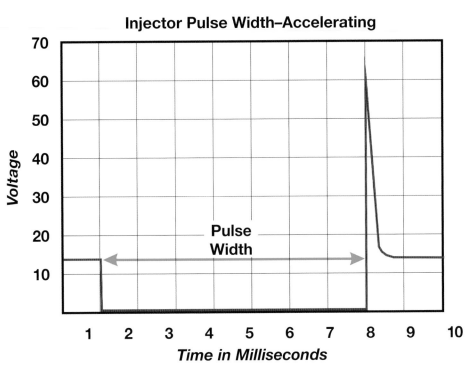

Injector Pulse Width–Accelerating

This graph illustrates how the pulse width is affected when the throttle is suddenly opened. The ECU reads inputs from its various sensors and grounds the injector for a longer period of time. This allows the injector to spray more fuel into the engine, making a smooth transition from idle to wide-open throttle. The pulse width for acceleration is 7 milliseconds and is similar to a carburetor's accelerator pump squirt of fuel into the intake manifold.

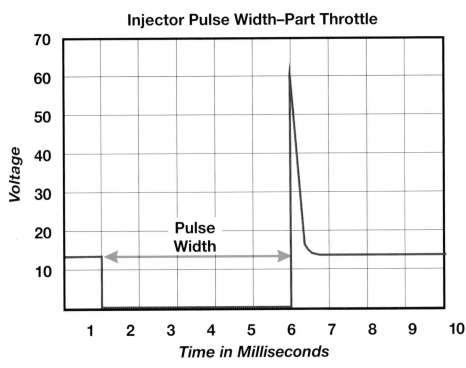

Injector Pulse Width–Part Throttle

After the engine has been accelerated, the throttle is closed partway to maintain steady cruising speeds. The injector pulse width is now set at 5 milliseconds for good fuel economy. Pulse width can also be modified for changes in outside temperature and altitude. This precise fuel control allows EFI motorcycles to perform better than older carbureted bikes.

of time. When the fuel injectors are turned on (called "on time"), they spray fuel into the engine. The amount of on time is called injector pulse width, and the longer this is, the greater the amount of fuel injected into the engine.

The graphs above illustrate what fuel injector on time looks like on a digital lab scope. These are snapshots of three engine operating conditions: idle, acceleration, and part throttle. These pulse width numbers are only used to illustrate basic operation of a typical EFI system. Actual fuel injector on time will be different and vary from one EFI system to the next.

INTERVIEW WITH AN ECM

W hile a carburetor may undoubtedly be a dumb hunk of aluminum, there are those who would argue an ECM (electronic control module) is nothing more than a dumb wafer of silicone with wires attached. To settle the matter, we searched for and found an ECM willing to be interviewed, and ready to answer questions about how electronic fuel-injection systems work. This onboard powersports ECM definitely has an attitude, but also has more smarts than most, so we're lucky to have this opportunity. In this Motorbooks Workshop series exclusive, the first ever "face-to-processor" interview, we got the chance to ask all the questions about EFI systems that everyone's been dying to get the answers to.

Motorbooks: Thanks, Mr. ECM, for agreeing to talk with us. We don't often get a chance to interview motorcycle onboard computers. Can you introduce yourself and give us a general description of what you do?

ECM: Thanks for having me. It's so great to hear that riders are interested in what I do. Some less enlightened people have unkindly referred to me as an overgrown calculator and while there is some truth to that description, it's not exactly true, since I do have more computing power than a calculator, though less than a typical laptop. I have really fast access to my memory and can perform close to a million calculations per second. Plus, I have a network of friends that supply me with information when needed. You see, I have connections—a bunch of sensors that feed me information on various engine-operating conditions. These sensors serve me at a moment's notice, acting like my own eyes and ears. It's discerning friends like these that allow me to keep things under control. I can also calculate fuel delivery and ignition settings that correctly respond to whatever the "nut" holding on to the handlebars might have in mind while riding the motorcycle I'm installed in.

Motorbooks: Hmm. That is impressive. Sounds like you don't often get enough credit. Why don't you take us through the steps you would typically go through while managing the engine and its various systems? For instance, what do you do when the ignition key is first turned to the ON position?

ECM: I take voltage readings from the engine coolant temperature sensor as well as the outside air temperature sensor. To illustrate, assuming the outside air and

Does Mr. ECM here have the computing power to manage his vehicle's fuel and ignition systems? Find out in the next section when you read the first interview with an ECM ever recorded. *Courtesy Alan Lapp, Level Five Graphics*

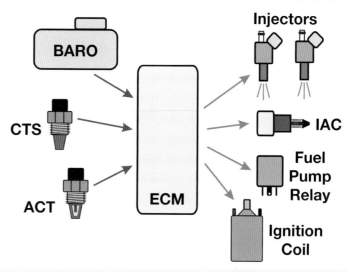

With the key in the ON position the ECM reads inputs from the BARO sensor, CTS (coolant), and ACT (intake manifold) temp sensors. With this information it can then calculate the injector on time, control idle speed, and turn on the fuel pump to prime the fuel system. This all happens in a fraction of a second from when the ignition key is turned to the ON position.

engine temperatures read 50 degrees F, I'll increase the injector on time, or pulse width, to add extra fuel to start the engine. But I also command the idle air controller, or IAC, to provide some extra air to the engine to increase its idle speed when it starts, otherwise the stupid thing would stall. I'll also check in with my barometric pressure sensor, or BARO, to determine what altitude I'm operating at, so I can fine-tune and match fuel delivery to atmospheric pressure. Oh, I almost forgot, I also have to turn on the fuel pump for a couple of seconds to prime the fuel system. I can't leave it running for safety reasons, unless of course, the engine is already started and stays running.

Motorbooks: Wow. That's a lot. I had no idea you were so busy when the engine starts up. I guess I just took engine starting for granted. Once the engine is running, is there anything else you do to control basic engine operation?

ECM: Yes. In fact, it often feels like my job is never done. Basically, to manage engine operation I must control four things: injector on time, ignition timing, engine idle speed, and fuel pump operation. However, please understand that these four functions are the bare minimum I must perform in order to keep the engine running smoothly. On liquid-cooled bikes I also control when the radiator fan is turned on—don't want a meltdown on my hands.

(continued)

Motorbooks: Gee, I had no idea. Sounds tough, but it sounds like you've found a way to work it all out smoothly. Let's get back to the reason for this interview—namely, how electronic fuel-injection systems operate. With the key in the ON position, what happens when the start button is pressed and the engine cranks over?

ECM: You're assuming that the idiot sitting in the seat flipped the kill switch off, but for the sake of argument we'll agree that it's off. As soon as the engine starts rotating, I receive pulsing signals from both the crank and camshaft position sensors. These signals let me know the engine is trying to start; so the first thing I do is turn the fuel pump back on. Since I know the engine is cold, I'll keep the injectors open a little longer to add extra fuel. Once the engine is warmed up, I'll use a camshaft position signal to determine which cylinder is about to open its intake valve. Then I'll pulse, or energize, individual injectors in the same firing order as the spark plugs in order to create an atomized cloud of fuel that will wait right at the intake valve, so that as soon as the valve opens, the fuel will get sucked into the cylinder. This strategy is called "sequential port fuel injection" because the injector firings are timed with each cylinder's intake valve opening.

Motorbooks: That's a lot of work to perform, and it sounds fairly sophisticated. But once the engine is started, is your job done? Can you kick back and relax? Or do you still have to pay attention to what's going on?

ECM: Well, that depends. If the rider lets the engine idle for a while engine temperature will increase. Then I have to shorten the injector pulse width so that less fuel is delivered. I'll also gradually lower the idle speed. However, if, on the other hand, the rider shifts into first gear, lets out the clutch, and rolls on the throttle, then I have to pay attention and really make things happen quickly, since I know that the engine will need more fuel—how much more fuel is where things get tricky.

I rely on four informational signal inputs to determine appropriate base injection on time, also known as pulse width. These include engine rpm from the crank sensor, cylinder identification from the camshaft position sensor, throttle position from the TPS sensor (sometimes referred to as rider demand), and engine load from the MAP sensor. These input signals allow me to adjust and control injector pulse width and ignition timing to match the fuel and air requirements of the engine at any given time.

Motorbooks: Wow. Don't you get stimuli overload? With all the information coming in from your sensors, how do you actually decide what action to take in response to either rider demand or engine power requirements?

ECM: Sometimes it's difficult, but I can handle it since I have help. I use a three-dimensional mapping program, sort of the equivalent of visual aids, that is burned into my electronic memory. As engine rpm increases, I simply fire the injectors so that their firing matches engine speed. At any given rpm, I can monitor the TPS, or MAP sensor, to determine the quantity of air entering the engine. Airflow is directly proportional to engine rpm and load (how hard the engine has to work to get the vehicle moving down the road).

Once the engine is started, three basic inputs—engine rpm, throttle position, and engine load—determine the base injector pulse width ("ON time") and ignition timing. The MAP sensor works like an electronic vacuum gauge, in effect telling the ECM how hard the engine is working. The TPS sensor sends the ECM rider demand information of how much and how fast the throttle is being twisted. The engine rpm signal is used to trigger the fuel injectors.

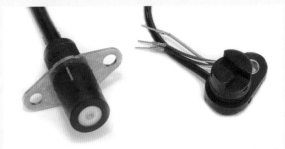

This Harley-Davidson crank sensor (left) and cam sensor provide the ECM with engine speed and cylinder identification information. The cam sensor (right) is used for the sequential fuel injection as it identifies which cylinder is approaching top dead center on its compression stroke. This allows the ECM to pulse only that specific injector just before the intake valve opens. The crankshaft sensor sends a speed signal to the ECM so it can trigger the fuel injectors and ignition coils. *Courtesy Harley-Davidson of Frederick*

ELECTRONIC FUEL INJECTION

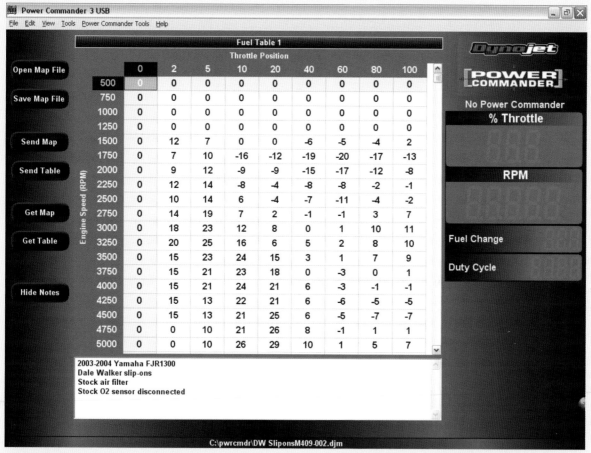

Power Commander 3 USB

File Edit View Tools Power Commander Tools Help

Fuel Table 1

Throttle Position

Engine Speed (RPM)	0	2	5	10	20	40	60	80	100
500	0	0	0	0	0	0	0	0	0
750	0	0	0	0	0	0	0	0	0
1000	0	0	0	0	0	0	0	0	0
1250	0	0	0	0	0	0	0	0	0
1500	0	12	7	0	0	-6	-5	-4	2
1750	0	7	10	-16	-12	-19	-20	-17	-13
2000	0	9	12	-9	-9	-15	-17	-12	-8
2250	0	12	14	-8	-4	-8	-8	-2	-1
2500	0	10	14	6	-4	-7	-11	-4	-2
2750	0	14	19	7	2	-1	-1	3	7
3000	0	18	23	12	8	0	1	10	11
3250	0	20	25	16	6	5	2	8	10
3500	0	15	23	24	15	3	1	7	9
3750	0	15	21	23	18	0	-3	0	1
4000	0	15	21	24	21	6	-3	-1	-1
4250	0	15	13	22	21	6	-6	-5	-5
4500	0	15	13	21	25	6	-5	-7	-7
4750	0	0	10	21	26	8	-1	1	1
5000	0	0	10	26	29	10	1	5	7

Open Map File | Save Map File | Send Map | Send Table | Get Map | Get Table | Hide Notes

POWER COMMANDER

No Power Commander
% Throttle

RPM

Fuel Change

Duty Cycle

2003-2004 Yamaha FJR1300
Dale Walker slip-ons
Stock air filter
Stock O2 sensor disconnected

C:\pwrcmdr\DW SliponsM409-002.djm

This Dynojet Power Commander, a two-dimensional fuel map, shows the percentage of throttle opening on the horizontal axes (top) and engine rpm on the vertical axes on the left. The map is divided into cells where a "0" value represents no change from stock fueling. Positive numbers represent an increase and negative numbers are a decrease in fuel at a given rpm and throttle opening. For example, at 2,000 rpm and 40 percent throttle opening, fuel has been subtracted from the stock base map by a factor of -15. A base map is provided with each Power Commander application and, depending on the make, model, and year of the motorcycle, fuel maps are available for specific exhaust systems and other performance components. *Courtesy Dynojet Research*

My fuel and ignition maps contain what are known as "look-up tables," where predetermined fuel delivery values are stored. From the information gleaned from the "look-up tables," I can calculate how long it is necessary to keep the injectors turned on and when to fire the spark plugs. I have to look up these values each time I pulse an injector or fire a spark plug, so I have to think and react pretty quickly. As you can imagine, things happen pretty fast on a high-revving engine. Did you know that an engine that is spinning at 5,000 rpm fires all the injectors and spark plugs 42 times per second? And that's nothing when compared to a high-revving sport bike at 14,000 rpm. Injectors are firing at a mind-boggling rate of 116 times per second. In fact, fuel injectors can't operate that fast so on these high-revving bikes a second set of fuel injectors are used, sometimes called shower or high-mount injectors.

Motorbooks: Life in the fast lane, huh? But I'm still a little puzzled about something you said earlier, when you talked about rider demand and input from the TPS sensor. Can you explain the relationship between these things?

ECM: Sure. The TPS or throttle position sensor is really the only input signal a rider has direct control over. Its varying voltage signal tells me what the rider is trying to accomplish in the horsepower and torque department. No matter how fast the throttle is twisted, I can react faster and provide the correct ignition timing and fuel delivery. In fact, I use the TPS signal to adjust fuel delivery much like an accelerator pump on a carbureted fuel system by providing an extra shot of fuel when the throttle is opened suddenly.

Let me give you some insight on this issue. Whenever the throttle is opened abruptly, a column of air moves through the intake manifold at high speeds. To prevent the occurrence of a "flat spot" during acceleration, gasoline must join with a moving blast of air before the intake valve opens. I can modify the length of time the injectors stay on, at a computer processing rate of more than 100 times

(continued)

ELECTRONIC FUEL INJECTION

Motorcycles use two types of EFI systems: speed density and alpha-n. The difference between the two is how they determine the load being placed on the engine. The alpha-n system uses two basic inputs, engine speed and throttle position. Rapid movement of the throttle along with increased rpm causes the ECU to lengthen the injector pulse width. Alpha-n systems were used early on as they only needed a moderate amount of computer processing power. The speed-density system uses three inputs: engine rpm, TPS, and intake manifold pressure (air density) to sense engine load. A manifold absolute pressure (MAP) sensor is connected to the intake manifold and operates like an electronic vacuum gauge. Speed-density systems also use a TPS sensor and can deliver fuel more accurately than the alpha-n systems.

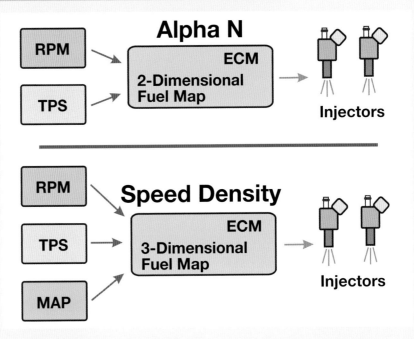

per second, so that when the throttle is whacked hard I have the exact amount of fuel waiting to mix with the blast of incoming air. Keep in mind that electricity still travels faster than any action either the rider or engine can perform, so keeping up with changing throttle positions, engine speeds, and loads is just not a problem for me.

Motorbooks: Well, that's understandable. Now that I know what a TPS does, I'm curious about something that used to happen quite often with older carbureted systems. When driving in the mountains, engines would run poorly and carburetors would have to be adjusted for higher altitude conditions. Do you experience a similar phenomenon, and if so, how to you deal with it?

ECM: I am happy to say that scenario is a non-issue for me. I simply have to read the input from my barometric pressure sensor, or BARO sensor, and then just adjust the fuel delivery to match the altitude the motorcycle is being operated at. The higher the altitude the motorcycle is being ridden at, the less air or oxygen available for combustion. Consequently, I simply shorten the injector on time and less fuel is delivered to the engine. This incremental adjustment is called fuel trim, and it provides the engine with exactly the right amount of fuel, regardless of the altitude the bike is operated at. Plus, I also use other sensors to trim or fine-tune fuel delivery. As an example, when the intake air temperature sensor notifies me the motorcycle is running on a hot day, I slightly reduce the amount of fuel delivered. On a cold day, I simply do the reverse—add a little more fuel.

Motorbooks: While all this electronic fuel control wizardry is occurring, how do you determine proper ignition timing or when to fire the spark plugs?

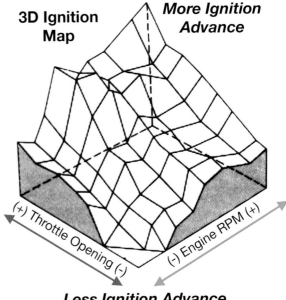

This three-dimensional (3D) ignition map illustrates how a typical EFI system controls ignition timing advance. At the lower left is throttle opening and on the right is engine rpm. As both throttle opening and rpm increase, the amount of ignition advance is increased (top of map). The reason the map has mountains and valleys is due to camshaft design, cylinder head flow, piston stroke, and exhaust system design. All of these factor into how much air flows into and out of the engine at any given rpm and throttle opening. As a result, the amount of spark timing changes with the conditions created inside the combustion chamber.

ELECTRONIC FUEL INJECTION

ECM: Again, I rely on information from my sensors. Depending on specific inputs I receive from my TPS sensor, engine speed or rpm, and MAP sensor, I either advance or retard ignition spark timing, depending on engine demand. For example, if the rider is operating the engine at part throttle combined with moderate engine rpm, I will adjust the ignition timing by advancing it for better fuel economy. If the throttle is opened suddenly, however, and engine rpm is low, then I adjust the ignition timing accordingly, by start it later (retarded timing) to prevent engine knock. Once the knocking stops I will advance ignition timing to ensure optimum horsepower production.

Motorbooks: You mentioned engine knock, the sound that an engine makes when fuel in the combustion chamber is exploding rather than burning. Does your system have a knock sensor, and if so, what does it do?

ECM: There is a knock sensor, and its sole purpose is to detect whenever the engine knocks, pings, or detonates. All of these conditions are bad and can cause severe engine damage. Once I receive a signal from the knock sensor, I slightly retard ignition timing until the knocking stops. In fact, I am smart enough to tell which cylinder is knocking, so I will only retard the spark timing for that specific cylinder. Once the ping or knock disappears, I'll immediately advance ignition timing again for better fuel economy and engine power.

Motorbooks: You haven't talked about oxygen sensors or catalytic converters yet. What's going on with these emissions devices and what's your roll in their operation?

ECM: Well, a catalytic converter, or "cat" as many people commonly call it, controls engine exhaust emissions that occur during two engine-operating conditions, idle and part-throttle. For the cat to work properly, the fuel-injection system must be able to average its air/fuel ratio to just slightly above and slightly below 14.7:1, the ideal proportional relationship of 14.7 parts of air to 1 part of fuel. To accomplish this, I use an oxygen sensor, which is located in the exhaust system between the engine and the cat. This sensor measures oxygen content in exhaust gas and as a result of these measurements produces a small signal voltage that

Pictured is the catalyst honeycomb substrate inside the BUB Seven muffler. These catalytic converters use more precious metals than stock mufflers to ensure that they meet CARB and EPA specifications while at the same time providing high-flow exhaust capacity. The catalysts flow 30 percent more exhaust gases than the stock cats from Harley-Davidson and provide an 11 percent increase in engine horsepower with the proper EFI fuel modifications. *Courtesy BUB Enterprises*

BUB Enterprises is the first aftermarket exhaust manufacturer to produce high-performance and EPA/CARB-compliant exhaust systems that use a catalytic converter for motorcycles. These 4-inch mufflers are available with the BUB Seven slash cut end caps in chrome or black Teflon and in TDX routing for the 2009 and 2011 FL Touring motorcycles. *Courtesy BUB Enterprises*

The oxygen sensor is the key to keeping the air/fuel ratio at 14.7:1 (14.7 parts air to 1 part fuel). This mixture allows the three-way catalytic converter to clean up what's coming out of the engine's exhaust.

(continued)

I receive. I then determine what fuel corrections to make to keep the air/fuel ratio averaging 14.7:1.

This scenario goes something like this: I inject fuel into the engine, sense exhaust gas oxygen, and compare it to what is needed for an ideal mixture and correct subsequent fuel delivery. This strategy is called closed-loop operation because it is an informational loop—sense, compare, and correct—get it? I should add that closed loop only takes place when the engine is hot and either at idle or part throttle.

Motorbooks: Okay, if that's how closed-loop operation works, is open-loop operation just the opposite?

ECM: Let's see, how can I explain this? OKay, remember how I only use closed-loop operation during idle or part throttle conditions? Well, I use open-loop operation for all other driving conditions. For example, cold or hot starting, accelerating, decelerating, etc. All of these modes of engine operation do not require an ideal 14.7:1 air/fuel ratio that I spoke of earlier. So the sense, compare, and correct form of informational loop is not used or necessary, hence the system is now operating in open-loop mode.

Motorbooks: I hear a lot these about auto-tuning and wide-band O_2 sensors. Can you explain how these work?

ECM: Auto tuning is not something that a stock ECM can do. Aftermarket ECMs and controllers do provide a way to continually tune the fuel maps as the motorcycle is ridden. It's just like closed-loop operation but with a twist. The stock O_2 sensors are replaced with aftermarket wide-band oxygen sensors. These sensors can measure air/fuel ratios in a wider range than the stock sensors. During an auto-tuning session the fuel system is always in closed-loop mode, as it constantly measures the air/fuel ratio and automatically adjusts the ECM's fuel map. Think of it as a dyno session complete with a skilled tuner in a box.

Motorbooks: Many manufacturers are offering throttle-by-wire and electronic traction control. Tell me about how you work with these systems.

ECM: The motorcycle I'm currently installed in just happens to have traction control and a throttle-by-wire

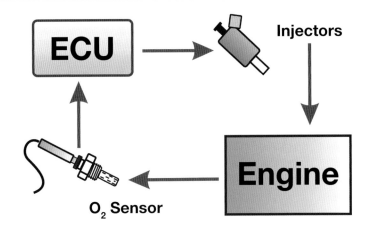

FEEDBACK LOOP

The informational "loop" consisting of "inject, sense, and control" works to maintain the correct air/fuel ratio required by the motorcycle's catalytic converter. Since the loop is endless, it's often referred to as a "closed loop" or "feedback loop."

Three components—an ECM, injector, and oxygen sensor—comprise a closed-loop fuel-control system. The informational loop of sense, compare, and correct takes place at part throttle or idle on most motorcycles and provides cleaner emissions. *Courtesy Bob's BMW*

system. Throttle-by-wire just replaces the mechanical throttle cables with an electronically controlled throttle. Operation is pretty simple. When the rider twists the throttle, it sends me a signal that lets me know what the rider is trying to do—essentially go faster, or slower. I use this information to control a small motor that opens or closes the throttle plates. I can smooth out rider demand by also controlling the speed that the throttle opens and closes.

I use traction control to keep the rear tire from losing traction from too much engine power. If the road is wet and the rear tire starts to slip, I analyze lots of info before I apply traction control—road speed, gear selection, lean angle, and throttle position are all evaluated

Dynojet's Auto Tune Kit for the Power Commander V provides a wide-band, closed-loop EFI tuning system. A target AFR map is loaded into the PC-V and the base map is modified as inputs are received from the Auto Tune module. This is like having a dyno tuner constantly tuning the fuel system as the motorcycle is ridden. Auto Tune is available with one wideband O_2 sensor, or for Big Twin engines, two wideband oxygen sensors to accommodate differences between cylinder fueling. *Courtesy Dynojet Research*

Pictured is a Harley-Davidson Throttle-by-Wire actuator. On motorcycles that use this system there is no direct connection from the rider to the throttle plate. When the rider twists the throttle grip on the handlebar, a signal is sent to the ECM, which in turn controls the throttle plate. The ECM takes into account how fast and far the rider is actually twisting the throttle but also considers other factors, including engine rpm, MAP sensor input, gear selection, and others. The end result is the ideal throttle opening for any riding scenario. *Courtesy Dynojet Research*

in a fraction of a second. If it think it's necessary, I can back off the throttle without the rider being aware of my actions and keep the rear tire from spinning.

And not to brag, but I should point out that not all ECMs have as many sensor inputs as I do, nor do they control as many vehicle systems as I do. I guess I'm just a little bit smarter than most ECMs.

Motorbooks: Great! Thanks for your time. I guess that wraps it up for now. I'd like to thank my audience, too, for being part of an exclusive interview with an electronic control module about how it manages a motorcycle's fuel and ignition systems. This is Motorbooks International signing off. Have a great day.

Sensor inputs to the ECM can be processed at an amazing rate of more than one million times per second. However, the rate at which ECM outputs change is much slower, only about 80 times per second. Because a rider can't open the throttle, accelerate, or change gears faster than the EFI system can process information, the operation of the engine-management system is seamless and invisible to the rider.

Motorcycles that use computerized engine-management systems have "good manners" when it comes to engine operation. Typically EFI engines: (1) start and run well either cold or hot, (2) accelerate smoothly, (3) get good fuel mileage, and (4) don't pollute as much as a carbureted motorcycle. As a result, electronically fuel-injected motorcycles offer better overall performance while exhaust gases coming from the tail pipes are often cleaner than the surrounding air.

(continued)

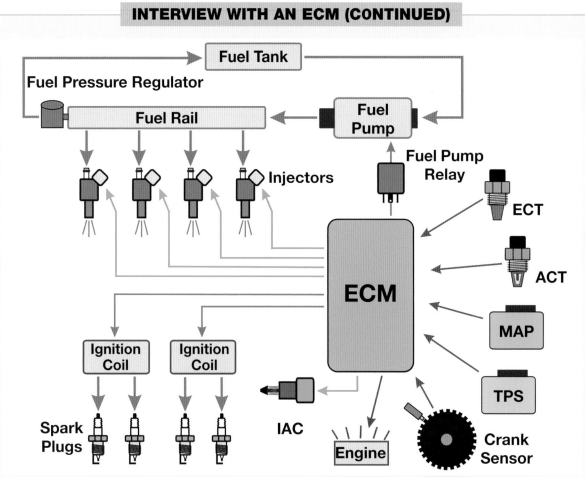

Illustrated is a basic engine-management control system where the ECM controls both the fuel delivery and ignition systems. The system can be divided into inputs (sensors) and outputs (actuators). The inputs are to the right of the ECM and include engine temp (ETC), air temp (ACT), MAP, TPS, and crank sensor. Outputs include the fuel pump relay, fuel injectors, ignition coils, idle control (IAC), and the check engine light. An electronic fuel pump pressurizes fuel in the fuel rail, which acts like a storage tank for the injectors. In the system shown, excess fuel is returned to the fuel tank via the fuel pressure regulator. When the ECM pulses the injectors, fuel is sprayed into the engine.

The ECM powers up the fuel pump via the fuel pump relay for about two seconds when the ignition is first turned on to prime the fuel system. As long as the ECM receives an engine rpm signal it keeps the fuel pump relay energized. As a safety measure in case of a crash that could cause the engine to shut off, the fuel pump is turned off automatically by the ECM, preventing a possible fire. Fuel pumps on most EFI motorcycles are located in the gas tank and in a few applications the pump is mounted somewhere on the frame under the tank.

One of four injectors on a Yamaha FJR1300. Each injector is sandwiched between the intake runner and a fuel rail. The fuel rail acts like a pressurized fuel storage tank. Excess fuel is returned to the fuel tank via the fuel pressure regulator. *Courtesy Twigg Cycles*

COMPUTER SENSOR TESTING

This next section covers how to test EFI system computer sensors. Many service manuals use a diagnostic trouble tree to determine if an EFI sensor is good or bad. Typically these charts are overly time-consuming and often the last step states, "Replace with known good sensor and retest," which is the first step a dealer takes, not the last. Swapping new sensors, until discovering which one is bad, is a common practice in both the powersports and automotive industries, and while some would call this "cheating" it is often the fastest way to fix the problem and move on to the next bike in line for service. Home-brewed technicians don't have this option because electrical parts (especially EFI related ones) are not generally returnable to the dealership.

Instead of blindly following the trouble tree chart in a service manual, there is a better way to test EFI-related sensors. We'll take a generic approach to sensor diagnosis because these components, whether on a car or motorcycle, work in a similar manner and the same basic testing procedures apply to typical motorcycle EFI computer sensors. It does help to use a factory service manual as some do have specific testing procedures for the sensors used on a particular manufacturer's EFI system. Most late-model motorcycles have the ability to produce EFI system diagnostic codes. In the past these were accessible only with dealer-only scan tools, but today many factory systems can be accessed by aftermarket scanners. The Internet is a good place to search for home-technician scan tools. If a scanner does show a trouble code (diagnostic fault code) for a specific sensor it should be considered a starting point for further diagnosis. Simply replacing the sensor indicated as "bad" by a trouble code will not work much of the time, and because these are not returnable to the dealer, will be expensive for the owner.

Following are some simple tests for sensors, including throttle position sensors, temperature sensors (both liquid and air types), oxygen sensors, manifold absolute, and barometric pressure sensors, knock sensors, and vehicle speed sensors.

THROTTLE POSITION SENSOR TESTING

Most throttle position sensors (TPS) used on motorcycles have three wires: power (5 volts), ground, and TPS signal that goes back to the ECM. A TPS sensor can be tested in either of two ways: by measuring

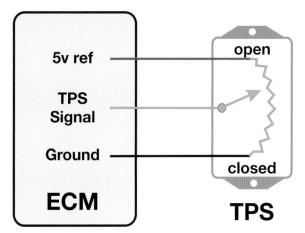

This is a typical throttle position sensor/ECM circuit. A TPS is simply a variable resistor, and as the throttle is opened, the TPS signal voltage increases, getting closer to the reference voltage of 5 volts. This increasing voltage indicates to the ECM that it should add fuel accordingly as the vehicle accelerates.

TPS sensors come in different shapes and configurations. Most are variable resistors and provide throttle angle, or position, to the motorcycle's electronic fuel-injection computer. Adjustment is critical on some bikes, and a service manual should be consulted for the proper procedure. *Courtesy Bob's BMW*

varying voltage or by varying resistance. Measuring TPS voltage on the signal wire is a more accurate method for testing because the ECM reads voltage as the TPS input and not a variable resistance from the TPS.

A service manual is helpful to identify the three wires at the TPS but is not necessary. By checking each wire using a digital voltmeter, the wires can be identified based on the voltage on each. To check for the presence of a TPS signal to the ECM and test the sensor, turn the ignition key to the ON position. Leave the TPS

Honda's 599 EFI motorcycle uses a TPS sensor to relay rider demand as the throttle is twisted open. The ECM not only knows how far the throttle is opened but how fast it can adjust fuel delivery accordingly. *Courtesy Twigg Cycles*

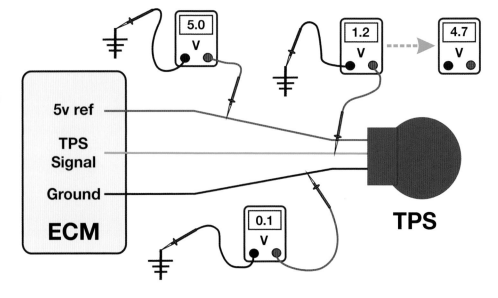

The TPS signal wire (green) should have a smooth transition from low voltage (throttle closed) to high voltage (throttle open). If the voltage skips around, the TPS is not working correctly and should be replaced.

sensor plugged in. Back probe each wire with a digital voltmeter. The three wires tested should have readings as follows:

- **Five-volt reference wire:** The ECM sends 5 volts to the TPS as a reference voltage. This voltage will not change when the throttle is twisted. If none of the wires at the TPS have 5 volts, check the fuses that

power the ECM. If the fuses are good, and the TPS wires to the ECM are okay as well, there may be a problem with the ECM.

- **Ground wire:** The TPS ground comes directly from the ECM. This wire should read close to 0 volts and will not change when the throttle is twisted. If it's higher than 0.02 volts the ECM may have a bad ground wire.

- **Signal wire:** The TPS sends a varying voltage signal to the ECM via the signal wire. With the throttle closed, voltage should be around 0.5 volts. As the throttle opens, voltage should gradually increase until it reaches around 4.5 volts at wide-open throttle. Inside the TPS is a variable resistor that changes resistance in relationship to throttle angle (opening). This resistor can eventually wear out over many miles of engine operation. Open the throttle slowly while checking the voltmeter reading. A steady increase in voltage without any "skipping" or jumping around indicates a good TPS.

TEMPERATURE SENSOR TESTING

Depending on manufacturer, engine temperature sensors may have different names, including ECT (engine coolant temperature), ET (engine temperature), CT (coolant temperature), and CHT (cylinder head temperature—on an air-cooled engine). Intake manifold temperature sensors operate in a similar manner and can be called ACT (air charge temperature), IAT, (intake air temperature), or MAT (manifold air temperature) sensors.

Both coolant and intake manifold temperature sensors can be tested in the same manner. The ECM sends a 5-volt reference signal to the temperature sensor. As the sensor's resistance changes, the voltage that the ECM reads changes as well. High voltage (around 3 volts) is interrupted as low temperature. Low voltage (around 0.5 volts) is for normal engine operating temperatures. Temperature sensors are typically equipped with two wires. To check a coolant or air temp sensor, turn the ignition key to ON and back probe both wires using a DVOM. One wire should read close to 0 volts since it is the temp sensor ground; the other wire should have between 0.1 and 4.5 volts, depending on the manufacturer and temperature of the sensor. On a cold engine, voltage should be approximately 3 volts or higher. Start the engine and watch the voltmeter reading as the engine warms up. Voltage should gradually start dropping to between 0.5 to 2 volts, depending on manufacture. If signal voltage drops fast or skips around, the coolant/air temp sensor is probably bad.

Engine or air temperature sensors can also be tested for internal resistance by unplugging the coolant/air temp sensor and using an ohmmeter. Measuring internal resistance is one indicator of a good temp sensor. In general, resistance should be high (thousands of ohms) when cold and lower when hot (below 2,000 ohms). See a service manual for exact resistance values vs. temperatures for a specific motorcycle.

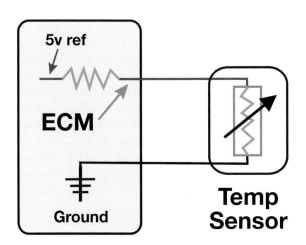

The ECM reads voltage at a point on the temp sensor's signal wire located just before the internal resistor (blue arrow). Depending on the sensor (air, coolant, or oil) this variable voltage signal is interpreted by the ECM as temperature. The higher the temperature, the lower the sensor voltage output.

Air temperature sensors work in a similar manner to coolant or oil temp sensors. The difference is the sensor's probe that may have holes, or cut-outs to allow airflow to come in direct contact with the sensor. The motorcycle's ECM uses intake air temperature to trim or fine-tune fuel delivery.

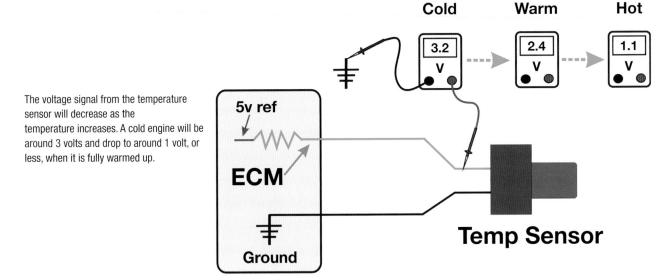

Cold **Warm** **Hot**

3.2 V — 2.4 V — 1.1 V

The voltage signal from the temperature sensor will decrease as the temperature increases. A cold engine will be around 3 volts and drop to around 1 volt, or less, when it is fully warmed up.

5v ref

ECM

Ground

Temp Sensor

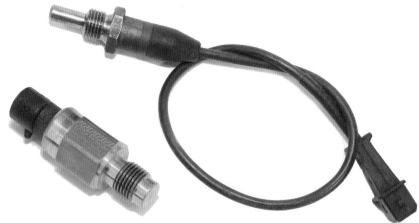

The Harley-Davidson (left) and BMW oil temperature sensors provide engine temperature information to the onboard computer. As engine temperature increases, injection pulse width is decreased by the ECM, resulting in a lean fuel mixture. Both sensors send a varying voltage to the ECM. *Courtesy Bob's BMW*

This Moto Guzzi uses a cylinder head temperature sensor. The sensor's probe is located inside an oil galley and uses oil temperature as an indication of engine temperature. Harley-Davidson uses a similar oil temp sensor. *Courtesy Bob's BMW*

OXYGEN SENSOR TESTING

Oxygen sensors used on automobiles and motorcycles are generally reliable and do not require maintenance. They can go bad and this is usually caused by problems with the fuel system or engine mechanical issues. For example, if the EFI system has a bad engine temperature sensor and produces too rich an air/fuel mixture, the excessive fuel can contaminate the O_2 sensor. An engine with blown head gaskets that causes coolant to leak in to the exhaust system can also damage an O_2 sensor. Also, racing gasoline that contains lead will cause the sensor to go bad. O_2 sensors generally don't wear out when used on motorcycles because they just don't rack up the miles that cars do. O_2 sensors on automobiles will last more than 100,000 miles with no issues.

Unlike other sensors with a fixed number of wires, O_2 sensors on motorcycles can have three or four wires. To test an O_2 sensor, the engine should be warmed up to normal operating temperature. To do this, don't just let the engine idle in your garage for a few minutes; go for a short ride. Gaining access to the O_2 sensor's wires is usually easier at the ECM wiring harness connector than at the O_2 sensor itself. Using the positive lead of a digital voltmeter, back probe the O_2 sensor's signal wire at the ECM. Connect the meter's negative lead to a good ground. Start the engine and maintain speed at 2,000 rpm for 60 seconds. If the O_2 voltage starts switching back and forth somewhere between 0.2 and 0.8 volts, the EFI system is in closed-loop mode. (For purposes of this test, it doesn't really matter if the system is in closed loop or open loop.)

Next, while watching the voltmeter, snap the throttle open. The O_2 voltage should immediately go up to 0.9 volts, indicating a rich mixture. Hold engine speed steady again, and then quickly close the throttle. This time, O_2 voltage should drop to 0.1 volt or less because the ECM has "cut-off" fuel to the engine, creating a lean mixture. How fast the O_2 sensor responds to the changes in exhaust gas oxygen, as well as the range of voltage displayed (0.1v to 0.9v), indicates whether the sensor is good or bad. A good sensor should be able to make voltage transitions instantly, while a lazy or worn-out O_2 sensor makes voltage transitions only slowly and won't be able to reach 0.9 volts no matter how rich the engine is running.

O_2 sensors without internal heaters are usually located as close to the engine as possible. This keeps the sensor hot enough to produce an exhaust gas oxygen content signal that is sent to the onboard computer. Most motorcycles use O_2 sensors that have an internal heating element. *Courtesy Bob's BMW*

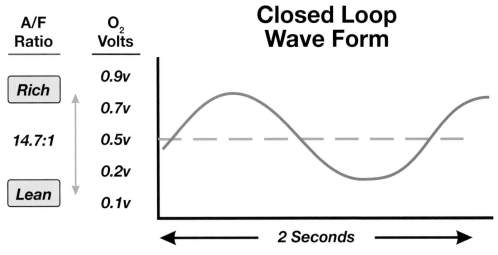

A/F Ratio	O_2 Volts	
Rich	0.9v	**Closed Loop Wave Form**
	0.7v	
14.7:1	0.5v	
	0.2v	
Lean	0.1v	

← **2 Seconds** →

This lab scope waveform shows an O_2 sensor switching between rich and lean air/fuel mixtures. Rich mixtures are indicated by sensor voltage readings above 0.5 volts, while readings below 0.5 volts are for lean air/fuel ratios. The switching voltage indicates that the fuel management system is in closed loop.

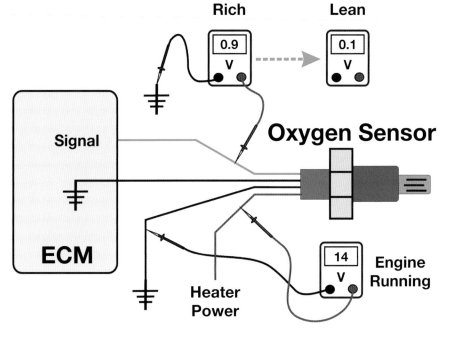

Rich   **Lean**

0.9 V   0.1 V

Oxygen Sensor

This four-wire O$_2$ has an internal heating element. The signal wire switches voltage from low (0.1), a lean mixture, to high (0.9), a rich mixture, with the engine in closed loop. With the engine running the voltage should switch repeatedly from low to high. The ECM provides a ground wire for the sensor. The heater wires do not usually go to the ECM. With the engine running the heater power wire is 14 volts, or charging voltage.

Signal

ECM

Heater Power

14 V **Engine Running**

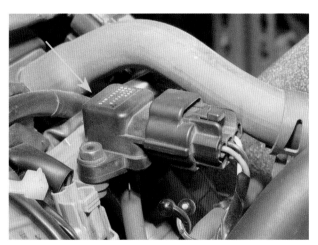

All MAP sensors are basically electronic vacuum gauges. They have three wires: power (5 volts) ground and a signal wire that indicates intake manifold pressure. Some MAP sensors are mounted remotely from the engine using a vacuum hose to connect to the intake manifold and others can be directly attached to the intake manifold (pictured). *Courtesy Twigg Cycles*

MAP AND BARO SENSOR TESTING

A manifold absolute pressure sensor (MAP) sensor is nothing more than an electronic vacuum gauge. Whenever the engine is idling, the negative pressure inside the intake manifold is high—around 20 inches of mercury. Once the throttle is open, the vacuum (negative pressure) drops until, at wide-open throttle, engine vacuum is at "0" Hg. The MAP sensor senses the engine vacuum and outputs a variable voltage signal to the ECM for processing. With input from the MAP sensor, the ECM can determine if there is a load on the engine. For example, if the throttle is held steady (highway speed at 60 miles per hour on a flat road) the engine is not working too hard. The MAP sensor lets the ECM know this and the correct amount of fuel is injected into the engine. When the throttle is opened all the way, the engine is now working to its maximum and MAP sensor input tells the ECM to add more fuel.

Similar in operation to a MAP sensor, a barometric pressure sensor (BARO) measures ambient air pressure (altitude) and then sends a signal to the ECM. Motorcycle manufacturers may use different names for a BARO sensor, including AAP (ambient air pressure, IAP (intake air pressure), or TIP (throttle inlet pressure). Often these sensors are located in the intake airbox near the air filter. The ECM changes the fuel and ignition timing parameters, depending at what altitude the motorcycle is being operated. Mountain riding requires a leaner fuel mixture because there is less oxygen available and the ECM changes the injector pulse width accordingly. Both MAP and BARO sensors have three wires: power (5 volts), ground, and the signal wire.

To test both MAP and BARO sensors, turn the ignition key to the ON position. Using a DVOM, back

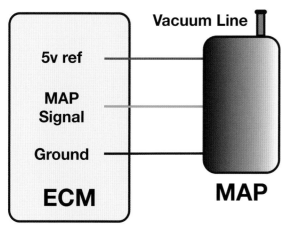

MAP and BARO sensors have three wires: power (5-volt reference), ground, and signal. Some MAP sensors have a nipple fitting to accept a vacuum hose in order to connect the sensor to the intake manifold.

probe all three wires. One wire should have 5 volts, one should be close to 0 volts (ground), and the last should be the signal wire. If there is no 5-volt reference at the sensor, check the wires going to the ECM. Use a hand vacuum pump to test MAP sensors. As you vary the vacuum pressure to the sensor, the voltage should change as well. MAP sensor voltage must be compensated for when testing at, or above, sea level since voltage readings will be slightly lower—about 0.2 volts for every 1,000 feet above sea level. BARO sensors won't have a vacuum nipple, so testing is just a matter of reading voltage with the ignition ON. Consult a service manual for voltage vs. altitude readings for a specific motorcycle.

KNOCK SENSOR TESTING

The Knock Sensor, or detonation sensor as it is sometimes called, has a piezoelectric crystal that generates voltage when subjected to mechanical stress. This crystal produces an electrical signal with a unique signature based upon engine knock or ping. When an engine knocks or pings under heavy acceleration, the knock sensor sends a signal to the bike's ECM. The ECM will retard the ignition timing in an effort to stop the knocking—a safety feature that can prevent damage to pistons and rings.

Following are some general diagnostic tests for knock sensors; however, a service manual should be consulted for specific tests, as these sensors can vary in their outputs. A good general test for this sensor is to disconnect it and probe the sensor wire with a digital voltmeter. Set the multimeter to read AC mv

(millivolts). Take a small hammer and tap on the engine case (near the sensor) while watching the voltmeter. The sensor should produce a small amount of AC voltage, usually less than 4 volts AC. Again, this test may not work on all knock sensors and a service manual should be consulted for specific testing procedures.

VEHICLE SPEED SENSOR TESTING

A vehicle speed sensor (VSS) provides a signal to the ECM to indicate the road speed of the motorcycle. The ECM then uses this information to control ignition timing and on some motorcycles operate secondary throttle plates. There are two types of VSS: AC pickup coil and Hall-effect switch. These speed sensors operate in the same manner as their "ignition" counterparts do when used in ignition systems. (See Chapter 4, "Ignition Systems," for an overview of testing methods used on speed sensors.)

FUEL INJECTOR OPERATION/TESTING

Fuel injectors are simply nothing more than electronic fuel valves that are controlled by the ECM. All fuel injectors are solenoids consisting of a coil of wire and

This Harley-Davidson vehicle speed sensor is located on the transmission and provides a signal to indicate road speed for the electronic speedometer and fuel-injection management system. *Courtesy Harley-Davidson of Frederick*

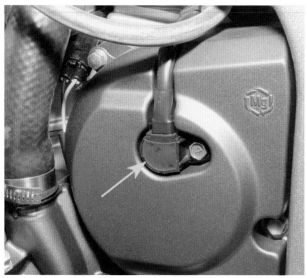

This Kawasaki ZZR uses an AC pickup type of vehicle speed sensor mounted on the transmission cover to send a varying frequency signal to the bike's ECM. Kawasaki uses dual throttle bodies to control throttle opening based on rider demand. Road speed input plus engine rpm, gear position, and rate of acceleration are used to prevent potentially extreme wheelies from becoming too exciting. *Courtesy Twigg Cycles*

While they might look different, all fuel injectors operate in the same manner. Each uses a coil of wire that acts as an electro-magnet when energized by the ECM. The length of on-time or pulse width determines how long the injector remains opens, and consequently, how much fuel is injected into the engine.

BMW was the first motorcycle manufacturer to widely use electronic fuel injection. The fuel injectors on this BMW air-cooled engine are located on the top of the intake runner. *Courtesy Bob's BMW*

moveable electromagnetic valve. When energized, the coil of wire acts like a magnet, causing the valve to open. How long the injectors are open (allowing fuel to be injected) is a function of the corresponding length of time the injectors are turned on by the ECM.

Manufacturers' service manuals usually provide resistance readings as the way to check if an injector is good or bad. A fuel injector's resistance can be measured using an ohmmeter; however, resistance readings will only confirm that the injector's internal coil is not electrically shorted or open. There are a number of better tests that will work most of the time to confirm indirectly that an injector is operating. The first three tests verify that the ECM is sending an injector pulse to the injector. The last test checks for mechanical operation of the injector.

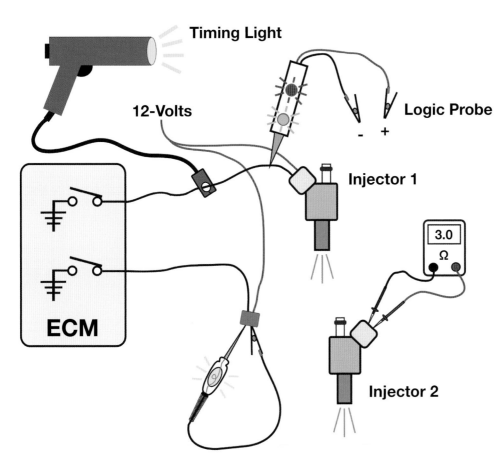

Timing Light

12-Volts

Logic Probe

− +

Injector 1

3.0 Ω

ECM

Injector 2

The ECM pulse signal is being testing on injector No. 1 by two methods: an inductive timing light and a logic probe. The injector is plugged in and the engine is cranking over or running—the timing light will flash and the logic probe will show a pulse signal. The pulse signal for injector No. 2 is being tested with a 12-volt test light. Injector No. 2 is also checked for an open or shorted internal coil with an ohmmeter. The injectors are supplied 12 volts, and the ECM switches the ground on and off, controlling the injector on time.

1. Unplug the injector and connect a test light between the two wires at the injector connector. Crank or start up the engine while watching the test light. If the light flashes, the ECM is sending an injector pulse to that injector.
2. Use an inductive ignition timing light to verify injector pulse. Clamp the timing light's probe around *one* of the wires going to the injector. Start or crank the engine and watch the timing light to see if it flashes. A flashing light provides confirmation that the ECM is sending an injector pulse to that injector.
3. Use a logic probe to verify the presence of an injector pulse signal from the ECM. Connect logic probe leads to the vehicle's battery and touch the probe to one of the injector wires (the injector should be plugged into its connector). Crank or start the engine and then watch the LED on the logic probe. If it flashes or pulses, the ECM is sending an injector pulse to that injector.
4. For a "low-tech" method, simply take a long screwdriver and touch the end to the fuel-injector

body and stick the other end (the handle, dummy) in your ear. If the injector is working, you'll hear a steady clicking from the injector. A wooden dowel or mechanic's stethoscope works just as well. This test doesn't work if the engine won't start because it's hard to hear the injector click over the noise of the starter motor.

IDLE AIR CONTROL TESTING

Idle air control sensors (IAC) are not really sensors at all—they are, in fact, actuators. The ECM controls these devices in order to change engine idle speed. Idle speed is increased by the ECM for cold starting and to help the alternator charge the battery or run accessories. Some IACs use a stepper motor to control the amount of air allowed into the engine, while others use an air bypass valve. In general, these actuators can be checked for resistance, but are difficult to test for actual operation. Using a computer scan tool (hand-held computer interface) is sometimes the only way to verify if the ECM and IAC sensor are functioning together correctly. Consult a service manual for proper testing procedures for specific motorcycles.

EFI PROJECTS

There are numerous modifications that can be applied to motorcycle electronic fuel injection. Why would an owner want to change the factor fuel injection? It depends on the motorcycle, especially if nonfactory parts have been installed. Aftermarket air filters, exhaust systems, and other mods all affect engine performance—either for the better, or worse. To avoid the latter, whenever a component is added to the engine that changes the amount of air flowing into or out of the engine, the EFI system's fuel delivery will have to be matched to the engine modifications. Some factory EFI systems accommodate these performance modifications to some extent, but many fall short in that the engine will run worse rather than better with a new exhaust system or high-performance air filter. Another instance

An idle air controller (pink arrow) receives a signal from a vehicle's ECM and adjusts engine idle speed. This idle IAC on a late-model Harley-Davidson is a stepper motor that is pulsed and opens a plunger in small increments. The pulses move a plunger that bypasses air around the throttle plates to increase engine idle. The TPS (yellow arrow) can be seen as well. *Courtesy Harley-Davidson of Frederick*

The idle air controller (yellow arrow) can be seen mounted on top of the left cylinder's intake manifold. This stepper motor can precisely control the amount of air bypassing the throttle plate to control engine idle speed. The TPS (pink arrow) sensor is also visible on the outside of the intake runner. *Courtesy Bob's BMW*

of wanting to modify the stock computer system's fuel delivery is if there are engine-performance problems with the factory system. Because the motorcycle must meet strict emissions requirements, their engine performance may suffer, especially at low speeds and part throttle. Adding aftermarket fuel system controllers can solve these issues. Modifying stock EFI systems is not as difficult as it sounds as the aftermarket has made vast improvements to its offerings over the years. Aftermarket EFI controllers (or even complete factory computer replacements) are well-engineered, come with complete instructions, and some type of technical support.

TYPES OF EFI CONTROLLERS

There are two common types of aftermarket EFI controllers available today. The most common is the so-called "piggyback" design. Dynojet, Dobeck, FuelPak, Cobra, and others use this style of controller. The other design is not really a design at all but a complete replacement of the stock ECU. ThunderMax, MoTeC, and other manufacturers offer ECUs that replace factory units. The piggy-back design operates like its name implies: It uses the stock ECU, intercepts the fuel-injector signal, modifies it by adding or subtracting fuel values, and sends it on the fuel injector. This type of fuel control relies on the stock EFI system's sensors and computer for basic operation. It piggybacks to the stock fuel-injector signal and changes it to create the desired fuel delivery table.

To review basic EFI operation, fuel injectors are either open (spraying fuel into the intake) or closed (no fuel delivery). All EFI systems power the injectors with battery voltage and the ECU grounds the injector (completing the electrical circuit) to energize it. The length of time that the ECU grounds the injector is called injector pulse width and it is measured in milliseconds, or one thousands of a second. Piggyback controllers receive power from the injector power wire and they measure injector pulse rate to read engine rpm. They also measure injector pulse rate over time. The pulse rate vs. time can be used by the controller to indirectly calculate several engine parameters, including acceleration, rider demand, and engine load. Using these two inputs (engine speed and pulse width), the aftermarket controllers modify the injector pulse width, either causing it to be longer (adding more fuel) or shorter (taking away fuel).

By contrast, a replacement EFI controller or computer does just that—replaces the factory computer. These systems are somewhat more expensive, but they can potentially offer more control over how the stock EFI computer operates. For example, if an owner wants to change idle speed on a bike that uses the stock computer to adjust engine idle speed, the replacement computer allows this type of adjustment.

Regardless of how they accomplish injector pulse width modification, companies that manufacture and sell EFI controllers have several common goals: to make more power over stock EFI systems, to compensate for

The Dynojet Power Commander (left) is a piggyback type of controller in that it intercepts the fuel injector signal from the motorcycle's ECU and modifies it. Zipper's ThunderMax takes a different approach and is a complete replacement for the stock ECU on many Harley-Davidson motorcycles. *Courtesy Dynojet Research and Zipper's Performance*

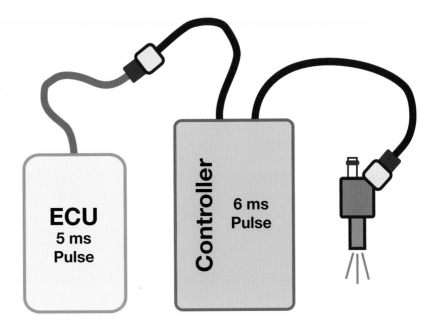

This is the sequence of events when a piggy-back type of controller is used with a stock ECU. In this example, the ECU calculates injector pulse width at 5 milliseconds for a given throttle position and engine rpm. The aftermarket controller intercepts the injector signal and modifies by adding more injector on time. The controller's output to the fuel injector is 6 milliseconds, one extra millisecond. This addition of fuel makes the difference between surging at part throttle or smoothing out the throttle transition between idle and part throttle.

engine modifications such as nonstock exhaust systems or other components, and finally to smooth out factory EPA-mandated EFI fuel-delivery engine-performance issues. Following are two EFI projects that modify the way fuel is delivered to the engine. We'll start with the originator of EFI controllers, Dynojet Research.

DYNOJET POWER COMMANDER PCIII AND PC-V

Dynojet's Power Commanders PCIII and PC-V are both piggyback controllers in that they work with the factory ECU to modify how fuel and ignition timing is delivered to the engine. In general, the PCIII is for motorcycles built from 2002 to 2009 and the PC-V is for bikes

Dynojet's Power Commander III (right) and PC-V offer owners the ability to take control of their motorcycle's fuel system. These piggyback systems can add or subtract fuel based on engine rpm and throttle position, are easy to install, and come with a variety of fuel maps that accommodate aftermarket exhaust systems and other engine-performance modifications. *Courtesy Dynojet Research*

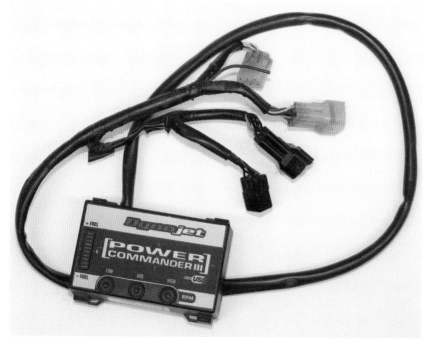

The PCIII for this installation has four connectors that will plug into the stock fuel injector wiring harness. The connectors are color coded (black and white) and correspond with the colors of the stock connectors. The only other wire is a ground wire that needs to be connected directly to the battery's negative terminal. *Courtesy Dynojet Research*

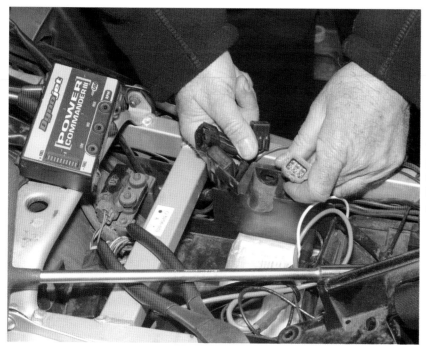

The PCIII will fit under the seat and the wiring harness must be threaded around and through the subframe of the motorcycle. Tie wraps are used to secure the wiring harness in place. *Courtesy Dynojet Research*

manufactured after 2009. Which Power Commander fits what years and models can be found on the Power Commander website, www.powercommander.com.

Installation for both the PCIII and PC-V is simple and straightforward. Each Power Commander comes with a custom wiring harness that is specific for installation on a particular motorcycle. Written instructions with photos are included with each unit. Following is an installation for the PCIII on a 2005 Yamaha FRJ 1300.

The PCIII and PC-V are similar in that when purchased they are supplied with base fuel maps that have been developed to provide an improvement over the stock ECU's map for many combinations of engine modifications. A zero map is provided for all motorcycles that is basically the same in that zeros are entered into the fuel table and no fuel correction is provided over stock settings. With the zero map loaded into the PCIII or PC-V, the Power Commander essentially does nothing regarding fuel correction. The zero map is a good diagnostic tool and can be used to determine if the stock ECU is causing an AFR-related problem or the fuel map in the controller. In addition to the zero map, a fuel map for the stock exhaust system and air filter is provided with each Power Commander. Depending on manufacturer, stock ECU maps are optimized for 60 to 70 percent of total engine performance. With a motorcycle completely stock, the Power Commander base map will increase performance levels to 85 to 95 percent. Once aftermarket parts are added to the engine, alternate maps may be found on either the CD that came with the controller or on Dynojet's website.

The two pairs of connectors are plugged into the stock wiring harness. Electrical contact cleaner should be used to remove dirt and corrosion from the connectors before plugging them together. The wiring tucks in behind the fuel rail and is held in place with tie wraps. *Courtesy Dynojet Research*

The PCIII can be adjusted using the buttons on the unit itself or a laptop. The "Mid" button has been pressed to increase the percentage of fuel to 4 percent over the values in the base map. Each LED on the light bar (at left) represents 2 percent. Two bars up from 0 is illuminated, indicating 4 percent additional fuel correction to the Mid fuel range on the map. *Courtesy Dynojet Research*

Dynojet is constantly updating their map database for specific motorcycles and it is not unusual to find maps for specific exhaust systems. The differences between brand A exhaust and brand B may be small; however, these differences will increase engine-performance optimization beyond the stock motorcycle's factory equipment. For example, listed are the maps for a 2009–2010 Suzuki SV 650 and SV 650 S:

- Zero map
- Stock exhaust, stock or aftermarket air filter
- Arata full exhaust, stock or aftermarket air filter
- Leo Vince high-mount full exhaust, stock or aftermarket air filter
- M4 high-mount slip-on, K&N air filter, airbox snorkel removed
- Two Brothers slip-on, stock or aftermarket air filter

The more popular the motorcycle, the more fuel maps available for specific years and models. For example, more than 136 maps are listed for 2009 Harley-Davidson FL touring models. These fuel maps encompass all manner of exhaust systems, slip-on mufflers, camshafts, air filters, big-bore kits, cylinder head modifications—the list is almost endless.

Another source for fuel maps is the Internet, particularly motorcycle forums. No matter the motorcycle, make, model, or year, there is an online forum comprised of members with the same or similar motorcycles. In addition to providing brand- and model-specific camaraderie, swapping lies about who's the fastest, parts, accessories, and riding gear, a great deal of technical information is usually available, including members' custom Dynojet fuel maps. Some forum members spend hundreds of dollars and many hours to have their bikes tuned on a dynamometer. If the forum community is large, chances are that a custom map exists that fits the combination of parts and modifications one is looking for. If asked nicely, most forum members willingly share their fuel maps with other members.

POWER COMMANDER V

The Power Commander V replaces the PCIII USB and is designed for 2009 and newer models. On more popular motorcycle models the PC-V may be available for years before 2009. Physically the PC-V is smaller than the PCIII, and the fuel mapping buttons have been removed. The PC-V functions much like the PCIII but has enhanced features that include the following: off-the-bike power supply directly from a computer USB port instead of using a 9-volt battery—a handy feature for "desktop" tuning. The PC-V has an input for a map switch and allows the

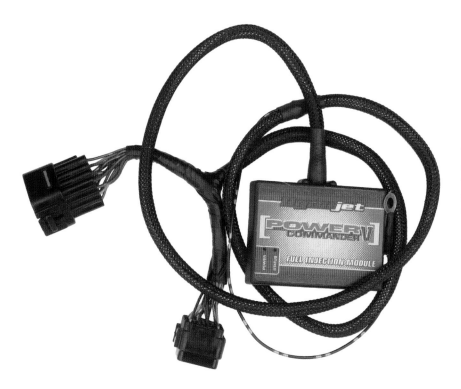

This Power Commander V will be installed in a 2003 Suzuki GSX R-1000. The PCV allows for fuel map adjustments based on gear selection and road speed. On a four-cylinder engine, with a six-speed transmission, as many as 24 separate fuel tables could be developed. *Courtesy Dynojet Research*

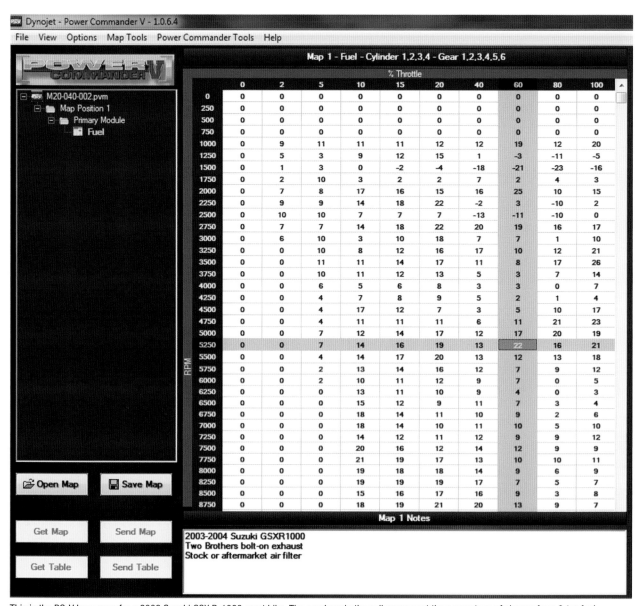

RPM \ % Throttle	0	2	5	10	15	20	40	60	80	100
0	0	0	0	0	0	0	0	0	0	0
250	0	0	0	0	0	0	0	0	0	0
500	0	0	0	0	0	0	0	0	0	0
750	0	0	0	0	0	0	0	0	0	0
1000	0	9	11	11	11	12	12	19	12	20
1250	0	5	3	9	12	15	1	-3	-11	-5
1500	0	1	3	0	-2	-4	-18	-21	-23	-16
1750	0	2	10	3	2	2	7	2	4	3
2000	0	7	8	17	16	15	16	25	10	15
2250	0	9	9	14	18	22	-2	3	-10	2
2500	0	10	10	7	7	7	-13	-11	-10	0
2750	0	7	7	14	18	22	20	19	16	17
3000	0	6	10	3	10	18	7	7	1	10
3250	0	0	10	8	12	16	17	10	12	21
3500	0	0	11	11	14	17	11	8	17	26
3750	0	0	10	11	12	13	5	3	7	14
4000	0	0	6	5	6	8	3	3	0	7
4250	0	0	4	7	8	9	5	2	1	4
4500	0	0	4	17	12	7	3	5	10	17
4750	0	0	4	11	11	11	6	11	21	23
5000	0	0	7	12	14	17	12	17	20	19
5250	0	0	7	14	16	19	13	22	16	21
5500	0	0	4	14	17	20	13	12	13	18
5750	0	0	2	13	14	16	12	7	9	12
6000	0	0	2	10	11	12	9	7	0	5
6250	0	0	0	13	11	10	9	4	0	3
6500	0	0	0	15	12	9	11	7	3	4
6750	0	0	0	18	14	11	10	9	2	6
7000	0	0	0	18	14	10	11	10	5	10
7250	0	0	0	14	12	11	12	9	9	12
7500	0	0	0	20	16	12	14	12	9	9
7750	0	0	0	21	19	17	13	10	10	11
8000	0	0	0	19	18	18	14	9	6	9
8250	0	0	0	19	19	19	17	7	5	7
8500	0	0	0	15	16	17	16	9	3	8
8750	0	0	0	18	19	21	20	13	9	7

Map 1 Notes

2003-2004 Suzuki GSXR1000
Two Brothers bolt-on exhaust
Stock or aftermarket air filter

This is the PC-V base map for a 2003 Suzuki GSX R-1000 sport bike. The numbers in the cells represent the percentage of change from 0 (no fuel correction) to either a positive number (more fuel added) or a negative number (less fuel than stock). The highlighted fuel cell represents the fuel correction when the engine is running at 5,250 rpm and throttle position is 60 percent open. In this example, the correction factor of 22 indicates that more fuel is being added over the stock fuel value for this throttle opening and engine rpm. *Courtesy Dynojet Research*

rider to switch between two internal fuel maps. A speed and gear input that allows for map adjustment based on gear position and speed. With this gear input the PC-V can have individual cylinder maps for each gear. For example, a four-cylinder engine with a six-speed gearbox could have 24 different fuel maps. The PC-V can make fuel changes from -100 to +250 percent (the PCIII USB had a range of -100 to +100 percent) and uses 10 throttle position columns instead of 9, like the PCIII. An analog input for a 0- to 5-volt signal (engine temperature, turbo boost, or other) that can be used to alter fuel mapping based on the input of this signal. This signal is programmed in the Power Commander Control Center software. The accelerator pump utility has increased adjustment and sensitivity ranges. Finally the PC-V can interface with Dynojet's Auto Tune kit that provides wide-band, closed-loop operation for the PC-V. This allows the PC-V to continually tune the fuel map based on target AFR set in the unit's base map software.

The Dynojet Power Commander PCV's small size makes it easy to install under the seat of most motorcycles. *Courtesy Dynojet Research*

These are the connectors from the PCV. The female connector (left) will plug into the stock connector for the fuel injectors. The male connector at right will plug into the stock EFI connector that used to go to the fuel injectors. With this connection the PCV will intercept the ECM's pulse width signal to the fuel injectors, modify it, and pass it along to the fuel injectors. *Courtesy Dynojet Research*

Because each PCV is ordered for a specific year, make, and model of motorcycle, the connectors to the stock wiring harness are plug-and-play. No cutting or splicing wires is necessary. *Courtesy Dynojet Research*

Here both the PCV and stock fuel injection connectors are plugged into each other. The only other wire necessary is a ground wire from the PCV to the battery negative terminal. *Courtesy Dynojet Research*

DYNOJET AUTO TUNE

The Auto Tune kit interfaces with the PC-V and uses a wideband oxygen sensor for automatic fuel mapping as the motorcycle is ridden. The Auto Tune module plugs into the PC-V. The only other wires are 12 volts for power and a ground. If the motorcycle has a factory oxygen sensor it can be removed and the Bosch wideband sensor can replace it. If there is no O_2 sensor, a bung (included in the kit) can be welded to the exhaust for the sensor. The Auto Tune system

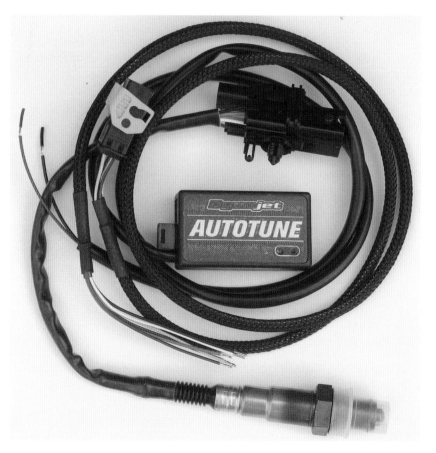

Dynojet's Auto Tune kit monitors the fuel mixture via a wide-band O_2 sensor mounted in the exhaust. It then sends this information to the Power Commander V and automatically corrects the air/fuel mixture while the motorcycle is ridden. *Courtesy Dynojet Research*

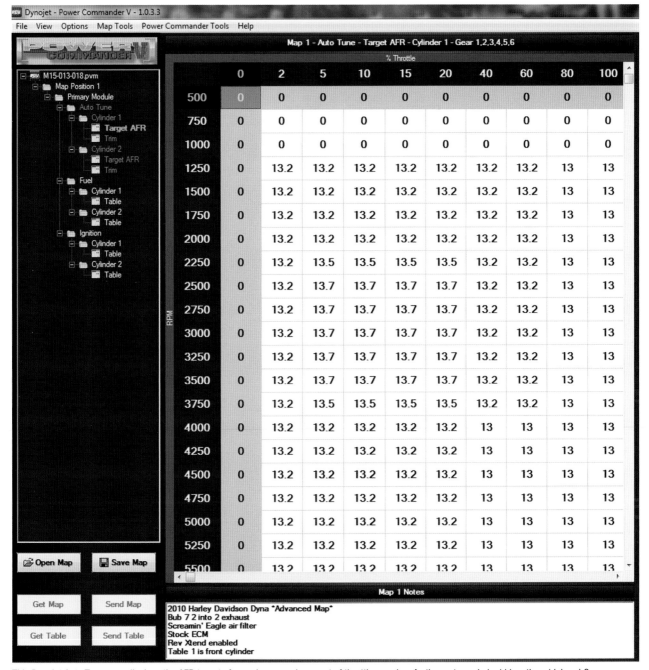

This Dynojet Auto Tune map displays the AFR targets for each rpm and percent of throttle opening. As the motorcycle is ridden, the wideband O_2 sensor and PC-V compare the actual AFR with the target AFR and adjust the base map until they match.

For example, when the engine is operated at 4,000 rpm and 20 percent throttle opening, the target AFR is 13.2. This number is based on the ideal AFR for a particular motorcycle as determined by Dynojet or an independent tuner based on dynamometer testing. The Auto Tune operation is automatic and works as the bike is ridden; however, if a dynamometer is used, the base map will be filled in more quickly. *Courtesy Dynojet Research*

uses the same technology that Dynojet's Tuning Link software uses for tuning air/fuel ratios on a dynamometer. A target AFR map is loaded into the PC-V. While the bike is ridden the wideband sensor sends a signal to the PC-V that is interpreted as the AFR for specific throttle openings and rpm settings. The PC-V then alters the fuel map to match the target AFR. The PC-V uses base maps like the PCIII, but with the Auto Tune module added fine adjustments of the fuel map are accomplished automatically. Big twin engines often vary significantly in their fuel requirements between front and rear cylinders and therefore require individual cylinder maps. The Auto Tune kit for Harley-Davidson motorcycles has two wideband O_2 sensors and the PC-V can map front and rear cylinders individually. The Auto Tune kit can be configured to run and correct AFR and fuel mapping at all times or, by using the map switch port on the PCV, the rider can switch between tuning mode and base map settings. Fuel maps developed by Dynojet come with preset AFR numbers that are the best overall settings. Once installed, the Auto Tune is like having a built-in tuner each time the bike is ridden.

The wires from the wide-band O_2 sensor are connected to the Dynojet Auto Tune module. Clear instructions and easily identifiable wires colors make it hard to get these connections wrong. *Courtesy Dynojet Research*

Here the Auto Tune module is connected to the oxygen sensor and ready to be installed under the seat. *Courtesy Dynojet Research*

The Auto Tune's power and ground connections are made using Posi-Lock connectors that are supplied with the Auto Tune kit. These make a clean, professional looking connection. *Courtesy Dynojet Research*

The Auto Tune module is plugged into the Power Commander V. Two-sided tape or Velcro can be used to mount both the Auto Tune and PCV modules. *Courtesy Dynojet Research*

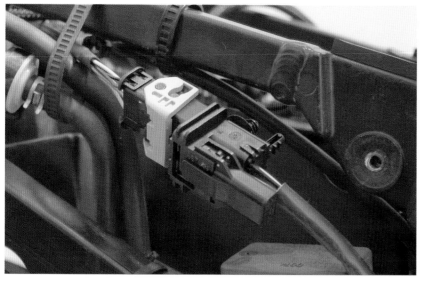

The Auto Tune wiring harness is plugged into the wide-band O_2 sensor harness. *Courtesy Dynojet Research*

Here both the PCV and Auto Tune modules are connected to the stock fuel-injection system. With the ignition key in the ON position, both have a green LED indicating that they have power and are ready to go. *Courtesy Dynojet Research*

THUNDERMAX EFI SYSTEMS

The ThunderMax line of EFI controllers are stand-alone replacements for Harley-Davidson factory ECUs. ThunderMax is engineered by Thunder Heart Performance and developed by Zipper's Performance Products. A complete ECU replacement overcomes the limitations of the stock system, including the Harley's Race Tuner software, and allows complete flexibility in setting engine parameters and fuel map tuning.

Unlike piggyback controllers that correct fuel mapping, the ThunderMax allows changes to other engine functions, including start fuel pulse, adjustable closed-loop air/fuel ratios and engine rpm targets, injector size compensation, automatic idle speed, acceleration pump simulation, ignition timing, rpm rev limits, throttle-by-wire control (2008 and up Touring models only), speedometer calibration, adjustable warm-up settings, diagnostic code output (Digital Tech scan tool

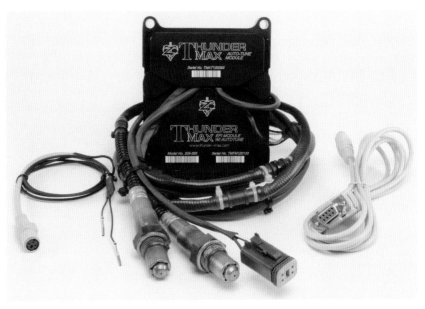

The ThunderMax Auto Tune module is bolted directly to the ThunderMax controller. This allows the system to operate in a closed loop mode as the system modifies the base map AFRs. Two wideband oxygen sensors are also included in the kit. *Courtesy Zipper's Performance Products*

Compatible), decal pop control, engine temperature alarm, live monitoring and recording, running statistics and logs, fuel map analysis, and others. More details can be found at www.thunder-max.com.

The ThunderMax EFI controller is an Alpha-N based system and uses engine rpm and throttle position to calculate basic fuel delivery and ignition timing. Unlike the stock EFI system, it does not use the factory MAP sensor. The ThunderMax uses more rpm and throttle position cells or blocks than the stock ECU uses in its look-up fuel tables—close to 2,000. Regardless of throttle position and engine rpm, there is a block on the look-up table to address the rider's demands for fuel. The abundance of rpm vs. throttle position information, plus a fast, onboard processor makes fueling and ignition control seamless to the rider. This design also makes fuel map tuning more straightforward and the system uses one less sensor input—one less thing to go wrong.

BASE MAPS

Because the stock ECU is replaced by the ThunderMax, there are no factory base fuel or ignition maps on which the Thunder Max ECU can use for basic operation. Instead, the ThunderMax must have a base map uploaded into the controller before it can be used. This is easily accomplished with Zipper's SmartLink software that comes with each ThunderMax product or can be downloaded from the company's website. Zipper's has an extensive library of base maps that they have developed using thousands of combinations of aftermarket parts on motorcycles at their dynamometer facility.

Zipper's base maps take into account engine size, engine family (TwinCam or EVO), throttle bore and injector size, exhaust system installed, muffler type and model, air cleaner, camshaft, cylinder head modifications, piston type, and other engine modifications. Zipper's continues to develop maps as soon as new aftermarket parts are available for Harley-Davidson motorcycles. If there is no base map that exactly matches the combination of engine modifications, the SmartLink software allows the base map to be adjusted by (+/-) 20 percent for fuel mapping and 10 degrees of ignition-timing

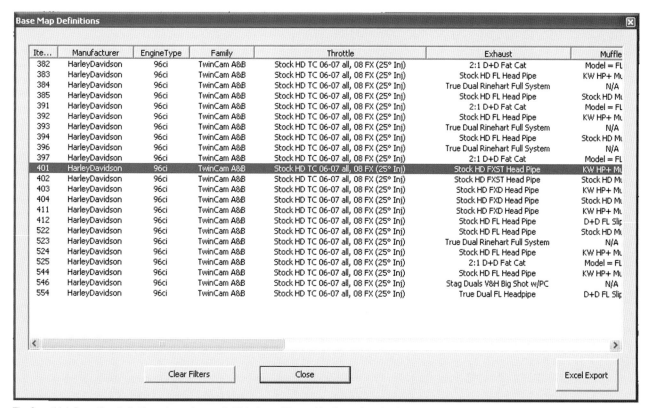

The SmartLink Base Map Definitions shown is a partial list of possible combinations of engine families, throttle and injector sizes, and exhaust systems for a particular motorcycle. Any of these base maps can be further modified to suit specific engine tuning requirements. Fuel maps can be uploaded into the ThunderMax controller. *Courtesy Zipper's Performance Products*

adjustments. Other engine parameters that can be adjusted, including idle adjustment, rpm limit, speedometer calibration, accelerator fuel enrichment, crank fuel, decal fuel cut (to prevent exhaust popping on deceleration), and engine temperature alarm (turns on check engine light if the engine overheats) are also easily adjustable with the click of a mouse.

Following is the general process for installing a ThunderMax on an XL Sportster and FXD Big Twin Harley-Davidson. Complete instructions for specific year and model come with each ThunderMax or are downloadable from their website. This is especially helpful if an owner is considering purchasing a ThunderMax and wants to see what is involved before making a commitment.

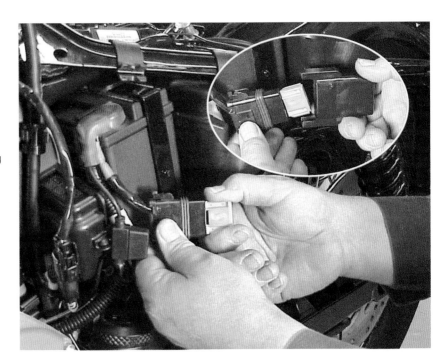

The main fuse must be removed before installing the ThunderMax. Disconnecting the Factory ECM with the fuse installed could cause damage. The fuse being removed is from an XL Sportster. *Courtesy Zipper's Performance Products*

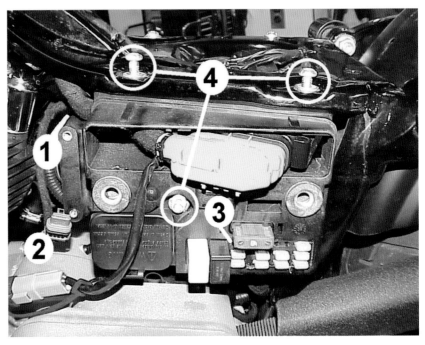

This picture is of an FXD, left side cover. Here are the steps for removing the ECM: (1) Unplug and remove the coil assembly from the ECM caddy, (2) slide the diagnostic plug forward to remove, (3) remove the ECM fuse—top left blue fuse, and (4) remove the ECM caddy bolts. *Courtesy Zipper's Performance Products*

The factory ECM is being unplugged on this XL Sportster. There is a connector tab that must be pressed to release the 36-pin connector from the ECM. *Courtesy Zipper's Performance Products*

Before installing the ECM connector, apply dielectric grease (provided with the kit) to the inside lip of the ThunderMax ECM. This will ensure the weather seal does not bind during installation. *Courtesy Zipper's Performance Products*

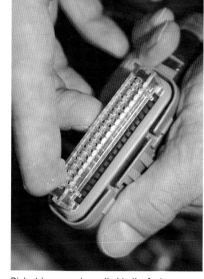

Dielectric grease is applied to the factory 36-pin connector. The grease should penetrate all the connector openings. Dielectric grease will improve conductivity between the ThunderMax and the connector. *Courtesy Zipper's Performance Products*

The ECM is being removed from this FXD. The caddy must be pulled away from the chassis to access the two ECM mounting bolts. Once the ECM is accessible, press the connector tab to remove the 36-pin connector. *Courtesy Zipper's Performance Products*

The factory O$_2$ sensors must be removed from this XL Sportster. The front sensor lead is routed behind the battery's positive cable and between the primary cover and foot peg. *Courtesy Zipper's Performance Products*

On the XL Sportster, the wide-band O$_2$ sensor harness is being routed toward the front of the engine between the left frame tube and the engine case. This is a tight fit and takes some patience. *Courtesy Zipper's Performance Products*

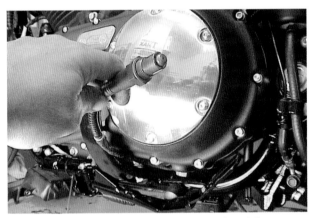

The XL's rear wide-band O$_2$ sensor harness is routed through the frame and then looped over the foot peg bracket toward the rear of the motorcycle. *Courtesy Zipper's Performance Products*

Here the front and rear O$_2$ sensors on the XL have been installed. Make sure to tighten the sensors in the exhaust pipes before securing the wiring harness to the frame with zip ties. The wires need to twist as the sensors are tightened. *Courtesy Zipper's Performance Products*

The rear O$_2$ sensor has been installed on the FXD and is just visible behind the rear exhaust pipe (arrow). *Courtesy Zipper's Performance Products*

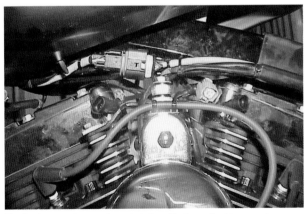

The front sensor harness is routed along the frame backbone and under the gas tank on the FXD. Check that the harness does not interfere with the gas tank when in position. Once the clearance is checked secure the harness with zip ties. *Courtesy Zipper's Performance Products*

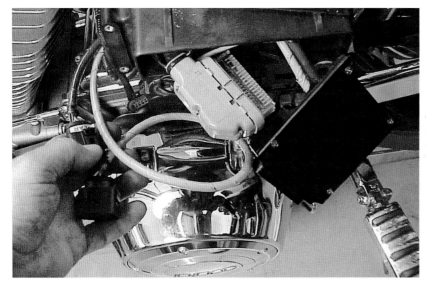

Apply dielectric grease to the front and rear O_2 sensor harnesses on the FXD. The harnesses are routed through the ECM caddy toward the front of the motorcycle. *Courtesy Zipper's Performance Products*

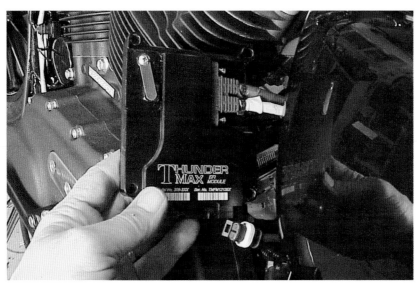

The installation on the FXD is almost complete. The oxygen sensor wires are plugged into the ThunderMax ECM. *Courtesy Zipper's Performance Products*

The ThunderMax software is installed into a PC or laptop by just inserting the CD. The software will automatically install. Just follow the instructions as they display on the monitor. *Courtesy Zipper's Performance Products*

Fuel mixture correction is but one of the numerous engine parameters that can be adjusted with the ThunderMax EFI system. The chart shows that at an engine temperature of 33 degrees F, the fuel system richens the air/fuel ratio (AFR) 59 percent over the base fuel map. As the engine warms up, the mixture is leaned out so when the engine temperature reaches around 220 degrees F, the fuel correction is only about 6 percent more than the base map. These changes offer better cold running characteristics over the stock ECU. *Courtesy Zipper's Performance Products*

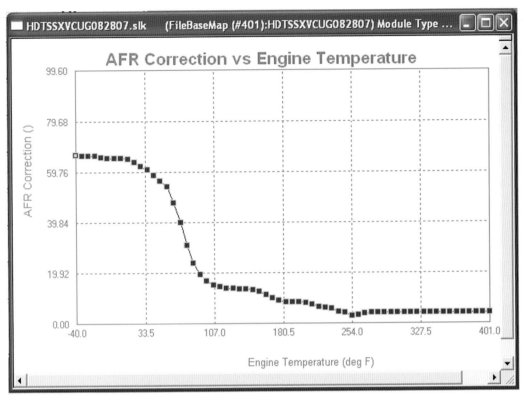

This ThunderMax fuel map is for the front cylinder on a Big Twin engine. This chart is only for a specific engine rpm, 2,816 in this case. There are fuel charts for engine rpm at 256-rpm intervals all the way from idle to redline. This type of detail produces fuel maps that offer superior performance over stock ECUs with factory fuel maps. The bottom axis of the chart is the throttle position in degrees of opening. The vertical axis is the percentage of change for fuel flow. As illustrated, the percentage change in fuel flow increases as the throttle is opened. *Courtesy Zipper's Performance Products*

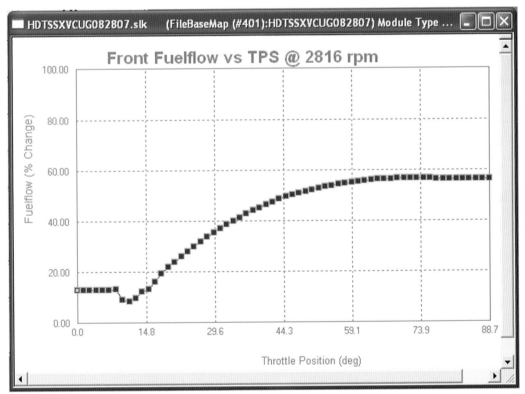

Chapter 6
Wiring Diagrams

This wiring diagram for a Yamaha FJR1300 is in color to make it easier to identify individual wires. Unfortunately, only numbers are used instead of component labels and a legend must be referred to often to make any sense of the diagram. In general, automobile wiring diagrams are much easier to read and interpret. For example, late-model Honda motorcycles are simpler to use than other powersports manufacturers—probably because they also make cars.

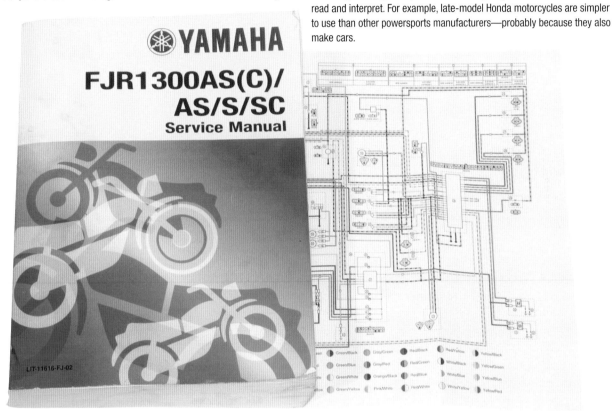

Taking a cross-country road trip when you were little may have been your introduction to reading a map. Your parents might have shown you a road atlas, and said, "We're here now, and after we drive for four days, we'll be there." Reading a wiring diagram is similar to reading a road map. Road maps illustrate how to get from point A to point B. However, instead of connecting interstates, highways, and roads, a wiring diagram shows major electrical systems, subsystems, and individual circuits, all interconnected. When a technician looks at a wiring diagram, the goal is to figure out why a circuit isn't operating, so destination points are replaced with power sources, controls, identification of and routes to load devices, and pathways for ground returns back to the negative battery terminal.

Wiring diagrams and road maps also have another feature in common—layers of detail. For example, if you look at a California road atlas, you won't be able to locate a street address in Santa Monica. You might find a city or town, but you won't find a specific route to an exact address. In order to find the exact location of a particular residence or building, you would need a detailed street map. The same is true (to a lesser extent) of wiring diagrams. On smaller or older motorcycles, wiring diagrams show the electrical system on one page. As motorcycles grew more complex and "car-like," wiring diagrams were categorized and separated into the major electrical systems and their subsystems (instead of an entire bike). This occurred, in part, due to the complexity of late-model motorcycles.

With so many electrical components, it was no longer practical to put everything on one wiring diagram on a single page. Honda's Gold Wing is a good example with its many subsystems: premium audio, satellite linked navigation, anti-lock brakes, and cold weather comfort package (heated grips, seats and backrests with individual rider and passenger controls). Honda uses individual wiring diagrams that each pertain to these specific electrical systems or subsystems. For example, if the heated pillion backrest isn't receiving 12 volts when the control is turned to HOT, and one wants to find out why, it can take several pages of wiring diagrams to map out exactly the path that power takes from the battery to the control and eventually the backrest. The diagram for the heated backrest will likely show you how power passes from the control to the heating element, but power to the controller might come from a relay located inside the fairing; consequently, a different wiring diagram might need to be consulted in order to determine how the relay receives power.

The secret to reading a particular wiring diagram is not found on the page or chart identifying all the electrical

Three Things

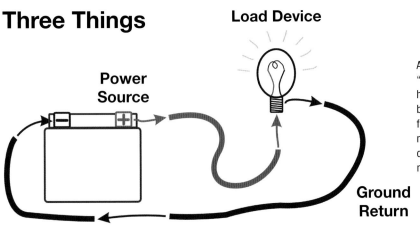

A light bulb powered by a battery illustrates the "Three Things" that all electrical circuits must have to operate. Electrical energy travels from the battery's positive terminal to the load device (the filament in the light bulb) and back to the battery negative, or ground terminal. If either side of the circuit (power or ground side) is open, the bulb will not light.

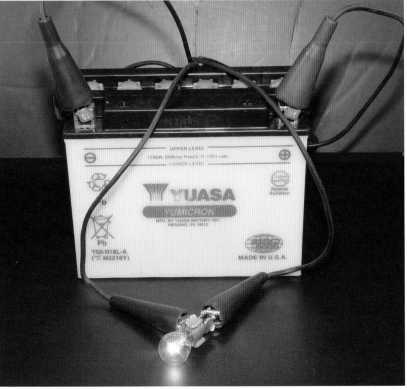

Here are the Three Things in action. The 12-volt Yuasa motorcycle battery's positive terminal provides power that is transmitted via a wire to the light bulb (red alligator clip). The bulb is "grounded" using the black alligator clip which is then connected back to the battery's negative terminal. Because the light bulb (load device) has both a positive and negative connection to the battery, the circuit is complete and the bulb lights. *Courtesy Yuasa Batteries, Inc.*

Identifying the Three Things on a wiring diagram with just one load device and a battery is easy; however, when faced with a mess of wires it's much more difficult to figure out what wires are what, regarding the Three Things. The ability to read a wiring diagram will make this process easier to digest.

symbols used. While this information is certainly valuable, it does not really tell you how to "read" a wiring diagram. The secret to deciphering a wiring diagram is to understand how a circuit or load device operates.

Every electrical circuit on a motorcycle has to have Three Things to operate: (1) a power source, (2) load device, and (3) a ground return. When the motorcycle's engine is not running the power source is the battery. As soon as the engine starts the power source switches from the battery to the motorcycle's charging system. The charging system and battery function as power sources and are extended throughout the entire motorcycle by way of wires and wiring harnesses. All wires that have 12 volts ultimately connect back to the battery's positive terminal, making them the power source for electrical components. Load devices are simply anything that does electrical work. A good example of a load device is a light bulb. This can take the form of a headlight, brake light, taillight, instrument light, or turn signal. Other load devices include the starter motor, onboard computer, instruments (speedo and tachometer), ABS braking system, heated grips, horn, and many others. In fact, the motorcycle's battery becomes a load device when the engine is running as it receives a charge (energy) from the charging system. The ground return completes the electrical path from the battery positive terminal, to the load device, and back to the battery negative terminal. Without the ground return, the load device will not operate just as it won't work without a power source.

Using the electrical road maps called wiring diagrams is not as difficult as it may seem. Identifying the Three Things in an electrical circuit is simply a matter of tracing the power source and ground return on the diagram. Every load device—motors, bulbs, relays, solenoids, and computers—requires a power source and ground return. In addition, load devices must be controlled. Some load devices are switched on or off by controlling their power source, while others are controlled by switching the ground returns on or off. Load devices may also depend on other load devices

Pictured are examples of load devices. The two black boxes are onboard computers, at right is a starter motor, and top center is a starter solenoid. Next to the starter motor (below and to the left) is an ignition coil. Light bulbs are near the coil and another smaller starter solenoid is at the lower left. All of these components require electrical energy to operate that include a power source and ground return. *Courtesy Twigg Cycles*

Here are the two power sources used on many motorcycles: the battery and alternator (Honda Gold Wing) or charging system. A smaller, off-road motorcycle may not have a battery and just use a simple charging system as an electrical power source. *Courtesy Twigg Cycles*

in order to operate, and some produce signals used by solid-state electronics that trigger other load devices as well. The process of figuring out how load devices are controlled must be determined by using a wiring diagram. This can get complicated, so to make it easier, we'll start out with some basic examples of circuit-wiring diagrams and then we'll add layers of complexity as we go. Understanding how these diagrams relate to the circuits they depict will help you when reading more complex motorcycle wiring diagrams.

Figure 1 is a simple wiring diagram showing a driving light circuit. The circuit consists of a battery, 15-amp fuse (used to protect the circuit), a switch (located on a fairing panel of the bike), and two lights. Note that the panel switch is in the open, or off position and the battery is not connected to the driving lights. This is common on wiring diagrams and switches are usually depicted as "open" or not switched on. To imagine the circuit in operation, one has to mentally "close" the switch. Now all Three Things are present in the driving light circuit and the lights are on. The positive battery terminal, fuse, switch, and wires connecting the battery to the driving lights make up the power side of the circuit. The driving lights are the load devices and the ground symbols are the ground returns for each of the lights back to the battery negative terminal. This wiring diagram is typical as it is not rendered in color. Some manufacturers may use color in wiring diagrams, but it is for purposes of identifying wire colors and not to show power or ground sides of a circuit.

The wiring diagram (Figure 2) is *not* typical of factory wiring diagrams. It shows the power side of the circuit (1) in red, which consists of the positive battery terminal, fuse, panel switch, and wires going to the lights. The fairing panel switch is in the closed (on) position and the positive side of the circuit has 12 volts at all points right up to the lights. The load devices or lights (2) are yellow, indicating that they are on. The ground return (3) symbols and wires are in black.

Reading this wiring diagram is easy for two reasons: The first is that the driving light circuit has been isolated and is not shown as a subcircuit of any other part of the overall lighting system. The second reason is that the wires and load devices are different colors—red for power, black for ground, and purple for load devices (bulb filaments). Unfortunately, most wiring diagrams do not provide any of these advantages and even late-model motorcycle diagrams may not isolate circuits to this extent. It's more likely they will be part of the overall lighting system. Color, if used at all in a wiring diagram,

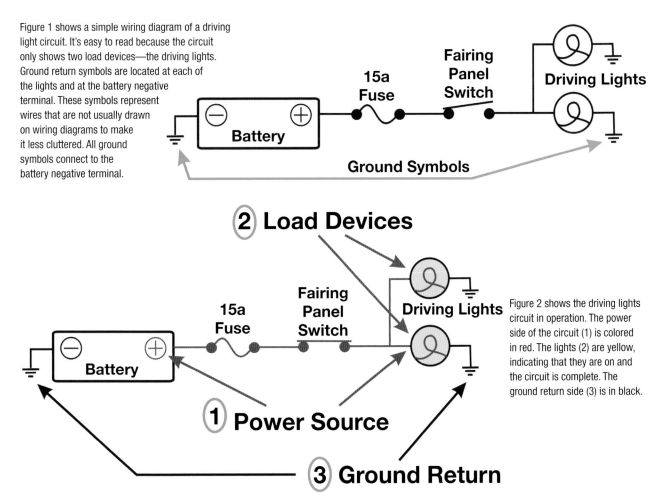

Figure 1 shows a simple wiring diagram of a driving light circuit. It's easy to read because the circuit only shows two load devices—the driving lights. Ground return symbols are located at each of the lights and at the battery negative terminal. These symbols represent wires that are not usually drawn on wiring diagrams to make it less cluttered. All ground symbols connect to the battery negative terminal.

Figure 2 shows the driving lights circuit in operation. The power side of the circuit (1) is colored in red. The lights (2) are yellow, indicating that they are on and the circuit is complete. The ground return side (3) is in black.

is used solely for the purpose of identifying individual wire colors, not to indicate power and ground sides of a circuit. In addition, wiring diagrams will not show a circuit in its on or off states.

While the wiring diagram in Figure 3 would never be used in a service manual, it does illustrate how when one of the Three Things in a circuit goes missing, the circuit doesn't operate and the driving lights are off. In this case, the 15-amp fuse has melted creating an open-circuit. Even with the panel switch in the closed position, the lights do not receive power and remain off. In the real world of electrical system diagnosis the only diagram that would be available is the one from Figure 1—a black-and-white diagram that does not show power, load device, or ground returns in color. Technicians must use their imagination to determine why the driving lights won't come on when the switch is in the ON position. The burned-out fuse is one possible reason for the nonoperational lights. Other possibilities include a bad switch that doesn't make contact, burnt-out

driving lights, bad ground return connections, or even a dead battery. A test light can be used to determine which of the Three Things is missing from the driving lights circuit as illustrated in the Figures 4 and 5.

The driving lights circuit depicted in Figure 1 does not truly represent reality (at least not the reality of motorcycle wiring diagrams). It is too simplistic and there is an inherent problem with its design that is simply solved by the addition of another component—a relay. Here's why: The wires in the circuit and fairing panel switch that control the driving lights would have to be heavy gauge in order to work reliably given the high amount of current that the lights require. Heavy-gauge wires are hard to route and the panel switch would have to be relatively large and thus take up extra space on the fairing. Instead of using a heavy-duty switch, a relay would solve these problems. The relay takes the place of the heavy-duty switch and provides the high-amperage connection between the driving lights and the battery. A panel switch would still be part of the overall circuit,

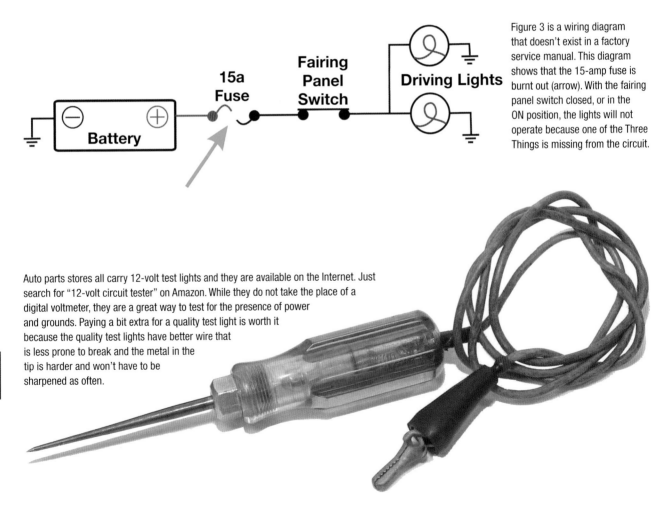

Figure 3 is a wiring diagram that doesn't exist in a factory service manual. This diagram shows that the 15-amp fuse is burnt out (arrow). With the fairing panel switch closed, or in the ON position, the lights will not operate because one of the Three Things is missing from the circuit.

Auto parts stores all carry 12-volt test lights and they are available on the Internet. Just search for "12-volt circuit tester" on Amazon. While they do not take the place of a digital voltmeter, they are a great way to test for the presence of power and grounds. Paying a bit extra for a quality test light is worth it because the quality test lights have better wire that is less prone to break and the metal in the tip is harder and won't have to be sharpened as often.

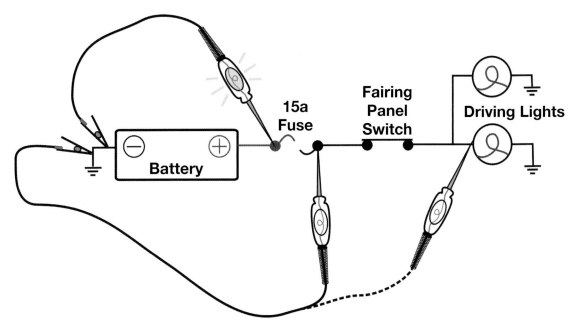

Figure 4 shows a test light connected to the negative battery terminal, where it can be used to locate the break in the power side of the circuit. As the test light's probe touches various sections of the power side of the circuit, it will light up as long as 12 volts are present. After the fuse, if the test light does not come on, it indicates that the fuse is burned out. Because the fuse, wires, and switch may be difficult to gain access to, the best place to start testing is at the driving lights themselves. If the test light were to light when touched to the power wire located at either one of the driving lights, the entire power side of the circuit is operating as it should and does not need to be checked further.

Figure 5 shows a test light connected to the positive battery terminal where it can be used to locate a break in the ground return side of a circuit. The test light will light up when probed anywhere along the ground side of the driving lights circuit, as long as there is no break between the load device and the battery's negative terminal.

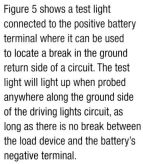

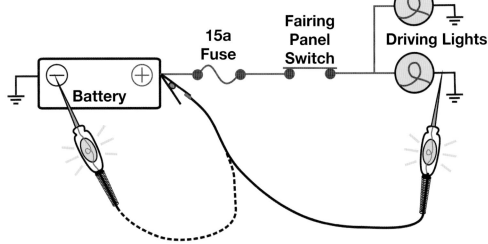

but now it only has to switch the low-amperage relay instead of the high-amperage driving lights As a result, the wires going to and from the switch, as well as the switch itself, don't have to be heavy-duty because the relay, instead of the switch, is controlling electrical current to the lights (see Figure 6).

The wiring diagram depicted in Figure 8 shows how the addition of another relay, controlled by the motorcycle's ignition switch, prevents the driving lights from being left on by mistake or with the engine not running. The purpose of Relay No. 1 is to connect power to Relay No. 2 (the same relay as depicted in Figures 6 and 7). Relay No. 2 can only receive 12 volts when the ignition key is in the ACCY (accessory) or RUN positions. If the key is in the LOCK or OFF positions, or removed from the ignition completely, no power is

Figure 6 shows that a relay has been added to the driving lights circuit. The relay now controls the high-amperage current that the lights need in order to operate (instead of the switch and wires depicted in Figure 1). The relay adds another load device to the circuit: the control coil located between terminals 3 and 4 of the relay. The 15-amp fuse supplies 12 volts to power the relay's control coil and the driving lights.

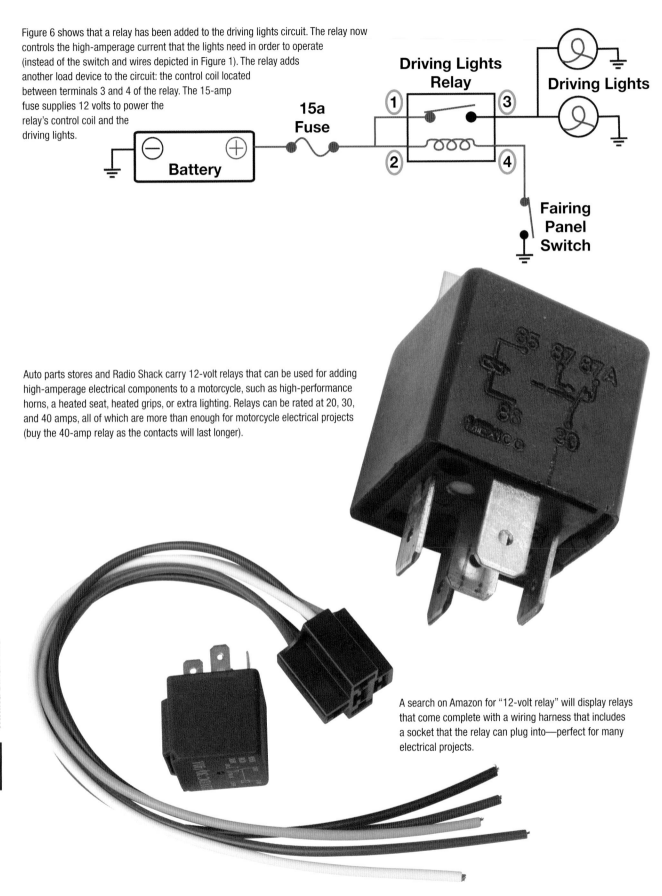

Auto parts stores and Radio Shack carry 12-volt relays that can be used for adding high-amperage electrical components to a motorcycle, such as high-performance horns, a heated seat, heated grips, or extra lighting. Relays can be rated at 20, 30, and 40 amps, all of which are more than enough for motorcycle electrical projects (buy the 40-amp relay as the contacts will last longer).

A search on Amazon for "12-volt relay" will display relays that come complete with a wiring harness that includes a socket that the relay can plug into—perfect for many electrical projects.

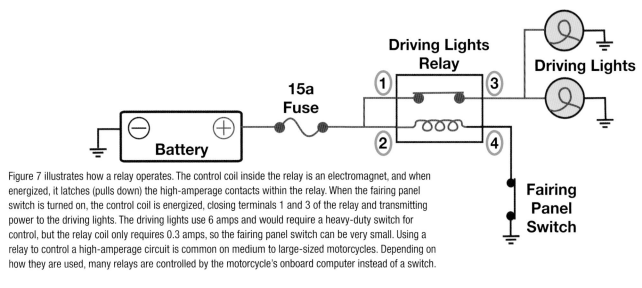

Figure 7 illustrates how a relay operates. The control coil inside the relay is an electromagnet, and when energized, it latches (pulls down) the high-amperage contacts within the relay. When the fairing panel switch is turned on, the control coil is energized, closing terminals 1 and 3 of the relay and transmitting power to the driving lights. The driving lights use 6 amps and would require a heavy-duty switch for control, but the relay coil only requires 0.3 amps, so the fairing panel switch can be very small. Using a relay to control a high-amperage circuit is common on medium to large-sized motorcycles. Depending on how they are used, many relays are controlled by the motorcycle's onboard computer instead of a switch.

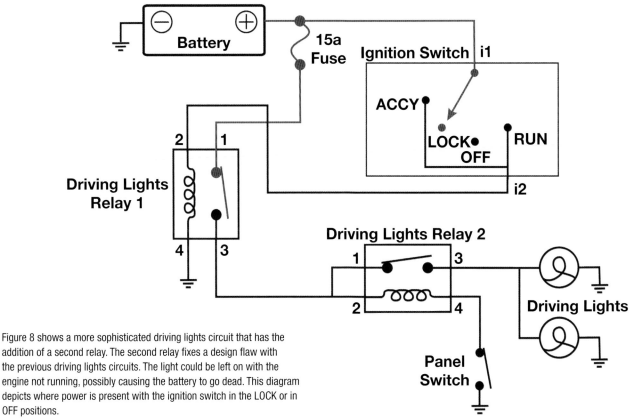

Figure 8 shows a more sophisticated driving lights circuit that has the addition of a second relay. The second relay fixes a design flaw with the previous driving lights circuits. The light could be left on with the engine not running, possibly causing the battery to go dead. This diagram depicts where power is present with the ignition switch in the LOCK or in OFF positions.

available at Relay No. 2. This prevents the driving lights from being left on inadvertently, even if the fairing panel switch is left on (see Figures 8 through11).

Figure 12 is a motorcycle horn wiring diagram that operates as follows. Starting at the top left portion of the diagram (1) Fuse F9 is a 15-amp fuse that powers half of the horn relay via a red with black stripe wire

(abbreviated as RED/BLK). The diagram provides additional information about Fuse F9, including its electrical state "Hot-At-All-Times," meaning that it is connected directly to the battery. The fuse location is also labeled "Front Power Distribution Box." To trace power from the battery to the front power distribution box another wiring diagram would have to be viewed.

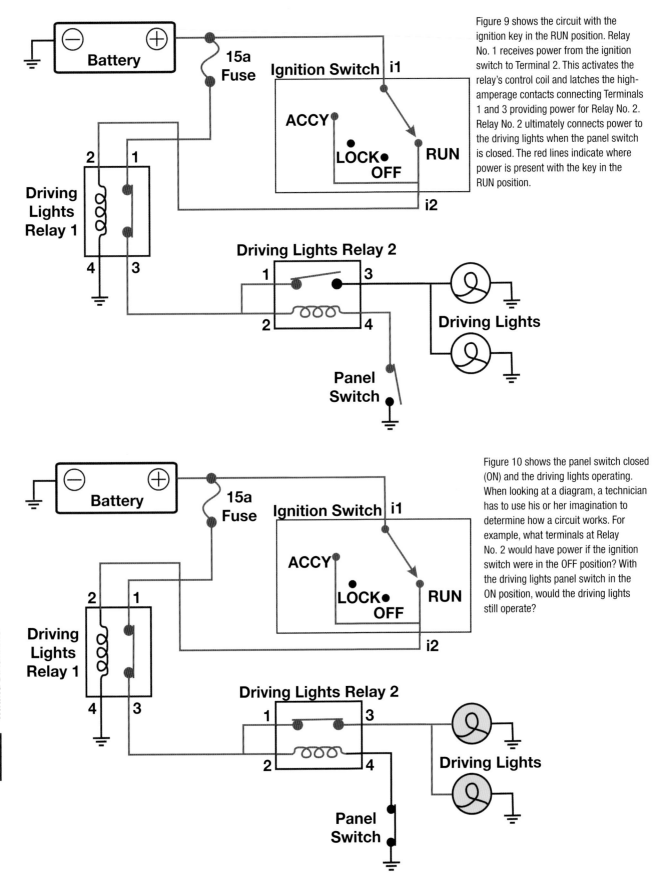

Figure 9 shows the circuit with the ignition key in the RUN position. Relay No. 1 receives power from the ignition switch to Terminal 2. This activates the relay's control coil and latches the high-amperage contacts connecting Terminals 1 and 3 providing power for Relay No. 2. Relay No. 2 ultimately connects power to the driving lights when the panel switch is closed. The red lines indicate where power is present with the key in the RUN position.

Figure 10 shows the panel switch closed (ON) and the driving lights operating. When looking at a diagram, a technician has to use his or her imagination to determine how a circuit works. For example, what terminals at Relay No. 2 would have power if the ignition switch were in the OFF position? With the driving lights panel switch in the ON position, would the driving lights still operate?

Figure 11 is how the two-relay driving lights circuit would appear in a typical factory service manual. Any color that is used would only be to identify the wire colors but not where 12 volts or power from the battery is present. All switches are usually depicted in their OFF, or open, position, and relays are in their OFF state (high-amperage contacts are not connected or are open). If the driving lights did not operate with the panel switch on, and the ignition switch was in the ACCY or RUN positions, a technician would start diagnosis by tracing power using a voltmeter or 12-volt test light. A good place to start is the 15-amp fuse and work toward Relay No. 2.

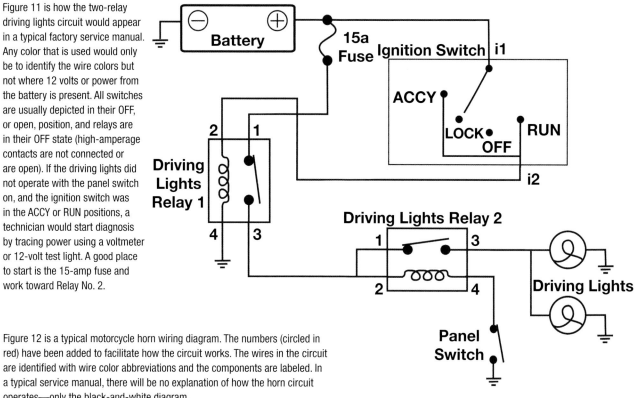

Figure 12 is a typical motorcycle horn wiring diagram. The numbers (circled in red) have been added to facilitate how the circuit works. The wires in the circuit are identified with wire color abbreviations and the components are labeled. In a typical service manual, there will be no explanation of how the horn circuit operates—only the black-and-white diagram.

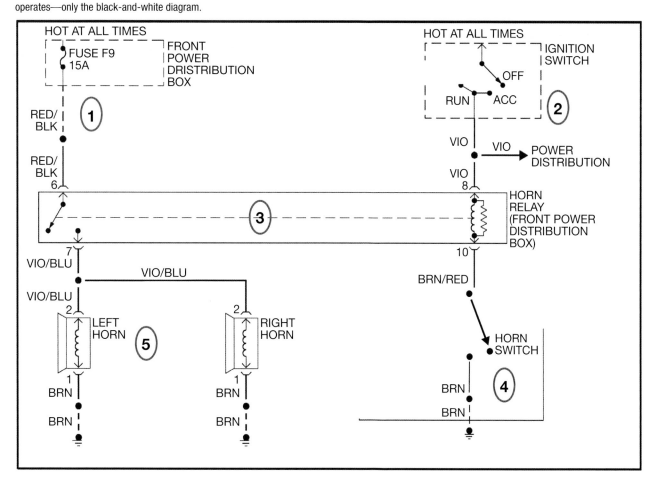

The ignition switch (2) is shown at the top right. Power to the switch is connected directly to the battery indicated by the "HOT AT ALL TIMES" label. In the ACCY and RUN positions, power will be present on the violet (VIO) wire. In the OFF position, the horn circuit will not operate because the relay's control coil has no power.

Number 3 in the diagram is the horn relay. The left side shows the high-amperage contacts that will power the horn. The right side is the relay's control coil. The coil will be activated when the horn switch is in the ON position but only if the ignition is on as well.

The horn switch (4) is at the lower right of the diagram. When the horn switch (button on the handlebars) is pressed, the brown-and-red striped (BRN/RED) wire is connected to the brown wire (BRN), which is ground. This activates the horn relay control coil that pulls the high-amperage contacts together.

When the horn button is pressed, the violet-and-blue (VIO/BLU) wire will have 12 volts and the horns will sound (5). The horn relay connects the RED/BLK wire to the VIO/BLU wire, completing the horn circuit. Both horns have a ground return via the brown (BRN) wire, as shown in the diagram.

The majority of 12-volt relays used on motorcycles operate in a similar manner as shown in Figure 13. Because they are commonly used on many years and models of bikes, the following example of a horn circuit (Figure 13) can be used as a guide for checking other relays. Following are the steps to check the relay.

1. With a test light connected to a chassis ground, or to the battery's negative terminal, the test light should light at Terminal 6 of the horn relay, which should always be "hot" or have 12 volts. If the test light did not light up, Fuse F9 should be checked.

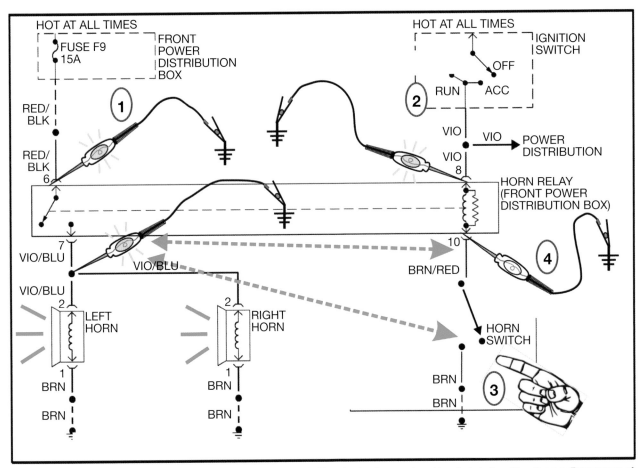

Figure 13 shows that a 12-volt test light can be used to test the horn circuit. The relay has four numbered terminals in the wiring diagram. For purposes of explanation, step numbers with test light connections have been added. Steps 1 through 3 test for the presence of 12 volts at the relay. Step 4 triggers the relay and bypasses the horn button.

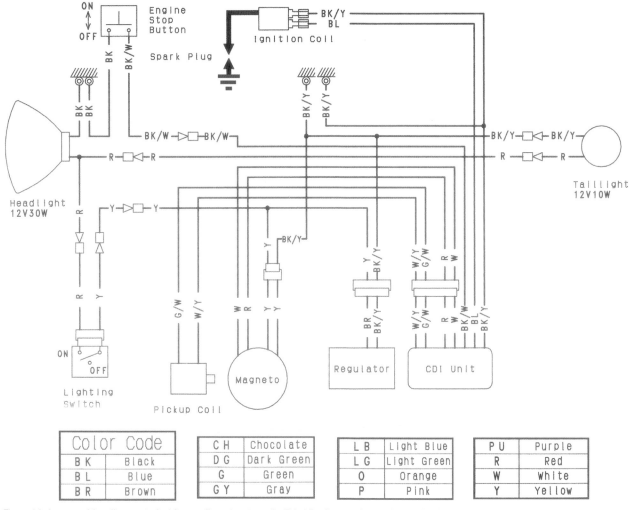

Color Code	
B K	Black
B L	Blue
B R	Brown

C H	Chocolate
D G	Dark Green
G	Green
G Y	Gray

L B	Light Blue
L G	Light Green
O	Orange
P	Pink

P U	Purple
R	Red
W	White
Y	Yellow

Figure 14 shows a wiring diagram typical for an off-road motorcycle. This bike does not have a battery, but instead uses a magneto as a power source for the ignition and lighting systems. The only load devices are a headlight, taillight, and ignition coil. The magneto has two pairs of wires. Each pair connects to a charging coil (not visible in the diagram). One charge coil powers the CDI ignition unit and the other is used for the lighting circuit. The head and taillight can be switched on or off via the lighting switch. The regulator adjusts charging voltage to 12 volts for the lights. Each wire is identified by its color, and wire colors are listed at the bottom of the diagram. Wires marked with two sets of letters have a solid color with a stripe. For example, if a wire's colors are G/W the wire is green with a white stripe or BK/LB is black with a light blue stripe. Wires that are only one color are marked with one set of letters. Before going on to Figure 15, try to identify the Three Things that make up the lighting circuit.

2. With the ignition key in the ON position, relay Terminal 8 should have power from the ignition switch. A test light connected to a ground will light up when connected as shown. If no power is present at Terminal 8, the wires going to the ignition switch should be checked, or check the power wire from the battery to the ignition switch.

3. When the horn button is pressed, Terminal 7 should also light up the test light and sound the horns. If the test light works, but the horns don't, the wires from the horn relay to the horns should be checked. Also, the ground return wires (BRN) should be checked for a bad ground.

4. The horn button can be bypassed by touching the grounded test light to Terminal 10 of the horn relay. The grounded test light will connect relay Terminal 10 to ground (just like the horn button). If the horns work using the test light to trigger the relay, but do not when the horn button is pressed, the horn button may be making poor contact to ground, or the ground wire is not connected to ground.

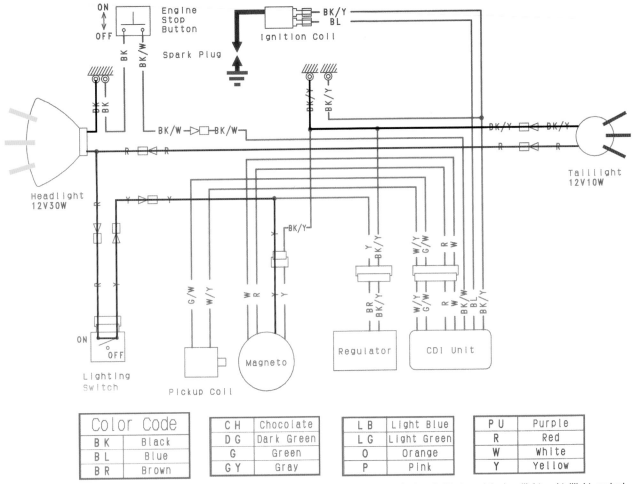

Color Code		C H	Chocolate	L B	Light Blue	P U	Purple
B K	Black	D G	Dark Green	L G	Light Green	R	Red
B L	Blue	G	Green	O	Orange	W	White
B R	Brown	G Y	Gray	P	Pink	Y	Yellow

Figure 15 highlights the lighting circuit. With the power side of the circuit shown in red, the ground return in black, and the headlight and taillight marked, it's easy to see the Three Things that make up a complete circuit. The yellow (Y) wire at the magneto is the power source. The lighting switch connects the yellow and red wires when the lights are switched on. Black-and-white wires are the ground return for both head and taillights. The ground wires use a symbol that is in reality the engine or motorcycle chassis. Before going on to Figure 16, try to locate the power source and ground return for the CDI Unit.

Note: Do not use a jumper wire in Step 4 to trigger the relay. While Terminal 10 on the horn relay is easily identified in the diagram, the actual relay with the wires connected may be much harder to identify. A jumper wire connected to the wrong relay terminal could cause an electrical short, melting fuses and burning wires. The reason a test light is used is that if the wrong terminal is grounded, the test light will just light up and not cause an electrical meltdown.

If the engine had no spark and the ignition coil had been replaced, the CDI unit, pickup coil, and wires connecting everything together could be the cause of the problem. The pickup coil can be tested at the CDI unit (wires highlighted in blue) using an ohmmeter or by measuring AC voltage (see the section "AC Pickup Coil" in Chapter 4, "Ignition Systems"). If the pickup coil

tests well, the CDI unit could be the cause of the no-spark condition. A new CDI unit is $482, and the dealer won't let you try one to see if your CDI unit is bad. Instead of guessing, and spending money, all the wires at the CDI unit should be tested. If they all have the correct electrical values and connections, the logical conclusion is that the CDI unit is bad and should be replaced.

The CDI unit receives power from the magneto via the white/yellow and green/white wires, indicated in red (see Figure 14). The ground return is the black/yellow wire as it connects to chassis ground. The black/white wire goes to the engine stop button (top left). If this wire were shorted to ground (when the engine stop button that is off the wire is grounded) the CDI unit will not produce a spark and the engine won't start. The last wire to check is the black wire that goes to the ignition coil.

If all the wires have what's supposed to be on them, then the CDI unit has everything it needs to work—so a no-spark condition would be caused by a bad CDI Unit.

By studying Figures 14 through 16, the entire off-road motorcycle's wiring diagram has been explained in detail. Unfortunately, in a real service manual there are generally no explanations or color-highlighted diagrams. Technicians have to use their imagination to isolate each circuit by identifying the Three Things that each needs to operate.

WIRING DIAGRAM EXERCISES

The most effective way to learn how to read and use a wiring diagram is to practice. With that in mind, the next several wiring diagrams are followed by a series of questions for you to answer. Write your answers down on a piece of paper as you look at each diagram. It may also help to draw the circuit that the question relates to. The correct answers to the questions and their analysis can be found at the end of this chapter. You may want to refer back to chapters on charging, ignition, or electronic fuel injection when answering some of the questions. The questions become progressively more difficult for each wiring diagram. Also, when taking tests in school, some of your teachers probably told you, "There are no trick questions." This is not the case here, as there are a few "trick" questions designed to make you think. Good luck!

As you can see the wiring diagram for this motorcycle (Figure 17) is more complex than the off-road bike in the previous wiring diagram and is pretty typical of a late

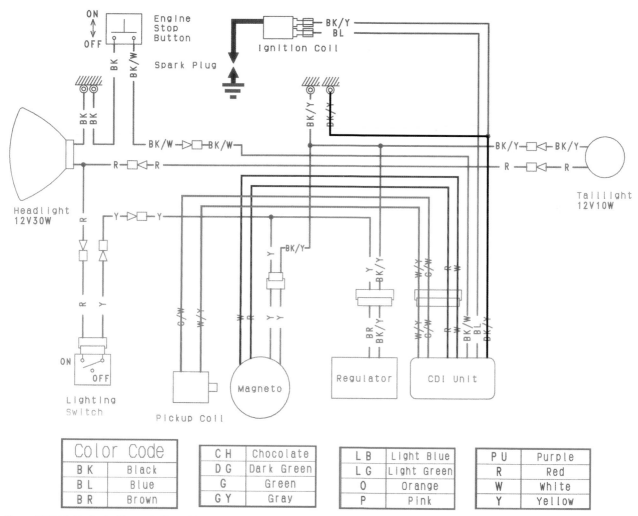

Color Code		CH	Chocolate	LB	Light Blue	PU	Purple
BK	Black	DG	Dark Green	LG	Light Green	R	Red
BL	Blue	G	Green	O	Orange	W	White
BR	Brown	GY	Gray	P	Pink	Y	Yellow

Figure 16 highlights the ignition control box (CDI unit) circuit. The ignition system uses an AC pickup coil (next to the magneto) to provide an rpm signal to the CDI unit (see Chapter 4 on ignition systems for more information). The CDI unit controls the ignition coil that fires the spark plug. The "Engine Stop Button" turns off the CDI unit to shut the engine off.

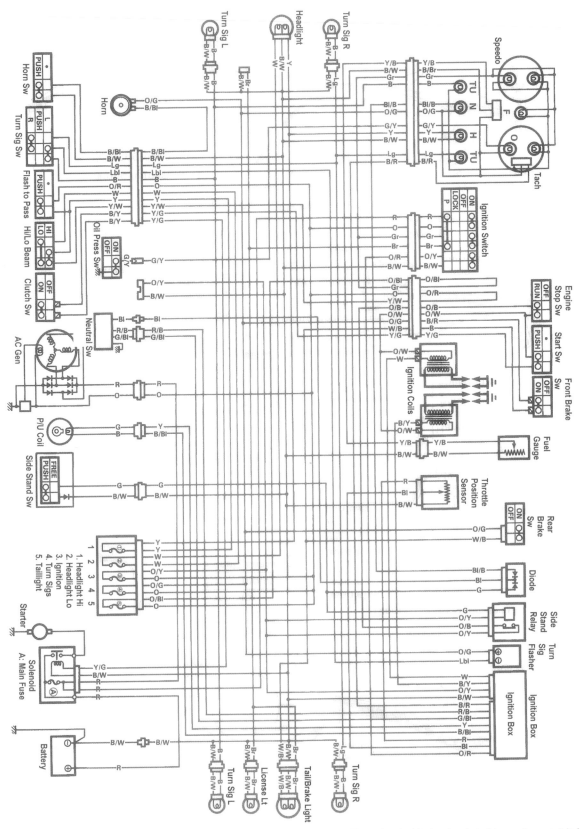

Figure 17 shows a typical Japanese motorcycle wiring diagram for a carbureted motorcycle. The entire electrical system is in this one diagram. It is fairly easy to read, though unfortunately that is not always the case. Some manufacturers don't label components, but instead use numbers, and the diagrams are so small you need a microscope to actually read one.

1990s motorcycle. Later model years of motorcycles may use more than one page to depict all the electrical circuits, as they won't fit onto one page. This bike is carbureted, but has electronic ignition and uses a throttle position sensor. A one-piece alternator with internal voltage regulator is used for the charging system. Five fuses distribute power to various components. There is only one relay used for the side stand. There is an interlock feature that prevents the engine from starting, unless the clutch is pulled in and the side stand is up. Lighting controls are standard, except there is a "Flash to Pass" European-style switch on the left handlebar control. Instruments are standard and include speedometer, tachometer, fuel gauge, and indicators for neutral, high beam, and turn signals. Wire colors are indicated by letters, as in G = green, Br = brown, Lbl = light blue, O/Bl = orange with a black stripe, and so on. To help in answering the questions related to the diagram a good visual aid is to draw on paper just the circuit that is being studied. This will help with removing all the other wiring clutter that tends to hide the circuit. Answering the following wiring diagram-related questions will help you sharpen your wiring diagram reading skills. Good luck again.

1. The four instrument lights are out when the key is in the ON position. The oil pressure light (marked with an "O") works. What fuse powers the instrument lights and what is the wire color at the ignition switch that provides power to the instrument lights?
2. You're trying to diagnose a no-spark problem. You have determined that there is no power at either of the ignition coils (orange/white wires) when the ignition switch is in the ON position. Trace the path that power takes from the battery to the ignition coils. Include what wires (colors), fuses, switches, and relays that are used.
3. The brake light does not come on when the front brake lever or rear brake pedal are applied (ignition is in the ON position). Trace power from the tail or brake light to the battery. Include wire colors and electrical components that are used.
4. With the key in the ON position, and the engine stop switch in the RUN position, the starter doesn't operate when the start switch (button) is pressed. How can a test light be used at the starter solenoid to make the starter motor operate?

Figure 18 is the wiring diagram for a fuel-injected, two-cylinder motorcycle. As you can see there are no labels used on the wiring diagram, but instead a numbering system is used to identify electrical components, connectors, buttons, switches, and relays. While this makes the diagram less cluttered, it also adds another step in reading the diagram, as a legend has to be consulted to make sense of what you're looking at. The ECM is located at the top of the diagram and each terminal, or pin, is numbered. Because the ECM is complex no circuits are shown in the diagram to indicate its inner workings. The same is true for the speedometer (14). The two fuel injectors are numbers 23 and 24 and located at the bottom center of the diagram. This motorcycle uses two spark plugs per cylinder and thus uses two dual-plug coils (5, top left). Various sensors are scattered through the diagram. Figure 19 is the legend for Figure 18 and all the components are identified by name and number. Understand this typical EFI wiring diagram will help you solve EFI-related problems. Have fun figuring out the answers.

1. This EFI system uses two crankshaft sensors. Both sensors are AC pickup coil types of speed sensors. How could you check the operation of both sensors at the ECM? You may want to refer back to the "AC Pickup Coil" section in Chapter 4, "Ignition Systems," to review how these sensors operate.
2. What is each of the four wires at the EFI relay used for? Where do they go and how is the relay controlled? To what components does the relay provide power?
3. The motorcycle has no spark. There is power to both ignition coils. When you connect a test light across the coil primary terminals there is no primary switching when the engine is cranked over. Both crank sensors produce AC voltage at the ECM, so they are good as well. Because the ECM not only operates the fuel injectors but also acts as the ignition module, it may be bad. A new one costs, well I won't say how much it costs, but it's a lot. The dealer can simply plug in a new ECM and see if that fixes the problem. You on the other hand don't have that luxury. Before replacing the ECM you need to make sure that it has all the power and ground inputs it needs to work. What ECM pins should you check to find all the power and grounds?
4. What are the three wires at the TPS sensor for? What should be on each wire with the key in the ON position?

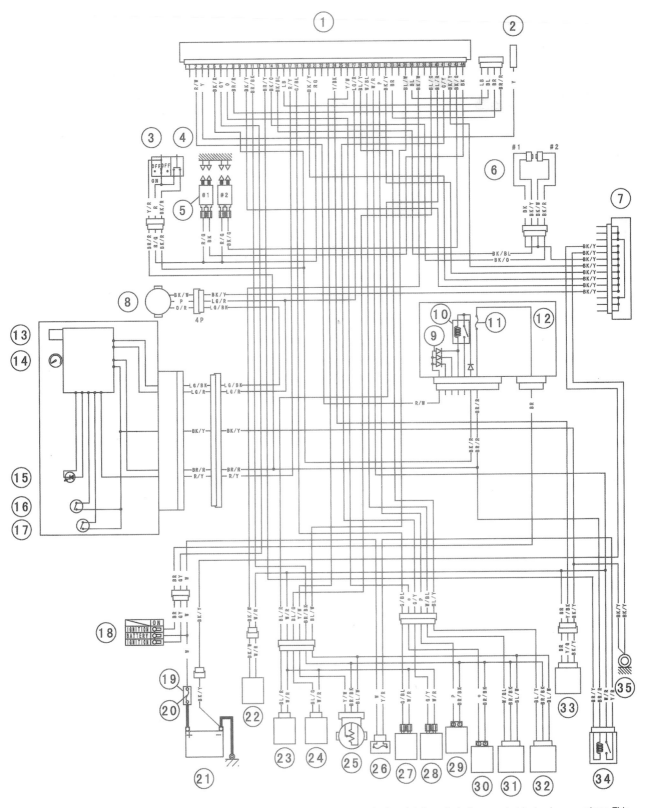

Figure 18 is a diagram of an electronic fuel-injected motorcycle. Some manufacturers don't place labels on their diagrams but instead use numbers. This adds another step in reading and interpreting this type of wiring diagram as each component has to be identified separately.

Number	Component	Number	Component	Number	Component
1	ECM	13	Instruments	25	TPS
2	Diag Terminal	14	Speedometer	26	EFI Fuse
3	Eng Stop Sw	15	Check Eng Light	27	ISC Valve
4	Start Button	16	Mode Sw	28	ISC Valve
5	Ignition Coils	17	Reset Sw	29	Air Temp Sen
6	Crank Sensor	18	Ignition Switch	30	Eng Temp Sen
7	Connector	19	Starter Relay	31	MAP
8	Road Speed Sen	20	Main Fuse	32	BARO
9	Interlock Diodes	21	Battery	33	Crash Sensor
10	Start Relay	22	Fuel Pump	34	EFI Relay
11	Ignition Fuse	23	Injector	35	Ground
12	Junction Bx	24	Injector		

Figure 19 is the legend for Figure 18. Refer to this table to identify the components in the EFI wiring diagram.

ANSWERS TO WIRING DIAGRAM EXERCISES QUESTIONS
Answers to Exercises—Figure 17

1. The taillight fuse (No. 5) powers the instrument lights. The wire from the fuse is orange/blue. At the connector located next to the ignition switch, the wire changes color to green, where it then goes to the ignition switch. From there it passes through a connector (below the instrument cluster) where it powers the four instrument bulbs.

2. Starting at the battery positive terminal, power follows the red wire to the starter solenoid, where it goes through the main fuse. From the fuse it comes out of the starter solenoid on the red wire (not the one going to the alternator). The red wire goes to the ignition switch. When the ignition switch is in the ON position, all the wires at the ignition switch will have 12 volts.

That was the easy part. There are now five wires coming out of the ignition switch all with power. Rather than trace each one, go to the orange/white wire at the ignition coils and work backward to the ignition switch. From the coils the orange/white wire goes to the engine stop switch. The RUN position on the stop switch is an orange/blue wire that goes to the side stand relay (top right of the diagram). The high-amperage contacts inside the relay pass power to the orange/yellow wire, where it goes to the No. 3 ignition fuse. Notice that the orange/yellow wire branches out in several directions. This clue indicates that this is a power wire feeding other components or circuits in the diagram. From ignition fuse (No. 3) the wire color is orange. This wire goes back to the ignition switch, other locations, and ultimately the battery positive terminal.

3. The brake light power wire is the white/black wire at the tail/brake light assembly. It goes to the rear brake switch and the front brake switch. From the rear brake switch the wire is orange/green and goes to Fuse 4 (turn signals). The front brake switch also gets power from the same fuse. Fuse 4 is powered from the orange wire that goes to the ignition switch. Power to the ignition switch comes from the red wire that goes to the starter solenoid and then on to the battery positive terminal.

4. The starter solenoid is just a form of 12-volt relay. A test light that is connected to ground, and then

touched to the black/white wire at the solenoid will trigger the solenoid and cause the starter motor to operate. The start switch does the same thing when it's pressed: It grounds the black/white wire at the solenoid. Caution: If you try this test on a real motorcycle make sure that the transmission is in neutral.

Answers to Exercises—Figure 18

1. Checking the crankshaft sensors on this motorcycle at the ECM is less time consuming than taking the engine case off where the sensors are located or trying to get to the wiring harness. The crank sensors (6) each have two wires. One from each sensor goes to the connector (7). The connector provides a ground for the crank sensors and other components. The other crank sensor wires go to the ECM on Pin 15, a black/blue wire and Pin 14, a black/orange wire. Notice that the crank sensor wires change colors at the connector at the crank sensor.

   By unplugging the ECM and connecting a digital voltmeter to ground and Pin 14 on the ECM wiring harness, one of the crank sensors can be tested. The voltmeter should be set to read AC volts. When the engine is cranked, the meter should indicate AC voltage to verify that the sensor is operating. ECM wiring harness Pin 15 would be tested in the same manner for the other crank sensor. Most service manuals provide crank sensor resistance values and these could be checked using the same ECM pins. See Chapter 4 for more information.

2. The wires at the EFI relay (34, located at bottom right of the diagram) are brown/yellow (relay control coil), brown/red (relay control coil), white/red (high-amperage contacts), and yellow/red also high-amperage contacts.

   To figure out how the relay is controlled (turned on or off) you need to trace the relay control coil wires. Power for the relay's control coil is on the brown/red wire that comes from the ignition fuse (11) that receives power from the ignition switch (18). To control the relay, the brown/yellow wire receives a ground signal from Pin 13 on the ECM.

   The yellow/red wire at the EFI relay is the power wire that switches it on. This wire comes from EFI fuse (26). At the fuse the wire is white and it goes directly to the main fuse (20) located at the battery (21). The EFI relay provides power to the fuel pump, fuel injectors, ECM, and ISC valves.

3. All powers and grounds to the ECM should be checked with the ECM plugged in and the ignition key on. Power to the ECM is on Pin 30, white/red wire from the ECM relay, and Pin 21 (red/green wire) that receives power from the engine stop switch (3), which in turn receives power from the ignition fuse (11). Pin 5 should have power when the starter is cranking. Pin 11 is the 5-volt reference to the some of the sensors and is supplied power by the ECM. ECM grounds are Pin 6, which goes directly to the battery negative terminal, and Pins 20 and 32 are grounds that connect to the ground connector (7).

   If all the powers and grounds are good, and the crank sensors are working, the only thing left at this point is a bad ECM.

4. The TPS sensor is number 25 (bottom, center of diagram). The black/white wire is the TPS ground and connects to ECM Pin 35. The brown/black wire is the 5-volt reference wire and goes to ECM Pin 11 (notice that this wire is also the 5-volt reference for other sensors). The yellow/white is the TPS signal wire and goes to ECM Pin 26. See Chapter 5 for more information on testing a TPS sensor.

Chapter 7
Electrical Projects

The key to installing electrical accessories is not to overtax the motorcycle's charging system. The Gold Wing alternator (left) puts out 1300 watts, enough to power just about anything added to a bike. Most motorcycles have a stator and rectifier type of charging system (right) and may not be up to running high-energy demanding accessories like driving lights or heated clothing.

Adding electrical accessories to your bike is a great way to make motorcycling more practical and fun. Extending your riding season can be easily accomplished by using heated clothing, including vests, pants, jackets, gloves, and even electric shocks. Knowing how lost you really are is even more fun with a GPS guidance system and listening to tunes on long stretches of interstate can be relaxing. There are many safety-related electrical projects that can make your bike more visible to other drivers out on the road, including flashing brake lights, extra taillights and running lights, super bright driving lights, and headlight modulators (pulsing headlight).

With so much aftermarket electrical accessories available, it's easy to get carried away and if the motorcycle's charging system can't keep up with all the electrical items installed the result will be a dead battery and dead motorcycle. What most riders don't realize is that once a motorcycle starts, the battery is no longer supposed to provide power to the electrical components. This is true for both factory-installed and owner-added electrical accessories. With the motor running, the charging system supplies power for everything, including charging the battery. If the

electrical power requirements exceed the charging system's capacity, the battery will make up the difference. This scenario will work for a while, but eventually the battery will become discharged, and when there is not enough power to run the fuel or ignition systems the engine will quit running.

Calculating electrical loads for the accessories that an owner wants to install and determining if the motorcycle's charging system can handle the extra power output requirements is something that should be considered before starting an electrical project. The following information regarding calculating excess electrical capacity comes from Powerlet Products (www. powerlet.com). More information on Powerlet and other companies featured in this chapter can be found in the Sources section at the back of this book.

HOW MUCH IS TOO MUCH?

A motorcycle's charging system is designed to power everything electrical that was installed at the factory and charge the battery at the same time. On most bikes the charging system has some extra electrical capacity built in for additional electrical accessories. This "extra"

Make	Model	Year	Fuel Delivery	Peak Charging Output
BMW	R1150RT	2003	Fuel injected	700 watts
BMW	K1600GS	2013	Fuel injected	580 watts
BMW	R1200GS	2013	Fuel injected	580 watts
Ducati	ST2/ST4	2002	Fuel injected	520 watts
Harley	FLT	1997 to 2005	Carbureted	650 watts
Harley	FLT	2006 to 2011	EFI & Carb	725 watts
Harley	Sportster	2008 to 2011	Fuel injected	478 watts
Honda	ST1300	2008	Fuel injected	740 watts
Honda	Valkyrie	2000	Carbureted	546 watts
Honda	GL1800	2012	Fuel injected	1300 watts
Kawasaki	Vulcan 1500	2000	Carbureted	377 watts
Kawasaki	Ninga 250	2008	Carbureted	266 watts
Kawasaki	ZX6R	2001	Carbureted	305 watts
Suzuki	Bandit 1200	1999	Carbureted	405 watts
Suzuki	V-Strom	2002	Fuel injection	360 watts
Yamaha	FJR1300	2009	Fuel injected	590 watts

Figure 1: This is a table that will give you a ballpark number for charging system output in watts for a variety of motorcycles. To find the specific output in watts for a given year, make, or model of motorcycle, check out the online motorcycle forums where someone has already done the research or an owner's manual. *Courtesy Powerlet Products*

electrical output from the charging system is what there is to work with to power whatever aftermarket electrical accessories the owner decides to install.

A motorcycle's excess electrical capacity is the charging system's output minus the normal operating loads. So exactly how many electronic gadgets can your motorcycle's charging system power? That depends on what year, make, and model of bike and ultimately how much electrical energy (measured in watts) the charging system can produce. To find excess electrical capacity, two numbers are needed: the charging system's output in watts and the total watts required for the stock electrical components. Watts produced by the charging system can be found easily in an owner's manual, service manual, or online at either the manufacturer's website or online forum. Finding the total watts consumed by the factory-installed components is a little more challenging. Some owner's manuals may list

wattage for each electrical component; however, if this information is not available the number will have to be estimated.

Figure 2 is a generic list of the number of watts required by typical components used in many motorcycles. In this example, 402 is the total number of watts needed to power all the factory-installed components, assuming that they are on all the time. The "on-all-the-time" loads total only 212 watts. Only the loads that are on all the time need to be used in the total watts calculation. Horn, brake light, and cooling fan are not used continuously so they don't need to be added to the total watts for the bike's electrical system. In addition, most motorcycles don't operate both high- and low-beam headlights at the same time so only one of these lights should be added to the total. Many large touring bikes have additional loads, including lighting, stereo radios, amplifiers, CD players, and heated grips, so make sure you include all of the items that could operate continuously while riding. In general, operating loads for carbureted bikes are around 195 watts and large fuel-injected models require about 285 watts.

To find the excess charging capacity, subtract the estimated factory electrical loads from the charging system's maximum output. The watts that are left over are what are available to work with for aftermarket electrical accessories. Exceeding the excess wattage for short periods of time is not a problem as the battery will make up the difference between what the charging system can produce and what the electrical accessories require. If the extra power is needed from the battery for long periods of time, however, the battery will eventually go dead and the engine will stop running

Another factor to consider is that a motorcycle-charging system will not produce anywhere close to its peak output with the engine at idle. For example, a Harley-Davidson Ultra Classic Electra-Glide will produce only 380 watts at idle. At 3,000 rpm (cruising

Component	Load	Use
High Beam	65 watts	Off with low beam
Low Beam	55 watts	Off with high beam
License Plate	5 watts	On all the time
Brake Light(s)	20 watts	Intermitent use
Tail/Running Lights	15 watts	On all the time
Instruments	2 watts	On all the time
Computer	25 watts	On all the time
Fuel Pump	60 watts	On all the time
Cooling Fan	60 watts	Intermitent use
Ignition	50 watts	On all the time
Horn	45 watts	Intermitent use
Total Watts	402 watts	
Total On All the Time	212 watts	

Figure 2: This table provides some basic numbers for calculating a motorcycle's normal operating electrical loads in watts. Some of the loads are on all the time, while others are intermittent. Most service manuals (and some owner's manuals) will give you more specific wattage numbers. *Courtesy Powerlet Products*

Example	Peak	Operating	Excess Capacity
Buell Blast	297 watts	195 watts	102 watts
Kawasaki ZX6R	305 watts	200 watts	105 watts
Ducati ST2/ST4	520 watts	285 watts	245 watts
Suzuki V-Strom	360 watts	285 watts	75 watts
Honda Valkyrie	546 watts	250 watts	296 watts
Vulcan 1500 FI	588 watts	340 watts	248 watts

Figure 3: Here are some examples of excess charging system capacity. As you can see, the number of watts available to run electrical accessories varies widely between motorcycles. In general, the larger the bike the more charging capacity it will have. *Courtesy Powerlet Products*

speed) the charging system makes 578 watts and above that the peak output is 589 watts. Take this into consideration if you plan on using electrical accessories when running the engine at low speeds.

As can be seen in Figure 4, heated clothing really adds up when you consider both rider and passenger. Add two electric vests or jackets and two pairs of heated gloves, and more than 250 watts can be reached easily. Another power user is auxiliary driving lights. If you want to light up a dark road like it's daytime, driving lights will do the job but can add significant electrical loads to your motorcycle's charging system. Notice the difference between standard halogen driving lights and the new, solid-state light-emitting diodes (LEDs), which use considerably less power than traditional lighting—almost less than half the watts. In addition to driving lights, LEDs are available for running, tail, brake, and turn-signal lighting. LEDs use less power, last longer (will outlast the normal life of the motorcycle), and are considerably brighter than conventional lighting. With so many new LED products in the marketplace, they are the way to go for all types of aftermarket lighting.

This Glenda LED light only uses 12 watts and outputs almost twice the light that a conventional incandescent light provides. The Glenda lighting kit comes with two lights and are designed to provide high visibility in fog or for oncoming drivers. *Courtesy Clearwater Lights*

Accessory	Watts
Heated Vest	70w
Heated Jacket	100w
Heated Gloves	30w
Heated Socks	25w
Heated Seat	20-50w
Heated Grips	30-50w
Halogen Lights	35-100w (each)
LED Lights	20-70w (pair)
Cell Phone	1-3w
Radar Detector	1-3w
GPS	2-6w
Portable Music	1-3w

Figure 4: This table shows how much power many common accessories require. By far heated clothing and auxiliary lighting are the big power users. Small items, including cell phones and portable music, are inconsequential. *Courtesy Powerlet Products*

ELECTRICAL PROJECTS

Part of motorcycle ownership, and indeed motorcycling, is customizing a motorcycle to fit the rider. Changing seats, control levers, handlebars, and foot pegs all make it fit better, and adding electrical accessories is no different. This chapter will address the addition of some of the more popular electrical accessories to a variety of bikes. Some projects are more complex than others and this section will provide the reader with a measure of what's difficult and what's not. These projects will be presented in a step-by-step format with written explanations where needed. Good-quality aftermarket products always come with illustrated instructions to make the job easier and they should be followed for specific products that are installed. Prices listed are as of early 2013 and website addresses are provided for all the projects where the current pricing information is available. Also, the approximate time required for each project is provided.

POSI-LOCK CONNECTORS

All of the electrical projects in this book require connecting wires to each other or to the motorcycle's battery. Soldering and electrical tape has been the traditional method to accomplish this task, but they have some drawbacks. Although not difficult to learn, soldering takes some degree of skill. In addition, wires that are soldered together are sometimes problematic to take apart if the connection is no longer needed.

For example, expensive driving lights are installed on a motorcycle, and when it's eventually sold the lights and wiring harness need to be removed to transfer to another motorcycle. Crimp connectors are popular, quick to make, and reliable; however, they cannot be removed and wires must be cut to undo connections.

There is a product that addresses all of these wiring connecting issues, Posi-Products No Crimp Connectors. They have been around since 1997, and if you're not familiar with how they work you're missing out on a really easy, foolproof way to make motorcycle electrical projects go more smoothly. Posi-Lock connectors require no crimping or soldering or tools of any kind—simply hand tighten the connectors to the wires and the connection is complete. On top of that, the connectors are reusable over and over. Posi-Lock connectors are available for various types of wire connections, including inline connections, splice or T connections, and others. The connectors are vibration resistant, perfect for motorcycle applications, weather resistant (some are even waterproof), and can withstand high temperatures if used near a motorcycle's engine. For more detailed information check out their website, www.posi-lock.com.

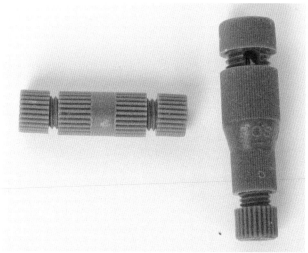

Posi-Lock inline connector (left) and Posi-Tap connector (right) do not require any tools to assemble. The connectors are vibration resistant and reusable. *Courtesy Posi- Products*

About ⅜ inch of insulation needs to be stripped off a wire that is going to be connected to a Posi-Lock connector.

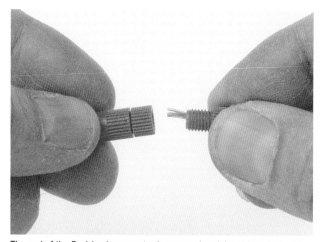

The end of the Posi-Lock connector is removed and the stripped wire is inserted. The bare wire is then screwed into the body of the Posi-Lock connector for a secure connection. *Courtesy Posi-Products*

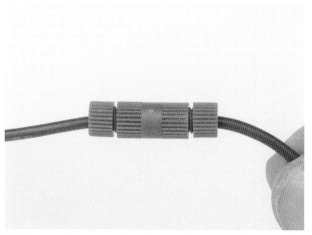

The in-line Posi-Lock connector makes a neat connection that can easily be taken apart. The connectors are available to accommodate wires ranging in size from 24 to 8 gauge. *Courtesy Posi-Products*

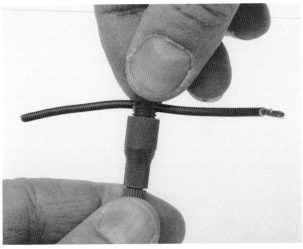

This wire has been inserted into a Posi-Tap connector. These connectors can splice wires into an existing wire without cutting it. Inside the connector is a sharp pin-like barb that pierces the inline wire making the connection. *Courtesy Posi-Products*

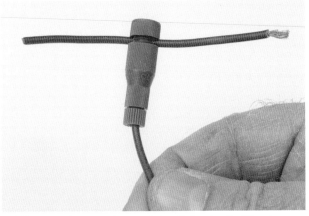

Posi-Tap connectors come in several sizes that work with different wire gauges. They are especially useful with trying to splice wires in a wiring harness, behind a headlight or under a motorcycle's seat. *Courtesy Posi-Products*

The Posi-Fuse Round Fuse holder works with glass fuses in lengths from ¾ to 1¼ inches long. Each end of the Posi-Fuse uses no-crimp technology to secure the wire. *Courtesy Posi-Products*

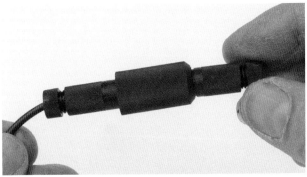

The fuse is held securely in place within the Posi-Fuse. A simple twist separates the fuse holder if the fuse needs to be changed. *Courtesy Posi-Products*

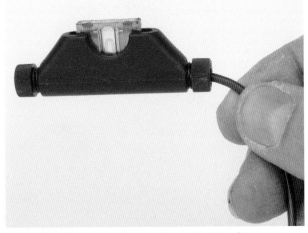

The Posi-Fuse Blade fuse holder uses the Posi-Lock no-crimp technology at each end. It works with ATC, ATO, and Mini Fuses and can accommodate 12- to 18-gauge wire. *Courtesy Posi-Products*

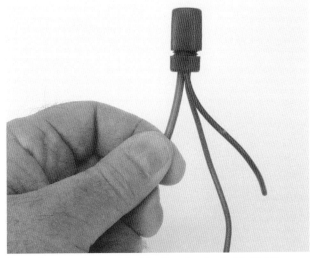

If more than two wires are to be joined together, the Posi-Twist can connect them with a secure connection. Even wires with different gauge sizes can be used with the same connector. *Courtesy Posi-Products*

Wires located under the seat of a motorcycle are protected from the elements. This not true of wires under the rear fender or behind a headlight. For these applications there are two choices: Posi-Tite (water tight) and Posi-Seal (weatherproof) connectors. Both work well for connectors that are exposed to the elements. *Courtesy Posi-Products*

INSTALLING A 12-VOLT RELAY

If you're at all interested in adding electrical accessories to your motorcycle you may want to consider the installation of a 12-volt relay. So what's a relay and why should you want to install one? We'll answer these questions as well as how to wire one up on a motorcycle.

The basic idea of a relay is to control a large amount of electrical current, or amperage, using a relatively small current. The best way to explain how this works is to use a starter relay (aka starter solenoid) as an example. To get the starter to operate and start the engine, the positive battery terminal needs to be connected to the starter.

Relays used on motorcycles come in all shapes and sizes, but they all basically operate the same. Some late-model bikes use as many as 10 relays or more.

Pictured is a starter solenoid (left) and small 12-volt relay (right). While these two components may look very different they perform the same function: controlling a high-amperage circuit using a low-amperage circuit.

The starter motor requires lots of electrical power to spin the engine fast enough to start it and the battery cable has to be large enough to provide the high amperage needed by the starter. It is possible to use a very large switch that would make this connection every time the engine was started, but battery cables and a heavy-duty switch would look stupid mounted on the handlebars—so a relay mounted under the seat and small start button are used instead. Figure 5 shows how the battery is connected to the starter motor through the starter relay when the starter button is pressed.

The starter relay and other motorcycle relays are electro-mechanical switches. When the start button is pressed on the handlebars, it completes a circuit to a coil of wire inside the relay. This control coil becomes magnetized as current passes through it. The magnetic force from the coil physically moves a switch contact that connects the positive battery cable directly to the

Figure 5: This cutaway of a starter solenoid, or relay, illustrates how it works. When the start button on the handlebars is pressed, the control coil becomes an electromagnet and pushes a plunger up where it touches the high-amperage contacts connecting the starter motor to the battery.

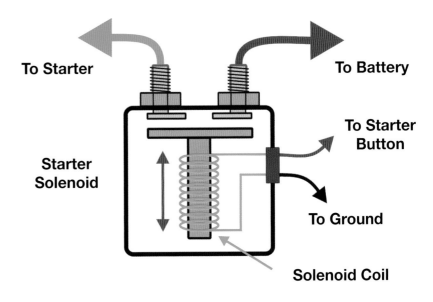

To Starter

To Battery

To Starter
Button

To Ground

Starter
Solenoid

Solenoid Coil

start motor, causing it to turn and start the engine. The control coil inside the relay only uses a small amount of current or energy, so the start button that controls the coil is small and uses light-gauge wires. Because of its size, the starter solenoid is usually located under the seat near the battery. Smaller relays used on motorcycle control other functions, including headlights, fuel pumps, ignition coils, brake lights, auxiliary lighting, horn, and more.

Installing a 12-volt relay is simply a matter of knowing how to connect it to the electrical component that it will control. We'll use the example of installing driving lights to illustrate how a relay operates and how to install one. In our example, the driving lights use 3 amps, or 45 watts each, for a total of 90 watts. Because a switch to control the lights would have to be heavy-duty, as well as the wires going to and from the switch, this is an ideal application for a 12-volt relay.

The small 12-volt relay works just like the larger starter relay. The high-amperage contact can be seen at the lower left. The relay control coil uses fine wire to create a magnetic field when energized.

This is a typical automotive-style 12-volt, 40-amp relay. Relays can be purchased at auto parts stores or Radio Shack and cost around $6.

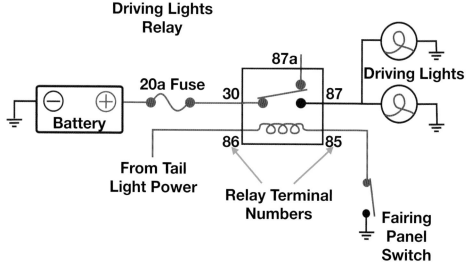

Figure 6: This wiring diagram shows how the relay controls the driving lights. The relay allows the use of a small fairing panel switch and also prevents the driving lights from being turned on when the ignition switch is off. Power from the battery goes to Terminal 30 of the relay. Power for the relay control coil is taken from the taillight's power wire, Terminal 86. The reason the taillight is used is to prevent the operation of the driving lights unless the engine is running (the taillight is not on unless the engine is operating). The relay is controlled by the panel switch, which is connected to Terminal 85. The driving lights are off because the panel switch is not on.

Figure 7: With the ignition switch turned on, the relay's control coil (between Terminals 85 and 86 in purple) can be activated via the panel switch. When the switch is "ON," it connects the relay coil to ground, completing the coil control circuit and turning the coil into an electromagnet. This moves or latches the high-amperage contacts inside the relay connecting Terminals 30 to 87 (87a is not used) and powering up the driving lights. When the key is turned off, the driving lights also turn off even if the panel switch is left in the ON position because the relay control coil will be turned off when it does not receive power from the taillight. This will help prevent a dead battery if the fairing panel switch is left on accidentally.

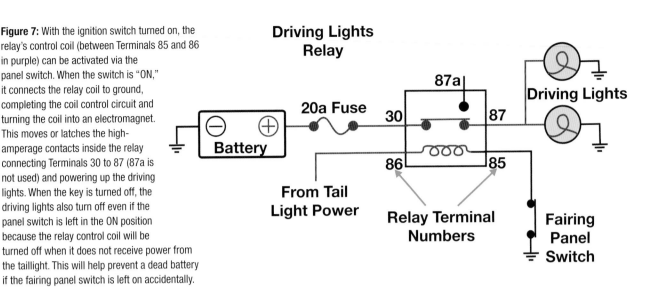

Twelve-volt, automotive-style relays are available from the Internet or at most auto parts stores. Just type "12-volt relay" into your favorite search engine and lots of choices will be displayed. Relays are also available with a wiring harness and may be listed as a "relay kit" on line. There are two common types: 5-pin and 4-pin and are sometimes called a "Single Pole, Double Throw" relay. They can be rated for 20, 30, and 40 amps with the latter being the most common rating. Motorcycles also use the same type of relay and they are common on many bikes.

Most 12-volt relays will have this diagram printed on them. This relay is rated at 30 amps but can take a 40-amp load for a short time. The "12VDC" and "14VDC" indicate that it is for use on a 12-volt system (14 volts when the engine is running). The terminal numbers are as follows: 85 and 86 are the relay control coil and should be connected to a power source and ground. Either 85 or 86 can be switched on/off to activate the relay. Terminal 30 is always 12 volts for whatever the relay is going to provide power for. Terminal 87 is "normally open" and connects to Terminal 30 when the relay is activated. Terminal 87a is "normally closed" and is connected to Terminal 30 when the relay is off and disconnected when the relay is on.

Here the relay pins are shown. Each is labeled with terminal numbers that are common on all 12-volt automotive relays. The placement of the relay pins is also standard.

If the relay is not part of a kit that comes with premade wiring, you can manufacture your own wiring harness to connect it. Crimp tools and spade connectors (available at auto parts stores) make for a clean installation. Use a crimp tool, not needle-nose pliers, to crimp the connector to the wire. The connectors can also be soldered if desired.

The spade connector will fit securely to the relay terminal pins. When all the wires are connected, duct tape can be wrapped around the connectors to keep them from touching anything metal like the motorcycle's frame or engine.

It's a good idea to provide electrical protection for any relay installation. An inline fuse (available at an auto parts store) should be located between Terminal 30 and the motorcycle's battery (or other power wire). If the power wire accidentally touches something metal like the engine or chassis, the fuse will keep it from melting and causing other electrical damage.

With the relay harness installed on the bike, the relay is plugged into the receptacle. Most motorcycles have enough room to install several relays under the seat.

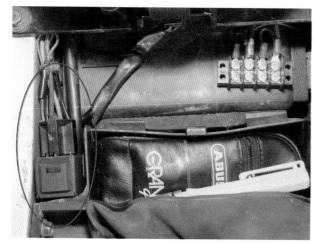

Here is the relay installed under a motorcycle's seat. Automotive relays are generally highly reliable and often last the life of the bike. Typical 12-volt automotive relays cost around $6 at an auto parts store, although they can be found for less online. Time for this project should be around one hour, depending on how difficult it is to access to all the wires involved.

The relay takes the place of the heavy-duty switch and provides the high-amperage connection between the driving lights and the battery. A panel or handlebar switch will operate the relay, and the relay will control the lights. The wires going to and from the switch, as well as the switch itself, don't have to be heavy-duty because the relay, instead of the switch, is turning the lights on and off.

HEADLIGHT/STARTER CUTOUT RELAY

On some older motorcycles the headlight will switch on as soon as the ignition key is in the ON position. It remains on even when the starter motor is trying to start the engine. While this works most of the time, sometimes when the temperature is low and the battery is not new the power used by the headlight is enough to keep the starter motor from turning fast enough to start the engine. A relay can be used to shut off the

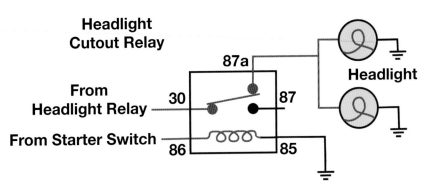

Figure 8: Terminal 30 is power from the headlight power source and is connected to Terminal 87a, which is normally closed (or on). When the starter motor is turning, Terminal 86 has power. With 12 volts to 86 and a constant ground at 85, the relay will connect Terminals 30 and 87 and disconnect Terminals 30 from 87a (shutting off the headlight). As soon as the engine starts and the starter motor is no longer operating, Terminal 86 will have no power and the relay opens and connects Terminals 30 to 87a powering up the headlight.

headlight when the starter motor is turning, allowing more amperage to be available to the starter. The wiring diagram in Figure 8 illustrates how relay Pin 87a is used to make a headlight cut-out circuit for starter motor operation. The cost of the relay is $6. Time for this project should be around one hour, depending on how difficult it is to access to all the wires involved.

CLEARWATER, GLENDA DRIVING LIGHTS

When riding a motorcycle, being seen by oncoming traffic is something in every rider's mind: "Does that SUV turning left really see me?" Anything we can do to make our motorcycles more visible increases our ability to manage the risk of riding in traffic. Adding extra lighting is the best way to be noticed, and for several years now LEDs have been available for tail, stop, and turn signal lights. LEDs offer advantages over standard incandescent bulbs, including more light output, vibration-proof design, bulb life of 50,000 hours, and they produce a "white" light that's very visible and use

less power than conventional lights. What has been missing, until now, are LEDs that can provide enough light to see by at night. Clearwater Lights makes the Glenda HPLED (high-powered LED) Motorcycle Light Kit that serves two functions: The lights allow oncoming drivers to see an approaching motorcycle and provide extra light for night riding.

For their small size (2 inches in diameter) the Glendas put out a high-intensity white light that stands out against any background. They are four to five times brighter than a halogen bulb. In fact, at full power they are too bright and can dazzle oncoming drivers, preventing them from seeing the bike's turn signals. To solve this problem the Glenda lights come with a dimmer control, allowing the rider to set the level of light intensity—lower for sunny days or a little higher for bad weather. The light kit also comes with a relay that automatically turns the lights to full power when the high beam is switched on. For nighttime riding, they produce the light output of a 50-watt halogen

Here are the components that come with the Glenda kit. The dimmer is on the upper right with the high-beam relay below. Mounting brackets are powder coated and hardware is stainless steel.
Courtesy Clearwater Company

bulb with a wide pattern that fills in areas where stock lighting is lacking.

The Glenda housings are made from machined billet aluminum and are powder coated for durability. Mounting brackets are either hard anodized or powder coated and use all-stainless-steel hardware.

Housings are available in red, orange, silver, blue, and black. Clearwater Lights makes kits for all brands of motorcycles each with a bracket specific for year, make and model. To give this new LED technology a test, we installed a set of Glenda lights on a 2005 Yamaha FJR. Following are the steps to install this high-quality kit.

Normally LEDs can't be dimmed like conventional bulbs. The Glendas use an advanced microprocessor to rapidly turn the LEDs off and on at a rate of more than 250 times per second. Our eyes cannot detect the lights switching and they appear dim instead. At full power they are switched on 100 percent of the time. *Courtesy Clearwater Company*

The fender attachment point on our FJR will be used to mount the bracket that the lights are bolted to. The lights are adjustable up and down via a curved slot in the bracket. *Courtesy Clearwater Company*

The brackets are fastened to the lights prior to mounting them on the side of the fender. We slightly tightened the fasteners as the lights will have to be adjusted once the bracket is mounted on the bike. *Courtesy Clearwater Company*

With a rider holding the bike upright on a level surface the lights can be aimed using a simple level. The housing should be 90 degrees to the ground. *Courtesy Clearwater Company*

Motorcycle engines vibrate so we are using Threadlocker from Locktite to keep the light mounting bolts from becoming loose and backing out. *Courtesy Clearwater Company*

Here are the Glenda lights mounted on the bike. The mounting bracket and light have a clean appearance and almost look like a factory-installed accessory. *Courtesy Clearwater Company*

Tie wraps are used to affix the lights' wires to the fork tubes. When routing the wiring make sure that you leave enough slack for suspension and steering movement. Brake lines are a good place to attach the wires. *Courtesy Clearwater Company*

Use a 12-volt test light to locate a switched power source and the wire that operates the high-beam circuit. These will be connected to the dimmer relay that comes with the Glenda wiring kit. *Courtesy Clearwater Company*

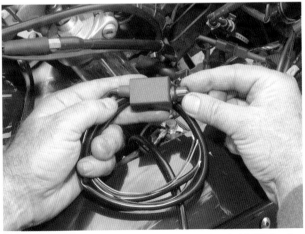

The Glenda lights use a rotary dimmer to adjust the level of light intensity. Light output can be modified to suit riding conditions and to keep from blinding oncoming drivers. *Courtesy Clearwater Company*

Because LED lights draw so little power (only 12 watts for the Glenda at full power) we made some of the connections using small crimp connectors. It's important to use the correct tool when crimping the wires. Don't use pliers as the wires can come loose. *Courtesy Clearwater Company*

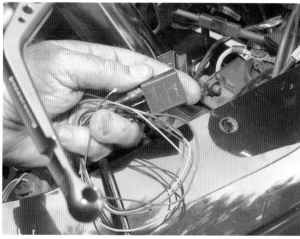

The relay that's included in the Glenda kit switches the lights to full power automatically when the high beam is switched on. Use of the relay allows the lights to be dimmed for normal riding and switched to full power when you really need to get noticed. *Courtesy Clearwater Company*

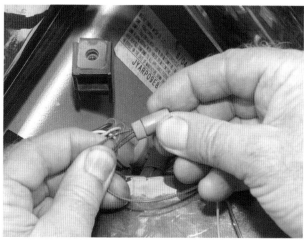

Wires from the dimmer switch, relay, and lights are 22-gauge. Posi-Lock connectors (provided in the kit) are perfect for connecting multiple wires together. They are water and vibration proof as well. *Courtesy Clearwater Company and Posi-Products*

We mounted the Glenda dimmer next to the hazard and heated grip switch on the left body panel of our FJR. *Courtesy Clearwater Company*

Here is how the Glenda lights look mounted on the FJR. The black anodized housings provide a clean look and complement the paint colors on most bikes. *Courtesy Clearwater Company*

The Glenda lights switched on and compared to the high-intensity discharge (HID) aftermarket lights on our FJR. When looking at the Glenda head-on they are exceptionally bright. At night they throw a wide beam of light that makes the sides of the road much more visible. The Glenda retails for $475 and took about two hours to install. In addition to these lights, Clearwater Lights also makes the "Krista" driving lights that lay down 180 watts of light while only using 36 watts of power, and for even more light, the "Erica" uses six LEDs that deliver 6,000 lumens of retina-melting power. *Courtesy Clearwater Company*

FLASHING BRAKE LIGHT
Electrical Connection 3rd Brake Light

Whenever you pull up and stop at a traffic light in heavy traffic you should be looking to see if the car or truck behind you is going to do the same. If you don't give this much thought you should reconsider riding in traffic or even at all. Rear-end collisions that involve motorcycles can be minor, amounting to a tipover or much worse. You might think, "That's why I have a brake light," but can that driver behind you see it? At night most motorcycle brake lights are readily visible but what about during the day—especially in bright sunlight? The Electrical Connection 3rd Brake Light offers an LED brake light bar that addresses the visibility problem nicely. LED lighting used for brake lights falls into three brightness categories: normal, pretty bright, and "I'm seeing red dots and my eyes hurt." The EC 3rd Brake Light is in the latter category. In addition to serving as a brake light, it can act as a running light as well. Check out The Electrical Connection website at: www.electricalconnection.com. We installed to see how it worked. Here's how the installation went.

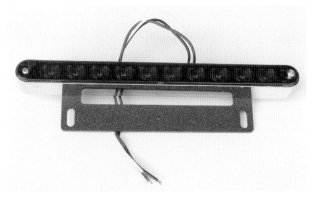

Here is what the EC 3rd Brake Light looks like. It consists of a 10-segment LED bar that is weatherproof and mounted in an ABS plastic chrome bezel. A license plate mount attaches the light to a license plate bracket. The bezel mounting holes are slotted to fit various configurations for license plate hole patterns. The unit is Department of Transportation (DOT) and Society of Automotive Engineers (SAE) approved and is available in either a red or clear lens. *Courtesy Electrical Connection*

With the license plate removed we see how the brake light will fit to the license plate bracket. The three wires from the light go through a hole in the fender and up to the tail section. The white wire goes to a ground (either the brake or taillight ground wire), the black wire goes to the power wire from the running lights, and the red wire connects to the bike's brake light power wire. *Courtesy Electrical Connection*

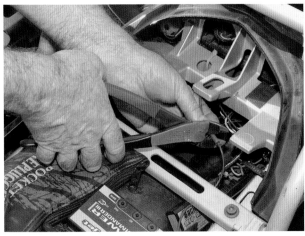

After running the wires through the rear fender and up to the tail section it is time to connect them to the motorcycle's electrical system. A 12-volt test light is a handy tool to locate the brake and taillight power wires and a ground. Since brake light operation is important, and electrical failure is not an option, we used crimp connectors to connect the wires. *Courtesy Electrical Connection*

Here is the EC 3rd Brake Light installed. The light bar looks good and blends in with the existing brake lights. In daylight we stood back from the rear of the bike about 100 feet and had a helper activate the brake light. It's highly visible and really stands out. Nighttime operation is almost blinding. *Courtesy Electrical Connection and RoadBike Magazine*

For the quality, the EC 3rd Brake Light with running light option is a bargain at $34.95. It's easy to install (takes about one and a half hours) and it attracts the right kind of attention on the road. All of the Electrical Connection's products are quality and assembled in the United States. The Electrical Connection also makes a plug-and-play wiring harness for Honda GL 1500 and 1800 Gold Wings as well as other lighting and wiring products for a variety of motorcycles. The Electrical Connection can be found at www.electricalconnection.com, 865-219-9192.

SUPERFLASH, LED BRAKE LIGHT FLASHER

For the last several years the use of LED lighting on motorcycles continues to grow. Marker lights, turn signals, and brake lights often come as stock items on some bikes, and even if your motorcycle doesn't use this technology you can easily add it yourself. LED brake lights have been available for motorcycles for some time

and several are featured in this chapter. The Electrical Connection (www.electricalconnection.com) offers a product called Superflash that works with any LED brake light, causing it to rapidly flash when the brakes are applied. While there are other brake light flashers on the market, the Superflash is unique in that it is adjustable for both the speed of the flash and the duration. For example, you can set the flash rate for rapid-fire bursts or slow steady flashing. The time for flashing can be one to five seconds. After the flash cycle is complete, the brake light is left on until the brakes are released by the rider. The Superflash is designed to modulate LED lights only, as standard, incandescent bulbs can't react quickly to being switched on and off. The unit measures $1\frac{7}{8} \times 1\frac{1}{2} \times \frac{1}{2}$ inches and will power 1.5 amps worth of LEDs. A plug-and-play model is available for the GL1800 Gold Wing. We installed the Superflash to see how it worked. Here's how the installation went.

The Superflash unit is small enough for an under-seat installation. The two blue pots with yellow dials adjust the flash speed and duration. *Courtesy Electrical Connection*

After referring to the factory wiring diagram, it's always a good idea to verify which wire does what. The test light lights up when the brakes are applied, confirming that this yellow wire powers the brake lights. This will be the input power wire for the Superflash. *Courtesy Electrical Connection*

The Superflash will control flash rate and time on this EC 3rd Brake light (also made by the Electrical Connection) but will also work on any LED brake light. *Courtesy Electrical Connection*

After identifying all the wires required for connection to the Superflash, jumper wires are used to temporarily connect the unit to the wiring on the motorcycle. This will verify that the brakes flash when applied and any incorrect connections are easily remedied before permanently soldering and taping the connections. *Courtesy Electrical Connection*

Any LED Brake Light

White
LED Ground

Black
LED Control

Superflash

Flash Duration ⊕

Flash Speed ⊕

Red
Brake Light
Input

Battery
Ground

Figure 9: The Superflash has three wires—black, which controls the LED brake light; white, which is the battery ground; and red, which is for the brake light power. The flash rate and time are adjusted by the electrical pots on the unit. *Courtesy Electrical Connection*

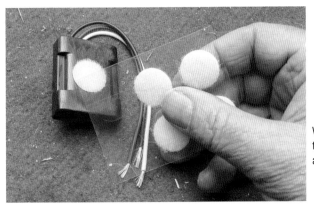

Velcro patches (available from a fabric store) are used to attach the Superflash to the rear fender well. The use of Velcro makes it easy to remove the unit for adjustments. *Courtesy Electrical Connection*

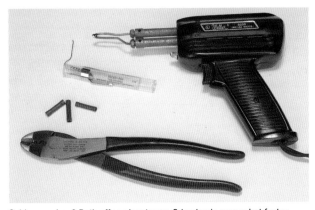

Solder or crimp? Both offer advantages. Crimping is somewhat faster but is harder to do on small-gauge wires. Soldering and tape is more durable and resists vibration. Because this circuit controls the brake lights we choose to solder the connections for added safety. *Courtesy Electrical Connection*

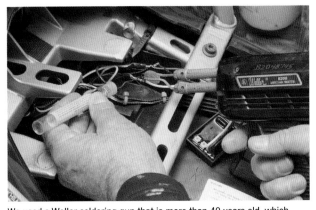

We used a Weller soldering gun that is more than 40 years old, which speaks volumes of the quality of Weller products. This model is still manufactured and can be purchased at hardware stores or Sears (sold under the Craftsman brand) for around $38, a good investment for electrical work on motorcycles or automobiles. *Courtesy Electrical Connection and Weller*

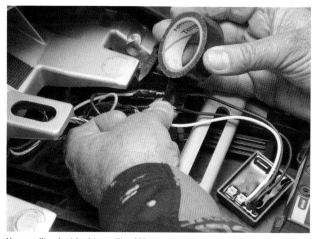

Use quality electrical tape (like 3M) to wrap the soldered connections. The tape will stand up to water, vibration, and heat and can be removed easily. *Courtesy Electrical Connection*

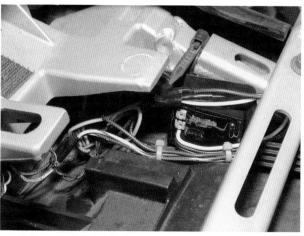

Here is the unit installed under the seat on our motorcycle. The two blue and yellow adjustment pots can be accessed to adjust the flash rate and how long the Superflash flashes the brake light. *Courtesy Electrical Connection*

The results of the rapid-burst flashing coming from the brake lights is attention-getting and really makes the rear of the bike highly visible when applying the brakes. Superflash sells for $34.95 and takes about an hour and a half to install. *Courtesy Electrical Connection*

POWER FOR YOUR TANK BAG

With all the electronic junk that I carry when I ride, having a 12-volt outlet inside my tank bag seems like a great idea. Powerlet Products makes this easy with their Luggage Electrix Connector and Cigarette Socket kit. A molded, flange mount SAE plug and anodized backing plate uses four screws to attach to the side of any tank bag. The external SAE connector can plug into a Powerlet plug, which are the same types, used on BMW, Triumph, and Ducati. I installed a panel connector on my FJR and the bag plugs into it while riding. Connecting the adapter inside the bag is an SAE/cigarette Y connector. Now I can power my cell phone, Autocom unit, bike-to-bike radio, or MP3 player while I ride—no more dead batteries. Powerlet has numerous types and styles of connectors to power just about anything you could want on a motorcycle. We installed the Luggage Electrix on both a RoadGear, and Cortech tank bag.

A tank bag is a great way to store items for long or short trips. This RoadGear Sport Tank Bag is a great way to hold all the stuff that you need to get to quickly. Maps, cell phone, iPad, MP3 player, gloves, helmet cleaner, and more.

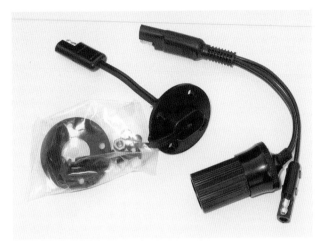

Here is the Luggage Electrix tank bag kit and interior Y connector. Black oxide, stainless-steel screws with stainless nyloc nuts are used to attach the inner backing plate to the tank bag. This will provide a water-resistant connection from the motorcycle's 12-volt electrical system to the interior of the bag. *Courtesy Powerlet Products*

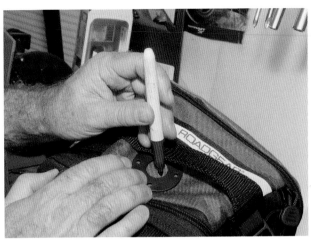

The first step is to mark the bag using the backing plate as a template. Choose an area of the bag that will be facing a power source on your bike. *Courtesy Powerlet Products*

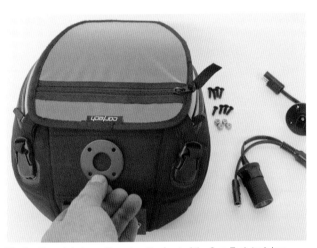

The backing plate is positioned on the front of the Core Tech tank bag.

A propane torch will be used to heat up some tools (nail and utility knife) to cut holes in the Cordura material for both tank bags.

A "hot" utility knife will make a clean cut through the bag's Cordura material. Heat from the blade will seal the edge of the material and keep it from fraying. *Courtesy Powerlet Products*

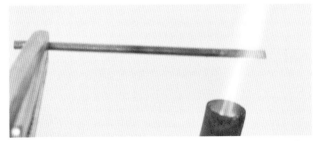

Heat the nail until it's glowing red. It will be used to poke screw-mounting holes in the tank bag. It will have to be reheated after making a couple of holes.

After the hole is cut for the adaptor the heated nail is used to poke holes in the bag for the Luggage Electrix's mounting screws. *Courtesy Powerlet Products*

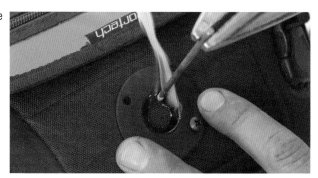

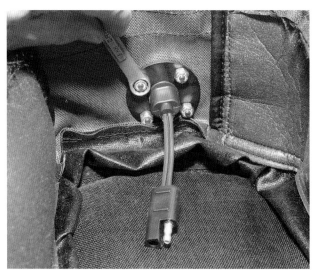

After installing the backing plate and adapter the nyloc mounting screws need to be tightened—you're almost ready for a 12-volt party inside your tank bag. The Luggage Electrix adapter comes with an SAE connector as shown. *Courtesy Powerlet Products*

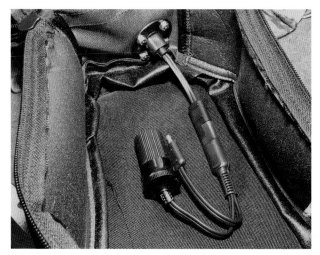

Two sources of power are available (SAE connector and cigarette lighter receptacle) with the Y connector plugged into the Luggage Electrix adaptor. Powerlet has numerous adapters to power just about anything that you use when you ride. *Courtesy Powerlet Products*

This motorcycle already had a power accessory socket to plug the tank bag into. Connecting the tank bag is simply a matter of plugging them together. As an alternative you can permanently install an SAE connector to your motorcycle's electrical system and plug the SAE plug directly into the Luggage Electrix adapter on the tank bag. *Courtesy Powerlet Products*

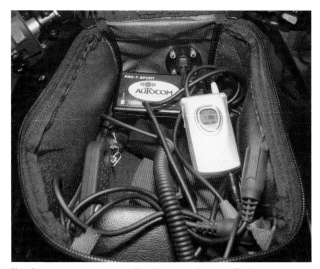

Now I can use my two-way radio, charge my vintage cell phone, or power up my music player during a ride. The Luggage Electrix Connector and Cigarette Socket sells for about $45 and takes around an hour to install. *Courtesy Powerlet Products*

INSTALLING HEATED GRIPS

No matter where you ride there will come a time when your hands will get cold. Even for riders who do not brave cold, 32 degrees F (or lower) winter riding, being able to warm your hands at the flip of a switch just make the riding experience more enjoyable. Heated handlebar grips have been around for a while and can extend the riding season for many motorcyclists. Another advantage of heated grips is that bulky winter gloves will only have to be worn in the coldest of weather. Lighter weight riding gloves allow for a better feel of the handlebar controls. The downside to many heated grips is that they use really hard rubber in their construction and are uncomfortable for long rides. The Symtec Hand Warmer Kits are not really heated grips at all but heating elements that fit under either stock or aftermarket handgrips. The heating elements offer two levels of heat and are easily installed on any ⅞-inch handlebar. The kit is made by Heat Demon and sells for around $50 (www.heatdemon.com). Installation takes about three hours. If you have never experienced riding with heated handgrips you will wonder how you ever rode without them. Following is an installation on a Kawasaki Versus.

Two switches are supplied with the kit. The metal toggle switch on the left has three positions: high, off, and low heat. The surface mount, rocker switch (right) has the same three-way functions but looks more "factory" in its appearance. The heating elements draw 36 watts on the high setting. *Courtesy Heat Demon*

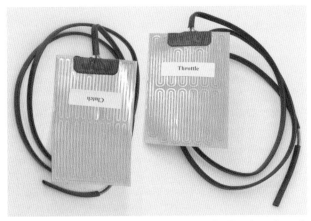

The Symtec Heat Demon Hand Warmer Kit has two heating elements made from flexible Mylar tape that attaches to the right and left handlebar tubes. The elements have a permanent adhesive backing to keep them in place. The throttle and clutch side elements are different, as can be seen by the pattern of wire in each. Heat transfer from the clutch side is rapid because the grip contacts the metal handlebar. The throttle side is insulated via the plastic throttle tube and the element doesn't have to produce as much heat. The end result is that both throttle and clutch grips heat evenly—a thoughtful design of the heating elements. *Courtesy Heat Demon*

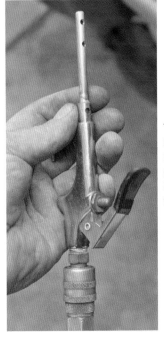

The best grip removal tool is a blowgun and compressed air. Removed using this method, the grips won't be damaged and can be used again—better than cutting them off with a razor blade.

The handlebar end weights have to be removed to be able to get the grips off the bar.

With the blowgun inserted part way into the grip, a quick blast of compressed air will loosen the seal between the grip and handlebar.

Inserting the blowgun into the other end of the grip will force it off the handlebar.

Denatured alcohol, lacquer thinner, or acetone all work well to remove residue from the bar.

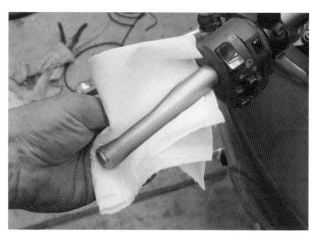

The surface needs to be clean for the heating elements to adhere to the handlebar. Be careful when cleaning the plastic throttle tube. If these chemicals are left on for too long they tend to "eat" plastic. *Courtesy Heat Demon*

The adhesive backing must be peeled off the heating elements. Keep fingers off the adhesive as much as possible so it will stick to the handlebar or throttle tube. *Courtesy Heat Demon*

Position the heating element carefully. Applying the element is a one-time operation, as it will tear if removed after being applied. *Courtesy Heat Demon*

Press the heating element firmly to the bar making sure that you have put pressure on the entire element. *Courtesy Heat Demon*

The clutch-side heating element has been positioned so that the wires exit to the front, just under the flash-to-pass button. The wires can be snug against the switch house so they don't get in the way of normal operation. *Courtesy Heat Demon*

On the throttle side, the heating element is applied to the plastic throttle tube. The wires need to be positioned so they exit at the front of the grip. *Courtesy Heat Demon*

Leave enough slack in the element wires so the throttle can be moved freely. A tie wrap can be used to secure the wires against the switch housing or farther along the handlebar. *Courtesy Heat Demon*

Here are the new Spider handgrips that will be installed over the heating elements. Having the option to use any brand of grip is a big incentive to choose the Symtec Hand Warmer Kit.

The new grips are designed for a ⅞-inch handlebar and look to be two different sizes. This is because the top grip will be used on the throttle side and has to fit the throttle tube. The clutch side grip just has to fit over the ⅞-inch bar.

Here the clutch side grip is being installed. A neat trick is to use some hair spray (scented or unscented) on the bar or heating element. This will make the grip slide easily onto the bar and act as a light glue to keep it from moving after it's installed. *Courtesy Heat Demon*

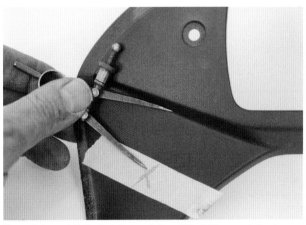

The switch needs to be installed next. One of the fairing panels has been removed and marked where the mounting hole is to be drilled.

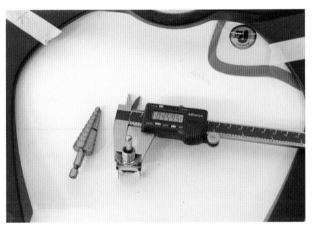

The diameter of the switch is being measured. At left is a stepped-hole drill. One of the steps will be slightly larger than the diameter of the switch.

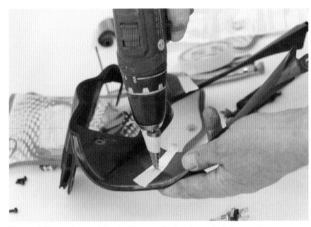

These drills work great in plastic or soft aluminum but do require some skill to use. Practice on another piece of material before trying to drill a hole in the fairing.

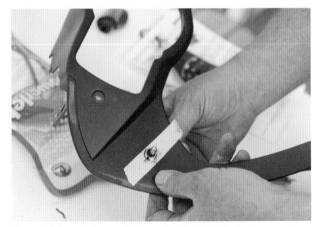

The switch is pushed through the newly drilled hole. It will be secured with a nut. It's a good idea to use Loctite on the nut to keep it from coming loose.

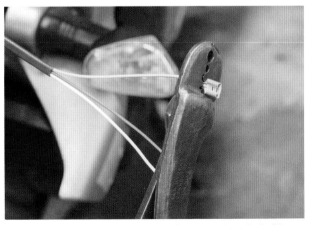

The heating element wires need to have crimp connectors attached to connect to the power switch.

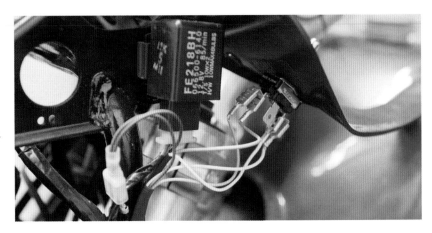

Shown is the underside of the switch. Power to the switch for both elements should connect to a key-on power source. This will prevent the grips from being left on when the engine is not running.
Courtesy Heat Demon

INSTALLING A MOTORCYCLE ALARM

A motorcycle thief surveys a row of bikes at a rally. Some of them have intimidating looking locks and others have a flashing LED light on the fairing, indicating an alarm in the armed mode. The thief chooses a motorcycle that has neither and breaks the ignition lock and rides off. Having protection for your bike is just common sense. The Gorilla 8017 Motorcycle Alarm offers protection for any type of motorcycle that has a 12-volt battery.

The Gorilla 8017 uses three built-in sensors that can detect tilt, shock, and battery current. The tilt sensor detects motion if the motorcycle has been lifted off its side stand. The shock sensor features two-stage sensitivity; a small disturbance like someone bumping the bike will sound a single chirp from the alarm. Moving the bike off a center stand or knocking it over will sound the alarm for 30 seconds. The current sensor detects if there is an electrical load on the battery—like if the bike is being hot-wired. Owners can choose from seven levels of alarm sensitivity, which can reduce the chance of false alarms.

The 8017 also has a pager key fob that can alert the rider if any of the sensors are activated. The LED display on the key fob even displays what sensor caused the alert. In fact, every function of the alarm can be monitored on the pager's LED screen from up to ½ mile away. In addition, the alarm features an adjustable 120-decibel Piezo siren that can emit five different tones in sequence when tripped. A flashing LED serves as both an alarm system status indicator as well as a visual deterrent to would-be thieves. For information on other Gorilla alarms, check out their website at www.gorillacyclealarm.com.

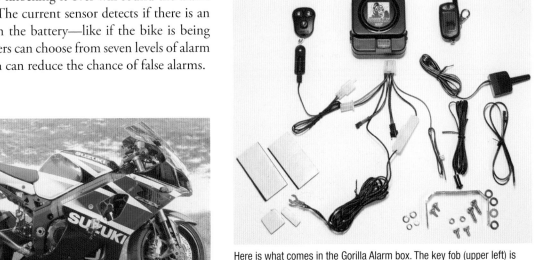

Here is what comes in the Gorilla Alarm box. The key fob (upper left) is for arming and disarming the alarm. The key fob on the right is for the pager function. Despite all the wires shown, only a power and a ground wire are connected to the motorcycle's battery. The other wires are for the tilt sensor and pager antenna and plug directly into the alarm controller.
Courtesy Gorilla Alarms

This Suzuki GSX-R1000 is a bike that gets stolen a lot, so installing the Gorilla Alarm was additional insurance against theft.

Here is the alarm controller. It measures 3 inches wide by 1.75 inches deep by 3.5 inches in height and can be mounted under a seat or in the tail section of many motorcycles. *Courtesy Gorilla Alarms*

The controller is being mounted using a Velcro strip (included with the alarm) under the seat of the GSX-R1000. Once mounted, all that's left to do is make the connection to the motorcycle's power and ground wires. *Courtesy Gorilla Alarms*

The two-way pager key fob can transmit back to the motorcycle from 100 feet, but it receives signals from a half mile away. Signals transmitted through buildings will shorten this distance. The pager fob can monitor every function of the alarm remotely and features five buttons to control alarm functions. *Courtesy Gorilla Alarms*

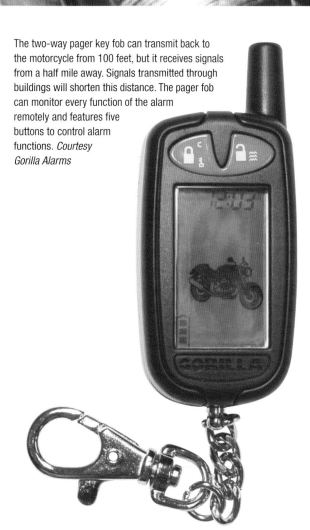

Here the power wire for the alarm is being connected using an existing stock connector that goes directly to the battery positive terminal.

The alarm's ground wire is being connected directly to the battery's negative terminal for a good ground.

Once the alarm is installed, a quick test with the key fob confirms operation. The tilt sensor should also be adjusted with the bike on its side stand and tested for sensitivity, which is adjustable on the alarm. *Courtesy Gorilla Alarms*

The pager should be tested away from the bike. Have a helper move the motorcycle off of its side stand or center stand to see if the sensitivity needs to be adjusted up or down. The Gorilla Alarm offers peace of mind for motorcycle owners. It's easy to install (less than 20 minutes for most applications), simple to use, and has a lot of features to keep your bike, well, yours. *Courtesy Gorilla Alarms*

INSTALLING A VOLTMETER

Few motorcycles come stock with an electrical system voltage gauge or display. This begs the question, "Why would anyone need one?" Well, there are several reasons. Having charging system voltage information for the rider is similar to a low oil level or oil pressure warning light. It's out of mind until the light comes on. Then the rider has the option of doing something about the warning—pull over or cross one's fingers and hope to make it home. It would be great to know that your charging system has quit working before the battery runs dead and you're stuck by the side of the road. Another use for voltage information is if electrical accessories have been added to the motorcycle. Heated clothing and extra lights may draw lots of power and if the charging system can't supply the power it will come from the battery—until it's dead. By monitoring system voltage riders can judge if they can run those 100-watt driving lights, their heated jacket liner, grips, and gloves all at the same time. If system voltage drops below around 12.5 volts, it's time to turn something off to keep the battery charged when riding.

Koso North America's CNC Voltmeter (Koso part number BH000K00) is a great way to monitor charging-system voltage when out on the road. The 10 colored LEDs provide voltage level information at a glance. It's easy to install (only two wires) and is small enough to be mounted on even small motorcycles. The voltmeter is priced around $45 and takes about an hour to install, depending on how hard it is to get to the wires involved. Here is how the installation went on a 2003 Yamaha FZ1.

Here what's in the box: the CNC voltmeter, two-sided tape, and two Scotch Lock wire connectors. The meter's wires are long enough to accommodate most installations. *Courtesy Koso North America*

A key-on power wire needs to connect to the voltmeter power wire. A key-on power wire can be located either using a factory wiring diagram or a 12-volt test light. The wire that gets power when the ignition switch is turned is a good one to connect to. The other wire from the meter goes to a good ground, which could be a wire, frame, or engine case fastener.

Two 3M Scotch Lock connectors are supplied with the CNC voltmeter. These can be used to splice into existing wires without any cutting or soldering. When closed, the connectors lock onto the wires making a good electrical connection. *Courtesy Koso North America*

The meter is mounted on top of the instrument display where it is easily seen. The CNC meter's small size (1.8 × 1 × .47 inches) allows for many mounting possibilities. As long as the lower, center LED is glowing green, the charging system is doing its job. If it is yellow or red, something is amiss and should be taken care of. *Courtesy Koso North America*

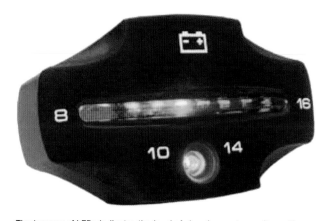

The top row of LEDs indicates the level of charging system voltage. The lower center LED acts like a go-no-go gauge—green is good, yellow is a potential problem, and red means do something. In general, green indicates 12 to 14 volts, yellow is below 12 or above 15, and red means too low or high a charging system voltage. *Courtesy Koso North America*

INSTALLING THE KOSO MINI 3

While more and more motorcycles now come equipped with a clock, there are many that do not. A few large touring bikes may feature the outside temperature displayed on the instrument panel, but few motorcycles come stock with a voltmeter that shows charging system voltage. Koso North America has come up with a gauge that has all three functions. They have been making quality gauges for motorcycles for more than 20 years and their Mini 3 Ambient Temperature/Clock/Volt gauge (Koso part number BA003130) displays time, outside temperature, and electrical system voltage. This is a simple electrical project that only has three wires to connect. The Mini 3 sells for about $100 and takes about three hours to install. The gauge is small enough to be mounted easily, even on smaller motorcycles. I installed the Mini 3 on a Yamaha FJR1300. Here's a quick look at how the installation went.

The Koso Mini 3 comes with two-sided tape, three Scotch Lock connectors for splicing into wires, and instructions (not shown). *Courtesy Koso North America*

The Mini 3 has a single button that allows the user to switch between the temperature, clock, and voltage displays. Its small size (2.4 × 1.2 × .48 inches) allows it to be mounted on most any motorcycle. *Courtesy Koso North America*

Finding a place to mount the Mini 3 is a matter of sitting on the seat and moving the Mini around until a location is found that allows the rider to easily see the display. I chose to mount it on the lower left fairing panel next to the hazard switch. Anytime an electrical device uses a button, it should be mounted on the left side of the motorcycle so it can be operated while riding. Because I wanted to mount it at an angle for better viewing, I had to manufacture a simple bracket. *Courtesy Koso North America*

I used a piece of 1.5 × ¹⁄₁₆-inch aluminum flat stock that I purchased at Home Depot. I only needed around 2 inches of the material for the gauge mount—plenty left over for other projects. *Courtesy Koso North America*

The aluminum is soft and is cut easily using a hacksaw. I cleaned up the edges after sawing with an aluminum file. Aluminum is a good material for project brackets, as it can be polished, sanded, or shot blasted to create different finishes. *Courtesy Koso North America*

To make the initial bend in the flat stock, I used a hammer (my favorite tool for working on motorcycles), and a vise. The aluminum bends without much effort and I got it bent to 90 degrees with a few blows of the hammer. *Courtesy Koso North America*

To get the bracket to bend past 90 degrees, I squeezed it in the vise to the desired angle. To determine the precise angle, I took the bracket out of the vise and held it where I wanted it mounted, sat on the seat, and "eyeballed" the angle. I repeated this process several times, bending the bracket a little each time until it was perfect. Unbending the bracket is problematic, and I did not want to have to make another bracket. *Courtesy Koso North America*

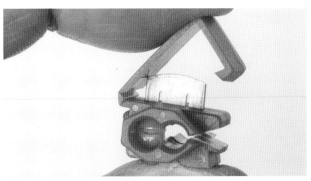

The Mini 3 comes with three 3M Scotch Lock connectors that are used to splice into the existing wiring on the motorcycle. No wire cutting is required and snapping the connector closed locks it in place. A wiring diagram can be used to identify what wires to splice into. The three wires are key-on power, ground, and a constant 12 volts. *Courtesy Koso North America*

I had already installed a key-on power terminal for another project and I used it to connect the Mini 3's key on the power wire and ground wire. The constant 12-volt wire should be directly connected to the battery's positive terminal. This will allow the meter to display the true electrical system voltage. *Courtesy Koso North America*

Here is the completed bracket mounted on the fairing panel. I used waterproof, two-sided tape to hold it in place. If the bracket needs to be removed, a single-edged razor blade is all that is needed. *Courtesy Koso North America*

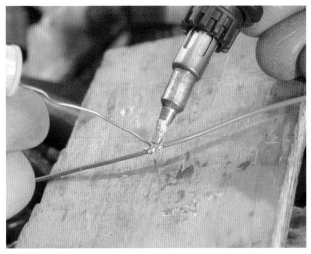

I had to extend two of the wires on the Mini 3, and I soldered these together and used electrical tape to insulate the soldered connections. *Courtesy Koso North America*

Here is the Mini 3 mounted on the bike. The display is easy to see in daylight, even bright sunlight. I can easily reach and work the mode button with my left hand while wearing riding gloves. *Courtesy Koso North America*

Here is what the backlit ambient temperature display looks like. The temperature range is from -11 to 140 degrees F. If you ride in cold weather and have never ridden with a temperature gauge, it really helps in anticipating what to change into or out of during a long ride. I did not ride with one for years but have had one in the last four years on whatever bike I've owned. *Courtesy Koso North America*

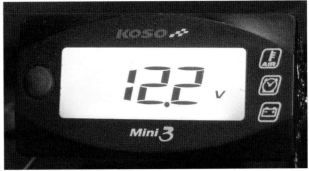

The voltmeter display range is 6 to 19 volts. Voltage above 15.5 or below 11.5 will cause the voltmeter to flash. A great feature of the Mini 3 is that the low-voltage warning can be programmed. I chose to set my low voltage warning to 12.5 volts. Anything below that indicates either a problem with the motorcycle's charging system, or too many electrical accessories are being used. This feature is especially useful on bikes that don't have a lot of excess electrical capacity. Without knowing what the system voltage is during a ride, too many electrical accessories can be turned on at the same time, possibly running the battery down. *Courtesy Koso North America*

INSTALLING A POWER OUTLET

Many riders use some type of electrically powered accessory when riding. These could include electric clothing, radar detectors, GPS units, cell phones, MP3

The Powerlet Socket Kit comes with a 24-inch lead (other lengths are available), fuse holder, and fuse. Wires are heavy-duty (16-gauge). The Powerlet socket is machined from aluminum and features a spring-loaded cap. *Courtesy Powerlet Products*

players, and even laptops. Getting power to all these gadgets can be problematic to say the least. Many of us suffer along with an SAE connector dangling between the seat and gas tank or elsewhere on our motorcycles. BMW has solved this problem for several years with a power outlet socket that comes stock on many of their motorcycles. Recently Ducati and Triumph have started using "BMW"-style power connectors on some of their bikes as well. Until recently these connectors were only available from BMW dealers for specific models or a plastic version from John Deer, the tractor guys. Powerlet Products (www.powerlet. com) manufacturers all kinds of electrical connections for motorcycles.

The company makes complete power outlet kits and a host of accessories and adaptors for connecting everything to everything else. Their model-specific kits include an anodized aluminum mounting bracket in gold, black, or clear (silver) and stainless-steel mounting hardware. They also make power outlets that are panel or handlebar mounted. Wiring harnesses use 16-gauge wire and waterproof ATO fuse holders. The Powerlet socket is machined from aluminum and has a spring-loaded cap to protect the socket from the elements when not in use. Well-written instructions are included and most kits make use of existing holes for mounting the bracket. Their kits typically don't include a male plug because there are several types to choose from. For the panel mount installation the Powerlet Socket Kit—24" (part number PKT-042-24) was used. It sells for $47. The Powerlet Basic Plug to SAE Connector (part number PAC-010-06) sells for $27. The Handlebar Outlet (part number PKT-081-54-B) sells for $140.

Each project should take around two to three hours, depending on how hard it is to get bodywork off and gain access to wiring. The Powerlet Socket Kit for panel mount is first.

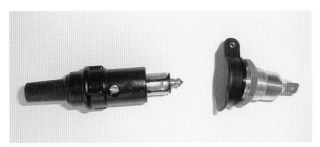

The Powerlet BMW-style plug is shown at left and Powerlet Socket at right. Other manufacturers use this style of plug, including Triumph and Ducati. *Courtesy Powerlet Products*

The Powerlet Basic Plug to SAE Connector (top) sells for $27. It's a great way to connect heating riding gear to the Powerlet Socket. Powerlet sells many versions of the socket and the one in the center could be used to connect a battery charger to the socket. *Courtesy Powerlet Products*

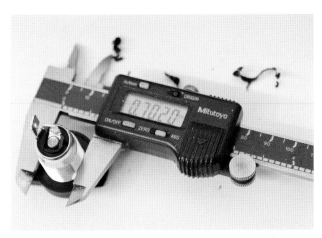

The Powerlet Socket's diameter (just under ¾ inch) is being measured. A ¾-inch hole will make a snug fit for the socket. *Courtesy Powerlet Products*

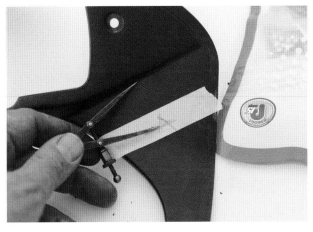

The fairing panel is marked for the mounting hole. Make sure it is in the correct place before drilling.

The masking tape makes a cleaner hole. The edges should be filed smooth before installing the socket.

The Powerlet Socket fits into the hole and is attached using a large nut that comes with the kit. Use thread sealer or silicone to keep the nut from loosening after installation. *Courtesy Powerlet Products*

The Powerlet wiring harness is connected directly to the battery. The inline fuse holder is visible just below and to the right of the positive battery terminal.

The Powerlet wiring harness needs to be routed from the battery to the socket. Zip ties can be used to keep it in place.

The Powerlet Socket is connected to the wring harness. *Courtesy Powerlet Products*

A rubber boot (supplied with the kit) keeps out dirt and moisture from the socket connections. *Courtesy Powerlet Products*

Here is the Powerlet socket in place on the fairing panel. It looks like a factory installation. *Courtesy Powerlet Products*

The Powerlet Handlebar Outlet comes in anodized black or chrome finishes. It makes a really clean installation, even on a cruiser. *Courtesy Powerlet Products*

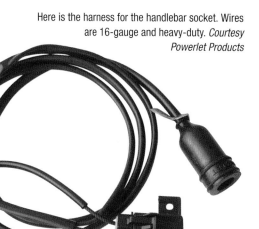

Here is the harness for the handlebar socket. Wires are 16-gauge and heavy-duty. *Courtesy Powerlet Products*

The Handlebar Socket is attached using Allen screws. Use Locktite to keep them from backing out. *Courtesy Powerlet Products*

Here, the Handlebar Socket is installed. All that's left to do is route and connect the wiring to the battery. *Courtesy Powerlet Products*

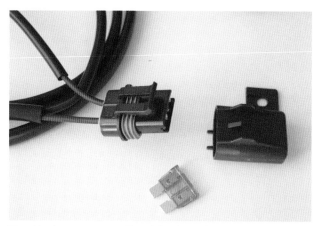

The wiring harness comes with an inline fuse holder and 15-amp fuse. This will protect the circuit in case the power wire touches a ground. *Courtesy Powerlet Products*

This fuse holder uses a spade-type, automotive 15-amp fuse. *Courtesy Powerlet Products*

The Powerlet wires are connected directly to the battery. *Courtesy Powerlet Products*

This end of the harness connects to the Powerlet socket. *Courtesy Powerlet Products*

Here is the Powerlet Handlebar Socket installation. Looks good on this Ducati Monster. *Courtesy Powerlet Products*

The Powerlet Socket is being tested with a heated clothing controller. The controller lights up so the connections are good. *Courtesy Powerlet Products*

LUNASEE HI-VIS WHEEL LIGHTING SYSTEM

When riding, being seen by the idiots driving cars and trucks may make the difference between enjoying motorcycling or taking a trip to the emergency room. This is especially true at night. There are many products that make riders highly visible from the front, including driving lights, headlight modulators, or high-intensity discharge (HID) lighting. In the rear, numerous flashing brake lights and LED marker lights are available. But what about lighting up a motorcycle from the side? For motorcycles sold in the United States, the Department of Transportation only requires side reflectors—amber at front and red on the back. Reflectors do just that: They reflect but don't provide a light source. Side marker lights can be installed, but they don't identify the vehicle as a motorcycle and tend to blend into the background.

The Lunasee Hi-Vis Wheel Lighting system is a unique product that addresses the issue of lighting up the sides of a motorcycle. Here is how the system works: A 4-millimeter-wide, phosphorescent pinstripe tape is applied to both sides of the wheels. The Light Emitting Rim tape (LERtape)is constantly excited by four (two for each wheel) high-intensity LEDpods that are mounted on the swingarm or front forks. As the wheels rotate, the

LERtape is charged by the LEDs and glows a florescent green that is highly visible. With the tape applied to the circumference of the wheel, the shape of the light is round and really makes a motorcycle stand out against any background. The Lunasee system provides active side lighting that clearly identifies a vehicle as a motorcycle in motion to other drivers. While not seen directly from the front or rear of the motorcycle, they are a real attention-getter from any angle to the side. The following images show how to install the Lunasee Hi-Vis Wheel Lighting system.

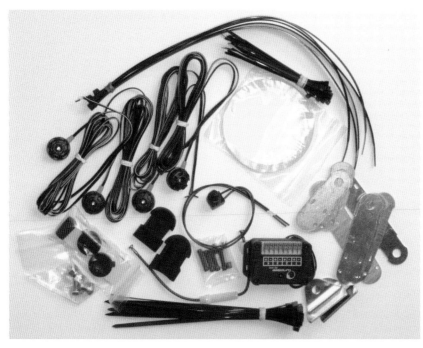

Here is what comes in the box of the Lunasee Hi-Vis Wheel Lighting System. The four LEDpods (middle left) can be mounted in a variety of ways to the forks or swingarm. An assortment of thin aluminum brackets are provided along with two-sided tape. With a little imagination, the pods can be positioned to direct their light toward the rotating wheel. *Courtesy Lunasee*

This is the Lunasee ASL 1000 lighting controller. It has two electrical connections, ground and switched 12-volt power. The orange terminals are for connections to the four LEDpods. *Courtesy Lunasee*

Pictured is one of four LEDpods. The pod lights charge the phosphorescent tape on the wheel. Because the light output is in the UV wavelength and direct viewing of the lights can damage eyes, be careful when testing the system. *Courtesy Lunasee*

The wheel must be clean for the LERtape to stick to it. Once the dirt and grime is removed, a quick wipe with some lacquer thinner (nail polish remover) will remove any cleaning residue. The wheel must be absolutely clean before applying the tape. *Courtesy Lunasee*

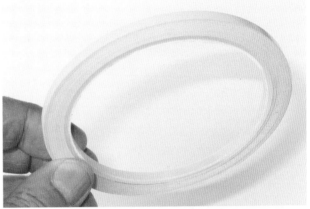

The LERtape is applied just like pinstriping tape. The adhesive on the tape will set in about 15 minutes and reach full adhesion strength in 72 hours. *Courtesy Lunasee*

Only a small section of LERtape should be positioned on the wheel to ensure that it will align with the edge of the rim. The tape can be repositioned to make small adjustments in alignments. The tape can be applied by hand as shown, or Lunasee makes a tape applicator tool that applies the tape evenly around the circumference of the wheel. *Courtesy Lunasee*

The rear swingarm on this Yamaha FJR provides an ideal location to mount the LEDpod. The pod is small enough to fit between the drive shaft, swingarm, and the wheel. *Courtesy Lunasee*

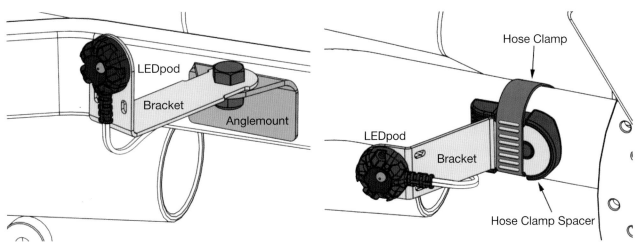

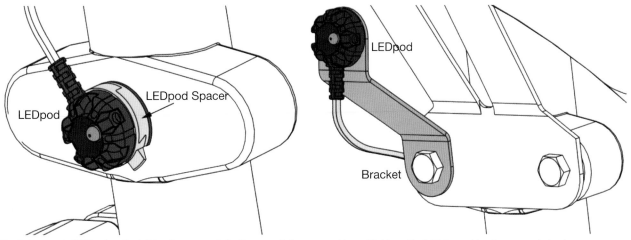

Options for mounting the LEDpods on a swingarm are shown. At left, a 90-degree mount uses two-sided tape to adhere it to the swingarm, and the bracket is bolted to the mount. On the right, a hose clamp and spacer is used to mount an aluminum bracket to one side of the swingarm. If mounting the pods on a motorcycle with a single-sided swingarm (BMW R 1200 GS and others) the fender can be used as a mounting point. The Lunasee website has lots of information about mounting options for various motorcycles. *Courtesy Lunasee*

The fork-mounted LEDpod on the left has been mounted with a supplied spacer and two-sided tape. To right, the pod has been mounted using an aluminum bracket bolted to a fender mounting bolt. A selection of aluminum brackets are supplied with the lighting kit. *Courtesy Lunasee*

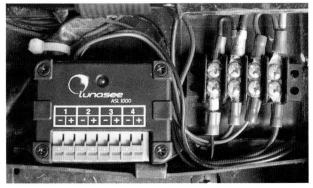

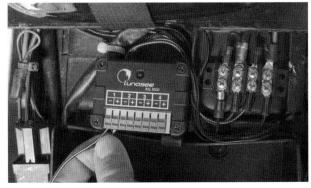

The Lunasee control box will need to be connected to a switched, 12-volt power wire and a ground. The motorcycle used for this installation already has a relay that turns on power with the ignition key. With a switched connection, the Lunasee controller will only power up with the ignition key on. *Courtesy Lunasee*

The LEDpods have two wires each. These are plugged into the controller in series. Port 1 and 2 must both be connected for the LEDpods to operate. The same is true for Ports 3 and 4. *Courtesy Lunasee*

Here is what the Lunasee wheel lights look like in action. This Honda GL1800 really lights up at night and is highly visible to motorists from any side angle. *Courtesy Lunasee*

With both front and rear wheels visible on this sport bike, the Lunasee wheel lights instantly indicate to drivers that they are looking at a motorcycle. Unlike a reflector that depends on light hitting it to become visible, the Lunasee wheel tape provides an active light source. Its green glow is highly visible from long distances. *Courtesy Lunasee*

OPTIMATE FLASHLIGHT

The Optimate Flashlight can provide needed light when working on your motorcycle in a dark garage or by the side of the road. *Courtesy TecMate*

Besides providing light, the Optimate flashlight has some additional functionality. If battery voltage drops below 12.4, a red LED on the side of the flashlight lights up to provide a "lo battery" warning. The flashlight will also indicate if the motorcycle's charging system is working as well. With the engine running, a green LED will light up when charging system voltage is above 14 volts. *Courtesy TecMate*

If you ride a lot at night, having a flashlight with you just makes sense. The Optimate, 6-LED flashlight comes with a 40-inch cord that has an SAE connector on its end. The flashlight fits easily into a tank bag or other luggage. *Courtesy TecMate*

POWER HUB

The PowerHub Power Distribution Module is sold by Twisted Throttle and provides fused connections for up to six electronic devices. Connections can either be on at all times or switch on when the motorcycle's ignition key is turned on. The PowerHub makes for a clean installation and is far superior to attaching multiple ring connectors to battery terminals. The PowerHub is rated for a total of 30 amps (360 watts). Each of the connections can handle up to 10 amps (120 watts), but the total number of amps

Here is what comes with the PowerHub: Velcro mounting strips (top), wiring harness for connecting the PowerHub, the PowerHub with the cover and base plate removed, mounting screws, and fuses. The connection to the battery's positive terminal has an inline, 30-amp fuse. *Courtesy Twisted Throttle*

This is the cover of the PowerHub. The unit measures 3.25 inches in length × 2.5 inches in width × 1.25 inches in height. A place is provided to label the electrical devices connected. The amps each device requires can be written down as well as if the circuit is switched on or is constantly on (C/S). The graphic at the top of the unit (+12VDC +VT GND) indicates the 12-volt power source, switched power (+VT), and ground inputs. *Courtesy Twisted Throttle*

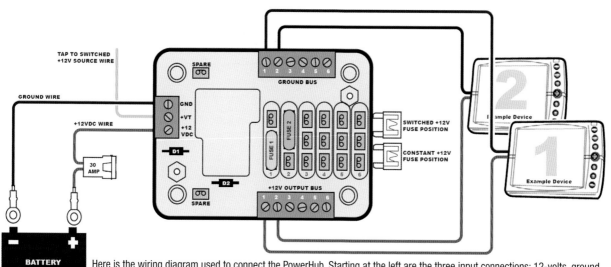

Here is the wiring diagram used to connect the PowerHub. Starting at the left are the three input connections: 12-volts, ground, and a switched input used to turn on the PowerHub's internal relay for the switched connections. The position of the fuse determines if a connection will be a constant 12 volts or switched on with the ignition key. There are two places where spare fuses can be stored as well. *Courtesy Twisted Throttle*

cannot exceed 30 if all of the six connections are used simultaneously. The following images show a typical installation of the PowerHub. Twisted Throttle (www. twistedthrottle.com) will be introducing the PowerHub2 soon. This new product will be slightly smaller in size and like the PowerHub will be compatible with CAN-BUS electrical systems, like those used on BMW motorcycles. Check out their website for details.

The yellow wire is connected to a power source that is switched on with the ignition key. On many motorcycles, the taillight circuit is a good place for a switch power source. Because this input will only provide power to the PowerHub's internal relay, it only draws about 0.3 or an amp and won't affect taillight operation. A Posi-Lock connector is provided for the connection. *Courtesy Twisted Throttle*

Here the switch input is verified using a 12-volt test light. With the key on, the test light lights, indicating that the correct connection has been made. *Courtesy Twisted Throttle*

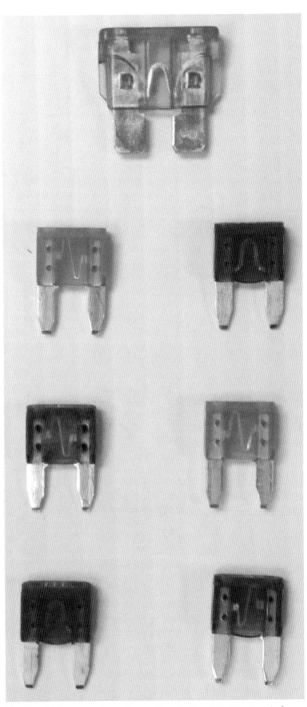

The PowerHub comes with a 30-amp fuse (top) and an assortment of other ATO mini-fuses, ranging from 2 to 10 amps. Before connecting electrical devices, check what each requires for amperage and select the appropriate fuse. *Courtesy Twisted Throttle*

Here is the PowerHub installed and connected to electrical accessories. In this installation only the switched outputs are being used. By moving the fuse to the Constant +12V terminals, the output will be on all the time. This clever design makes it easy to quickly change how power is delivered from the PowerHub. *Courtesy Twisted Throttle*

This is a side view of the PowerHub and the six terminals for the groundside are shown. The stripped end of a ground wire is inserted into the holes and a screw terminal is tightened to connect the wire. *Courtesy Twisted Throttle*

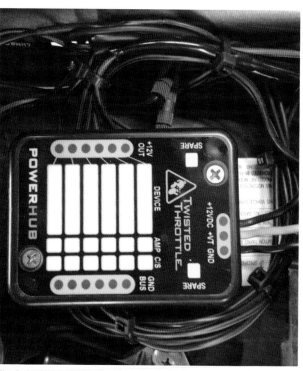

The PowerHub with the cover installed. Trying to connect six electrical devices directly to the battery leaves a mess of wiring and is confusing to work on. The PowerHub installation looks like it came from the factory or was installed by a pro. *Courtesy Twisted Throttle*

SQUADRON WIDE-CORNERING LED LIGHTS

If you only ride at night, occasionally factory lighting is good enough on most motorcycles. But if you ride for hours at a time in the dark, nonfactory lighting up front can make the experience safer. Baja Designs manufactures lighting for all types of vehicles, including cars, trucks (both on- and off-road), and motorcycles. LED technology as applied to motorcycles has been around for about 10 years and it continues to improve. It is superior to conventional lighting that uses halogen bulbs, especially in the power-consumption department and offers more lumens per watt of electrical power. We tried out Baja Design's Squadron Wide-Cornering LED Lights. The company makes dozens of motorcycle lighting products. Check out their website at www.bajadesigns.com. The following images show the installation of their Squadron Wide-Cornering LED driving lights on a Honda Gold Wing GL1800.

Baja Design's Squadron LED light measures 3x3x2.7 inches in length, making it ideal for use as an auxiliary driving light. Output is 4,300 lumens, which is more that an HID light of similar size. The design features a single layer solid core copper circuit board with active thermal management to keep the electronics cool. The housing is made using aircraft grade aluminum and the light only weighs 12 ounces. Power required is 42 watts per light and LED life expectancy is 49,930 hours, so basically the lights will outlast the life of the motorcycle. *Courtesy Baja Designs*

The Squadron light is available in four configurations: spot, wide cornering (pictured), flood, or a combination of spot and wide cornering. The hard-coated, polycarbonate lenses are easily changed by removing four Allen screws. At right, the four T6 Bin Cree XM-L2 LEDs can be seen. *Courtesy Baja Designs*

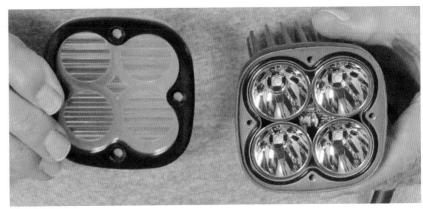

The Squadron lights are far too bright to be used at full power all the time as they will blind oncoming drivers. The PWM dimmer box and key fob provide a means to adjust the output of the Squadron lights. The key fob provides the user with 18 levels of adjustment for the low-beam output. Once the desired level is reached, the key fob is no longer needed as the electronics "remembers" the power setting level. When the high beam is operated, the dimmer box instantly powers the lights to full power. *Courtesy Baja Designs*

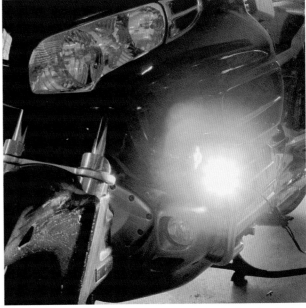

On this Honda Gold Wing GL1800 the Squadron lights are mounted on the crash bar. Baja Designs sells various mounting options for the Squadron lights. The black anodized aluminum housing gives the lights a factory-installed look. *Courtesy Baja Designs*

It's difficult to appreciate just how much illumination the Squadron lights project on to the road. Using the spot lens, the light projects more than 650 feet. The wide-cornering lens disperses the light pattern, and while the forward projection is somewhat shorter, the light illuminates the sides of the road and allows the rider to see into a corner before the motorcycle is turned. *Courtesy Baja Design*

Sources

Thanks to the following motorcycle dealerships and manufacturing companies for help with the images and information contained in this book. Their kind assistance made this a better book both from technical as well as artistic perspectives. All of these dealers and manufacturers offer great products and services for professional and do-it-yourself technicians alike. Contact information is listed for each company. Check out their websites.

their meeting place creates what we call the "BMW Environment." And it's what sets Bob's apart from all other BMW motorcycle dealerships.

Bob's BMW Motorcycles
10720 Guilford Rd
Jessup MD 20794-9385
301-497-8949
www.bobsbmw.com

BOB'S BMW

Bob's BMW is one of the most respected BMW motorcycle dealerships in North America and the winner of several awards for overall excellence, customer satisfaction, and community service. From its convenient location near Columbia, Maryland, Bob's serves riders throughout the Washington, D.C., Baltimore, and northern Virginia region.

Beyond the local level, Bob's is a destination of choice for BMW enthusiasts from far and wide, thanks largely to the thriving mail-order parts business, which, since 1981, has become nationally renowned as the BMW rider's prime source for parts, accessories, and apparel—and not only to owners of new models, but also collectors of classic and vintage BMWs too. There is even an on-site Vintage Museum at Bob's featuring rare bikes and artifacts that illustrate the complete history of BMW motorcycling.

Bob's BMW is more than just a full-service dealership in the conventional sense. There's a feeling about the place: where the special camaraderie shared among the many BMW riders who make Bob's

BATTLEY CYCLES/BATTLEY HARLEY-DAVIDSON

Battley Cycles/Battley Harley-Davidson is the Baltimore-Washington, D.C., area's only multiline dealer representing the most storied brands in the motorcycle industry. Battley's is the longest serving dealer in the area for BMW and Ducati and has been a Harley-Davidson and Yamaha dealer for more than 25 years. Battley Cycles was the first Buell dealer in the world and it still has the first production Buell RR1000 in its collection of vintage motorcycles.

Battley has been involved in all facets of motorcycle racing since the late 1970s and the company's sponsored riders have won numerous national championships. Battley's involvement in racing plus factory training has enabled its service department staff to always stay current with state-of-the-art technology in motorcycling. Whether it is building a big-inch H-D motor or blueprinting a Ducati, we have the expertise to make it happen. We have the most advanced performance tuning center in the area and are equipped with an infrared gas analyzer and Dynojet Dynamometer. H-D technicians are factory trained to program Dobeck Performance products, like their Gen3 controller, Dynojet's Power Commanders and Harley-Davidson's Screamn' Eagle Pro Race Tuner.

Visit Battley if you are in the Baltimore-D.C. area.
301-948-4581
www.battley.com

HARLEY-DAVIDSON OF FREDERICK

Harley-Davidson of Frederick is a full-service Harley-Davidson and Buell dealership. Its Harley-Davidson–certified service department offers quick bay services while you wait, Maryland state inspections on all brands, dyno testing for all brands, and highly trained and certified technicians. In addition, Harley-Davidson of Frederick offers an in-house, full-service, high-performance, and customer fabrication machine shop featuring state-of-the-art equipment and a talented crew of dedicated professionals.

With a newly expanded showroom, the company can show and sell more new and used motorcycles than ever before. It also has a huge selection of MotorClothes and collectibles, as well as parts and accessories to personalize your ride. Harley-Davidson of Frederick has recently started converting two-wheeled motorcycles to trikes and services them as well.

No matter what your motorcycling needs, chances are they can help. The Harley-Davidson of Frederick team is dedicated not only to exceeding the highest standards of professionalism and technical achievement but to unparalleled customer service as well.

Harley-Davidson of Frederick
5722 Urbana Pike
Frederick, Maryland 21704
301-694-8177
www.hdoffrederick.com
info@hdoffrederick.com

TWIGG CYCLES

Twigg Cycles celebrates its 83rd year in 2014. H. William Twigg sold his first bicycle in 1932 and established Twigg Cycles as an Indian motorcycle franchise in 1936. The family-owned and -operated dealership has carried 42 brands since that time, including Matchless, ATS, CS, Jawa, Triumph, BSA, Airel, Zundapp, Ducati, Benneli, American Eagle, Wizzar, and BMW. Today they sell Yamaha, Suzuki, Kawasaki, and Honda. In addition to motorcycles, they carry watercraft, including Polaris and Sea-Doo.

Twigg Cycles has satisfied thousands of customers in the Maryland, Pennsylvania, and West Virginia area. Twigg Cycles provides every customer with guaranteed satisfaction above and beyond their expectations and creates an environment of friendliness and superior quality for maximum enjoyment of the unique motor sports lifestyle offered by its people, products and services.

Twigg Cycles, Inc.
200 S. Edgewood Drive
Hagerstown Maryland 21740
301-739-2773
www.twiggcycles.com
sales@twiggcycles.com

YUASA BATTERY INC.

Yuasa Battery, Inc., has been manufacturing motorcycle batteries in the United States to uncompromisingly high standards since 2000. It is the largest American manufacturer and the largest distributor of batteries for motorcycles, snowmobiles, scooters, all-terrain vehicles, and personal watercraft. In addition to its vast replacement business, Yuasa is the preferred original-equipment supplier to many of these same markets. By producing batteries that generate more power, last longer, and require minimum maintenance, Yuasa Battery has achieved a leadership position in small engine starting batteries. Continuous research and development, along with unvarying standards of manufacturing quality, will help maintain its position as market leader around the world.

www.yuasabatteries.com

DYNOJET RESEARCH

Dynojet Research is uniquely positioned to support its customers worldwide. Partnerships with industry-leading companies in more than 56 countries ensures that local technical support for the customer is always available. This continued commitment to being a world-class supplier has led to more than 5,600 dynamometer installations worldwide. These installations include OEM manufacturers, importers, exhaust manufacturers, tuners, race teams, dealers, service shops, and motorcycle and ATV magazines. Furthermore, our dynamometers are officially licensed with the following race organizations:

Established in 1972, Dynojet is a research-and-development company, employing more than 100 people in Montana, Nevada, Holland, Germany, and United Kingdom. In addition to manufacturing dynamometers, Dynojet Research develops after-market performance products and diagnostic tools for the motorcycle and automotive industries. Dynojet designed the first, single-roller, inertia, chassis dynamometer for motorcycles in 1989. Shortly thereafter, Dynojet developed a computer interface and software package and began selling the first Model 100 motorcycle chassis dynamometer.

The Model 100 proved to be affordable, reliable, accurate, and above all, consistent. This was the case not only from one measurement to the next but also from one Dynojet dynamometer to another, enabling communication and sharing of test data. The success of the Model 100 led to further developments in chassis dynamometer technology.

800-992-4993
www.dynojet.com
www.powercommander.com

ZIPPER'S PERFORMANCE PRODUCTS

The year 2011 marked the 30th anniversary of Zipper's Performance Products. Zipper's was formed from a deep passion for racing Harley-Davidson motorcycles. The Zipper's team has developed an extensive line of products and services that propelled racers to five national titles and many world records, Development of racing parts led to the manufacturing new components to improve reliability, performance, and the overall riding experience for the Harley-Davidson enthusiast.

Today Zipper's offers hundreds of aftermarket components for every rider. These products include Redshift cams, ThunderMax EFI systems, and complete, pre-engineered engine kits. Zipper's Performance solutions are available through a worldwide network of dealers.

410-579-2828
www.zippersperformance.com
www.thunder-max.com

POWERLET

Powerlet offers a line of high-quality products tailored to the powersports industry. With more than 220 wiring products to choose from, Powerlet power adaptors can make connections to any battery-powered vehicle.

Products range from prepackaged socket kits that mount easily into a panel or frame boss, to adaptive and power cables ready to power any type of appliance. Based on the accepted industry standard, Powerlet is your source for powering appliances.

Our products permit riders to power everything from GPS units to radar detectors to heated gear, all directly from their motorcycle or power sports vehicle, further enriching the riding experience. Our lines of Luggage Electrix products enable riders to power stock luggage, bags, or tail trunks. Once our electrical connector is installed on a piece of luggage, riders charge and power appliances with ease and have the simplicity of one simple point to disconnect power from the vehicle.

It is all about the ride and enriching that experience with peace of mind products is what we refer to as being Powerlet Equipped. Kits start at $29.95 to $124.95. Cables start at $7.95 and Luggage Electrix products start at $24.95. Increase your riding comfort and get both you and your vehicle Powerlet Equipped today.

Powerlet products can be purchased at many fine resellers of motorcycle accessories or purchased direct on line.

Powerlet
5520 Chicago Road
Warren, MI 48092
877-752-7835
www.powerlet.com
marketing@powerlet.net

TECMATE

TecMate has been developing and manufacturing unique electronic products for the powersports and niche vehicle sectors for more than a decade. TecMate's product range includes unique precision tools, OptiMate advanced battery-saving chargers, plus various OptiMate cable and powered accessories. TecMate's products are used and recommended by many important vehicle manufacturers around the globe. OptiMate battery chargers now also charge, test, and maintain lithium (LiFe Po4) batteries.

TecMate North America
1-1097 North Service Road East
Suites 1 & 2
Oakville, ON L6H 1A6
Canada
905-337-2095
www.tecmate.com

RICK'S MOTORSPORT ELECTRICS

What began as a small motorcycle salvage business in the late 1970s has grown to a well-recognized, highly reputed brand name in the aftermarket powersports industry. Rick's Motorsport Electrics offers a full parts line of charging, starting, and ignition components for Asian and European street bikes, ATV/off road, snowmobiles, and watercraft. Rick's provides a high-quality, cost-effective alternative to OEM parts for home technicians and dealers alike. Many of Rick's components are direct plug-in replacements for original equipment. The company also provides many universal-fit parts for obscure powersports vehicle applications. Rick's Motorsport Electrics offers a one-year part replacement warranty on all motorsport parts, excluding CDI boxes.

Rick's Motorsport Electrics strives to stay on top of industry trends and is constantly adding new products to its line. The company's success comes from its extensive knowledge and 25 years of expertise in the motorsport industry. The inventory targets electrical parts that are in high demand by motorsport enthusiasts everywhere. Rick's has instructional videos on the YouTube channel, RicksElectrics's. Check out the website for details.

Rick's Motorsport Electrics, Inc.
30 Owens Court, Unit 2
Hampstead, NH 03941
800-521-0277
603-329-9901
www.ricksmotorsportelectrics.com
Info@RicksMotorsportElectrics.com

NGK SPARK PLUGS

When you require the best, count on the world leader in spark plug technology—NGK Spark Plugs. NGK offers the highest quality products for virtually every vehicle application. Count on NGK spark plugs to deliver the finest quality products and customer service. NGK has built a reputation for quality and reliability, and a commitment to excellence continues to be the driving force behind the company's advanced research and development programs. With state-of-the-art manufacturing, inventory, and distribution facilities, NGK is dedicated to providing customers with world-class products and services.

In North America, NGK is headquartered in Wixom, Michigan, and maintains manufacturing, inventory, and distribution facilities in Irvine, California; Sissonville, West Virginia; and Chicago, Illinois.

NGK Spark Plugs (USA), Inc.
46929 Magellan Drive
Wixom, MI 48393
Customer service and technical support:
877-473-6767
www.ngksparkplugs.com

FLUKE CORPORATION

Fluke Corporation is the world leader in the manufacture, distribution, and service of electronic test tools and software. Since its founding in 1948, Fluke has helped define and grow a unique technology market, providing testing and troubleshooting capabilities that have grown to mission-critical status in manufacturing and service industries. Every new manufacturing plant, office, hospital, or facility built today represents another potential customer for Fluke products.

From industrial electronic installation, maintenance, and service, to precision measurement and quality control, Fluke tools help keep business and industry around the globe up and running. Typical customers and users include automotive and powersport technicians, engineers, and computer network professionals—people who stake their reputations on their tools and use tools to help extend their personal power and abilities. The Fluke brand has a reputation for portability, ruggedness, safety, ease of use, and rigid standards of quality.

Fluke Corporation
P.O. Box 9090
6920 Seaway Boulevard
Everett, Washington, 98206-9090
800-44-Fluke (443-5853)
www.fluke.com

BUB ENTERPRISES

BUB Enterprises is all about performance and no one exemplifies this better than Denis "BUB" Manning, who at the age of 22 built his first motorcycle streamliner. In 1970, Manning built the world record–breaking Harley-Davidson streamliner that was ridden at 265 miles per hour by the late Cal Rayborn. He has designed and built streamliners for Harley-Davidson, Triumph, and Norton and has owned 6 of the 11 fastest motorcycles in history. In 2004, Manning and daughter-in-law, Delvene Manning, began the International Motorcycle Speed Trials by BUB as an annual event to provide a venue for motorcycle land speed racing. In 2006, at his third annual BUB Speed Trials, Manning and the "Seven" streamliner crew recaptured the elusive title of "World Fastest Motorcycle" with a world record speed of 350.884 miles per hour. His streamliner, piloted by Chris Carr, was also the first motorcycle to go over 350 miles per hour. With the support of the industry, Manning has advanced the sport of motorcycle land speed racing and in October 2006, fresh from his world record run, he was inducted into the AMA Motorcycle Hall of Fame.

BUB Enterprises manufactures high-performance exhaust systems for Harley-Davidson, Honda, Kawasaki, Suzuki, Triumph, and Yamaha in their 15,000-square-foot, state-of-the-art manufacturing facility in California. BUB is the first exhaust manufacturer to produce a street-legal, high-performance catalyst system for Harley-Davidson FL models. The BUB "Seven" meets California emission requirements and is EPA sound compliant.

> 800-934-9739
> bub@bub.com
> www.bub.com

HEAT DEMON

In 1989, Symtec developed its first heated product with a snowmobile thumb warmer. Soon, they were manufacturing a full line of heated aftermarket products for the powersports industry under the Heat Demon brand as well as completely customized OEM heating solutions from LCD warmers to heated grips. Throughout their history, Symtec has emphasized innovation and integration, constantly improving and perfecting its process and heating solutions.

In 2010, Symtec's founder sold the company to Riley Harlan, who revived our company's approach and core values. The entire organization, including the Heat Demon brand, went through a rebranding as part of a larger effort to move our products into the future. With new facilities in Minneapolis, cutting-edge equipment, and revamped internal control systems, Symtec has turned out more inventive and reliable solutions than ever before.

From grip warmers to heated seats, we've worked with a number of major powersports vehicle manufacturers to take cutting-edge heating solutions from ideation to production. Through an inventive process of continuous improvement and fine-tuning, Symtec can take any idea to completion.

> Heat Demon
> 124 Osborne Road NE
> Minneapolis, MN 55432
> www.heatdemon.com

BAJA DESIGNS

The people behind Baja Designs live and breathe off-roading, and the products reflect that passion. Baja's engineers have finished the grueling Baja 1000 more than 15 times, both on a bike in the competitive pro class and in class 16 and class 1 cars. They also take numerous multiday Dual Sport trips throughout the year. In fact, you never know where in the world they will show up on their motorcycles, ATVs, UTVs, and buggies. Baja's engineers are well-known throughout the industry as the gurus of off-road lighting. Since they are in Southern California, they are able to test with all of the factory motorcycle teams along with some of the biggest names in the truck and buggy classes. They use racer feedback and their own vast experience to develop the best off-road products on the planet. In addition to off-road applications, many of the lighting products can be used for street riding. On or off the road, the design and manufacturing of the best lighting possible is Baja's passion.

Baja Designs, Inc.
185 Bosstick Boulevard
San Marcos, CA 92069
800-422-5292
www.bajadesigns.com
info@bajadesigns.com

LUNASEE

Lunasee was created in 2005 by two bicyclists with a mission of changing safety for cyclists and other two-wheeled vehicles primarily through its core patented lighting technology. The goal was to create a brand associated with integrated, stylish, aesthetically pleasing, yet functional products designed to enhance safety and visibility. The company maintains several patents around its innovative technology. Lunasee high-quality and well-designed products provide a unique combination of style and safety for riders of all types.

Lunasee Hi-Viz Wheel Lighting systems use the latest LED and photoluminescent components to create a simple yet remarkable lighting system that uses the specially formulated LunaGLO tape, applied directly to a wheel's rim. As the wheels rotate, the LunaGLO tape is charged by four hidden high-intensity LEDpods, one each mounted on the frame or forks and targeted at the tape. The glowing tape creates continuous rings of light without any wires or lights attached to the wheels—simple and remarkable.

Lunasee sells to dealers, e-commerce retailers, distributors (both domestically and internationally), and through its website. The company is based in Greenville, North Carolina. For more information, or to order, visit our website or call us.

Lunasee LLC
1800 N. Greene Street
Suite F
Greenville, NC 27834
252-353-4354
www.lunasee.com

TWISTED THROTTLE

Twisted Throttle LLC is located in Exeter, Rhode Island, and is a dealer, distributor, and manufacturer specializing in motorcycle riding apparel and bolt-on equipment that provides protection and increased comfort for adventure riding, commuting, and long-distance travel. Brands that we distribute include SW-Motech/Bags Connection, R&G Racing, Barkbusters, Macna, MRA Windscreens, Kaoko, Interphone, and more. Additionally, Twisted Throttle designs and manufactures 100 percent waterproof military-spec dry luggage under the DrySpec brand and rugged LED auxiliary driving lights under the Denali brand. A staff of more than 35 includes MSF instructors, track day veterans, dual sport and adventure enthusiasts, and vintage racers. Twisted Throttle prides itself on its customer service and support, by riders for riders.

    401-284-4200 ex. 8412

    www.twistedthrottle.com

ADIRONDACKS & BEYOND MOTORCYCLE SAFETY

Adirondacks & Beyond specializes in Motorcycle Safety Foundation riding classes and suspension upgrades. Located in upstate New York in Lake George, they are an easy, one day ride from New York City, northern New Jersey, eastern Pennsylvania, Vermont, New Hampshire, and Maine. The company is the Northeast's pre-eminent, aftermarket motorcycle suspension shop and specializes in suspension modifications for large touring bikes, sport tourers, and dual-sport motorcycles. If your motorcycle has factory suspension, and you ride lots of miles, you're missing out on what aftermarket suspension can offer. Adirondacks & Beyond offers suspension upgrades using Race Tech or Traxxion suspension components. Give them a call to discuss how your motorcycling experience can be enhanced by tailoring your suspension to your specific needs and how your ride.

    Adirondacks & Beyond

    7 McGowan Circle

    Lake George, New York 12845

    518-796-8186

    www.adkmc.com

KOSO NORTH AMERICA

Koso is synonym for quality and performance. The company designs and has manufactured high-quality gauges and accessories for more than 20 years for aftermarket and major OEM companies. Pushing the limit further by continuously improving and developing new products is Koso's main goal. In order to reach that goal, Koso works with the best engineers and testing equipment available. They are proud to be the leader in digital technology and to offer to customers the best and most reliable products on the market.

    Koso North America

    Order line: 877-777-0604

    Technical line: 450-359-0604

    www.kosonorthamerica.com

CLEARWATER LIGHTS

Clearwater Lights are high-powered, fully dimmable LED lights that provide longer life and lower power consumption than other light systems. The innovative, patent-pending technology behind Clearwater Lights was born out of frustration with existing incandescent filament bulb technology. Incandescent bulbs, including halogen, rely on a high-resistance wire that glows when electricity flows through it. The light output is just a byproduct, so more than 90 percent of the power to a halogen light is wasted in heat. There had to be a brighter way.

Join the many serious riders who are experiencing the Clearwater Lights advantage.

Clearwater Company
11305 Sunrise Gold Circle, Suite D
Rancho Cordova, CA 95742
916-852-7029
www.clearwaterlights.com
sales@clearwaterlights.com

POSI-PRODUCTS

In 1997 Posi-Products started with the introduction of the Posi-Lock No Crimp Connector in just one size, 12–18-gauge in-line splice. Today Posi-Products manufactures six patented No Crimp Connector Brands: Posi-Lock In-Line Splice, Posi-Twist Non In-Line Splice, Posi-Tap T-Taps, Posi-Seal In-Line Weather-Tite, Posi-Tite In-Line Water-Tite, and Posi-Fuse In-Line Fuse Holders.

Wires are connected by twisting the connector by hand—with no tools required. They disconnect just as easily and are reusable. Unlike crimp-type connectors, Posi Lock connectors will not pull out or vibrate loose even under a harsh environment. Our products are sold in more than 40 countries worldwide, including markets for automotive, motorcycles, power sports, GPS, telematics, security, and military applications.

Corporate distribution centers are located in Missouri and Hong Kong. We sell direct on line to all markets worldwide. Our products may also be ordered through our distribution network.

Posi-Products, Inc.
PO Box 3111
St. Augustine, FL 32085
www.posi-products.com

DAYTONA TWIN TEC

Daytona Twin Tec LLC manufactures a range of high-tech feature-rich electronic engine controls, diagnostic tools, and tuning aids for Harley-Davidson and other American V-Twin motorcycles. They have a simple philosophy: do one thing and do it well.

They offer the most complete coverage of ignition and fuel-control systems for Harley-Davidsons, from Shovelhead to 2014 Twin Cams, plus a complete line of diagnostic tools and tuning aids.

Daytona Twin Tec LLC
933 Beville Road, Suite 101-H
South Daytona, FL 32119
386-304-0700
386-304-9502 fax
sales@daytona-twintec.com
www.daytona-twintec.com

GORILLA CYCLE ALARMS

Gorilla Cycle Alarms are the most compact and effective motorcycle alarms on the market today. With most motorcycles, installation takes less than 30 minutes and can be done with common hand tools. No matter what you ride, rest assured you're protected by the best in the industry. The choice is clear, protect your bike with a Gorilla Cycle Alarm.

2011 East 49th Street
Los Angeles, CA 90058
323-585-2852
www.gorillacyclealarm.com

Motorcycle Consumer NEWS

AMERICAN IRON MAGAZINE

American Iron Magazine is a Stamford, Connecticut–based American motorcycle magazine specializing in the coverage of American-made motorcycles, including Harley-Davidson, Indian (motorcycle), and Big Dog Motorcycles. *American Iron Magazine* (or AIM) contains columns by editor-in-chief Buzz Kanter, editor Chris Maida, and female motorcyclists Genevieve Schmitt and Stephanie Feld, as well as standard tech articles by featured writers Donny Peterson and Tom Johnson. Typical articles include how-to stories on motorcycle repairs and maintenance, classic bikes, custom builds, motorcycle reviews, motorcycle product and accessory reviews, events, the Hog Helpline for tech questions, and recommendations on routes for motorcycle enthusiasts.

Launched in 1989 in California, *American Iron Magazine* was purchased by magazine publisher Buzz Kanter's TAM Communications in 1991 and moved to Connecticut, where it is published today. In 2008, the staff of *American Iron Magazine* launched an online version for classic motorcycle enthusiasts named *Classic American Iron Magazine*. Limited to topics related to American-made motorcycles pre-1984, *Classic American Iron Magazine* features an online magazine format as well as an active bulletin board forum.

TAM Communications, Inc.
1010 Summer Street
Stamford, CT 06905
203-425-8777
877-693-3577
www.aimag.com

MOTORCYCLE CONSUMER NEWS

Motorcycle Consumer News is the monthly consumer resource for unbiased reviews of motorcycles and related aftermarket products and services. Combined with in-depth technical features and top-notch investigative reporting, it is considered "The Bible" for serious motorcycle enthusiasts. Unlike other powersports publications, *MCN* has no advertising and relies only on reader subscriptions as its source of income. This allows them unprecedented editorial freedom to write the "truth" regarding how well a product or service really works—or doesn't. If you want to know what brand of jacket, gloves, riding pants, bike-cleaning products, electronics, tires, helmets, and a whole host of other motorcycle-related products are best and how they compare to the competition, this is the magazine that is unafraid to tell it like it is.

In-depth reviews for new motorcycles lets readers know before they buy what they're getting for their money. Columns on "Mental Motorcycling" and motorcycle design trends make for interesting and informative reading. A quarterly "Used Bike Value Guide" can make purchasing a second-hand motorcycle a more enjoyable experience. The monthly column "Proficient Motorcycling" provides readers with valuable riding skills tip and techniques. Bulletins regarding factory recalls and letters from manufactures and readers all add value for motorcyclists.

Editorial information:
Motorcycle Consumer News
PO Box 6050
Mission Viejo, CA 92690-6050
949-855-8822
www.mcnews.com
editor@mcnews.com
Subscription information:
Motorcycle Consumer News
PO Box 37191
Boone, IA 50037-0191
888-333-0354
MCNcustserv@cdsfulfillment.com

Index